ERNEST LAPOINTE AND QUEBEC'S INFLUENCE ON CANADIAN FOREIGN POLICY

JOHN MacFARLANE

Ernest Lapointe
and Quebec's Influence
on Canadian Foreign Policy

UNIVERSITY OF TORONTO PRESS
Toronto Buffalo London

© University of Toronto Press Incorporated 1999
Toronto Buffalo London
Printed in Canada

ISBN 0-8020-4487-5 (cloth)

Printed on acid-free paper

Canadian Cataloguing in Publication Data

MacFarlane, John, 1963–
Ernest Lapointe and Quebec's influence on Canadian
foreign policy

Includes bibliographical references and index
ISBN 0-8020-4487-5

1. Lapointe, Ernest, 1876–1941. 2. Canada – Foreign relations –
1918–1945.* 3. Canada – Politics and government – 1921–1930.*
4. Canada – Politics and government – 1930–1935.* 5. Canada –
Politics and government – 1935–1948.* 6. Cabinet ministers
– Canada – Bibliography. I. Title.

FC581.L36M33 1999   970   C99-930023-7
F1034.L34M33 1999

This book has been published with the help of a grant from the Humanities and
Social Sciences Federation of Canada, using funds provided by the Social
Sciences and Humanities Research Council of Canada.

University of Toronto Press acknowledges the financial assistance to its publishing program of the Canada Council for the Arts and the Ontario Arts Council.

FOR DIANE

Contents

Acknowledgments

This work began at the Université Laval, and I am grateful to those who offered useful comments: Réal Bélanger, Richard Jones, Alain Laberge, Denyse Légaré, Jocelyn Létourneau, and H.B. Neatby. I would also like to thank several others who have helped improve this book, including my family, Emily Andrew, Gerry Hallowell, Diane LeBel, John Parry, and Cameron Pulsifer.

Throughout this book I make references to earlier works by Canadian historians. Often I challenged their interpretations, but this book would have been impossible without their work, and these historians have provided an excellent foundation for the study of Canada's past. For every questionable interpretation with which I have disagreed I always found much more with which I agreed, and it would be unfair of me not to acknowledge their contribution.

ERNEST LAPOINTE AND QUEBEC'S INFLUENCE ON CANADIAN FOREIGN POLICY

Introduction

A democratic political system must allow for a certain amount of public participation in decision making. When the population, as in Canada, includes a significantly large minority group with a definitely distinct *mentalité*, the government cannot rely simply on majority rule to decide questions that clearly divide the two groups: the minority will feel that it is not heard in the decision-making structure, that it has no voice.[1] Recognizing a minority group, without giving the majority the impression that its voice is somehow less equal, is not easy.

Many attempts by governments to include the minority voice have left both the minority and the majority unsatisfied. The reactions to the Meech Lake Accord and the Charlottetown constitutional agreement have illustrated the dangers that Canadian governments face. On the one hand, when the mostly French-speaking population of Quebec rejected the Charlottetown proposals, it did so because it believed that its views had been ignored and that the deal left it, 'as usual,' with little or no influence at Ottawa. On the other hand, when the mostly English-speaking population of the other provinces and territories opposed the same agreement, it did so because it was convinced that Quebecers had received too many concessions and that the arrangement would allow the minority, 'as usual,' to dominate the federal government.[2]

These contradictory interpretations of Quebec's influence have affected the writing of the country's past, particularly the writing that refers to the 'national unity prime minister,' William Lyon Mackenzie King. Many francophone historians have described the governments of King as having ignored Quebec's interests, while many anglophones complain that King allowed Quebec to dominate Canadian policy.[3] Other historians portray him as the leader who divided Canadians least, ensuring unity by skilfully reconciling the interests of the minority and the majority. Frank Underhill wrote in 1950 that dividing Canadians least was an accomplishment not to be underestimated, for 'perhaps this is as much as we shall ever be able to say, for a long time to come, about Canadian unity.'[4] King the generous (or politically astute) anglophone is increasingly recognized as the Canadian leader who most effectively incorporated the minority voice at Ottawa.[5]

When historians estimate Quebec's influence on the governments of Mackenzie King, it might be expected that they would refer often to the prime minister's relationship with Ernest Lapointe. His official titles, minister of marine and fisheries (1921–4) and minister of justice (1924–6, 1926–30, and 1935–41), do not reflect Lapointe's entire contribution. Until his death in 1941 he was known unofficially as King's Quebec lieutenant, but this term has been applied to so many people with such widely varying roles that it is inadequate to describe sufficiently what he meant to King.[6] Although Lapointe represented Quebec anglophones in cabinet and occasionally defended French Canadians outside Quebec, he devoted most of his attention to representing the francophones of Quebec.

Lapointe's role led him continually to questions of foreign policy where differences between anglophones and francophones were most obvious, and most explosive, particularly concerning the dominant theme of the period – the status and responsibilities of Canada in the British Empire. Because historians often consider that maintaining unity on these questions was King's greatest achievement, one might expect that Lapointe's influence – certainly recognized by his contemporaries – would have been analysed in detail.[7] Surprisingly, historians have paid less and less attention to the King–Lapointe relationship.

This study attempts to determine, with as much precision as possible, how and how much Lapointe influenced King's foreign policy from 1921 to 1941. Two elements are crucial here. First, how much did Lapointe's presence, his views, and his actions change the direction of Canadian policy from the course that King, without him, would have charted? Second, how did Lapointe attempt to impose his views on the prime minister? Did he have to rely on King's granting him influence, or did he have control over certain groups and certain questions? Determining Lapointe's influence on King will reveal much more than how one man – Lapointe – shaped the country's foreign policy. Both King and Lapointe (particularly between 1921 and 1938) were more followers than leaders of public opinion, and determining with precision the influence of

Lapointe will provide an excellent indication of francophone Quebec's influence on Canadian foreign policy.

Lapointe and the Historians

H.B. Neatby, King's official biographer, wrote the most influential and still the best account of the prime minister's career. Focusing on his subject, he complained in 1976 that francophone historians spoke too much about Lapointe, to the detriment of King. He supported this argument by pointing out that Lionel Groulx, in *Histoire du Canada français*, had four references to Lapointe in the index and none to King.[8] Applying the same criterion to other books, we find that it is Lapointe, not King, whom Canadian historians have neglected. The works of six anglophones writing about foreign relations and the Department of External Affairs at that time contain, on average, for each mention of Lapointe – who was omitted by two – seven references to King, who was secretary of state in the department (and two to the undersecretary of state, O.D. Skelton).[9] Lapointe is even less present in works by francophones, who seem to be even more affected than anglophone historians by the current tendencies to prefer social history over political and biographical studies – particularly studies of politicians in Ottawa. No historian has written a biography of Lapointe's full career, while there are over twenty biographies of King – almost all written by anglophones.

In general, francophone historians see Canada as an association of two distinct nations and consider that Quebec had little or no say in Canadian foreign policy during the period. The anglophone majority decided all policies and completely eclipsed the minority voice, they argue, most notably concerning the decision to go to war in 1939.[10] Lionel Groulx wrote that in 1939 anglophones, 'réservant presque unanimement leur plus haute allégeance et leur premier amour à l'Angleterre et prêts à entrer dans toutes ses guerres,' saw Canadian foreign affairs differently from francophones, who were equally unanimous in knowing no other 'patrie' than Canada.[11]

Quebecers have had various reasons for denying that Lapointe had significant influence at Ottawa. René Lévesque concluded that although Lapointe 'had the knack of keeping crowds interested and [had] a lot of flair and colour,' he could do little at Ottawa, where French Canadians have inevitably been 'kept outside the inner circles that had to do with financial policy' in the federal cabinet.[12] Pierre Trudeau argued that the system was adequate but that Lapointe was not: 'With the sole exception of Laurier, I fail to see a single French Canadian in more than three-quarters of a century whose presence in the federal cabinet might be considered indispensable to the history of Canada as written.'[13] Whether they claim that Lapointe was a puppet of the majority or another francophone who failed to make himself indispensable, almost all francophone writers – even those who refer to a King–Lapointe government – agree that he did not impose Quebec's voice in Canadian foreign policy.[14]

Anglophone historians can be divided into two groups. The first group, seeing Canada as one nation and considering that the majority should decide policy, feels that Quebec had too much influence. When describing external affairs they have been concerned primarily with Canadian or, more exactly, British Empire defence, arguing that King was too preoccupied with national unity and let Quebec dominate Canadian policy.[15] T.B. Slobodin argues that when King decided foreign policy he 'usually sided completely with French Canada' and found that 'catering to Quebec all those years had only made it intractable, had only made tougher the already fibrous cocoon in which Quebec was wrapped.'[16] For these authors, the regrettable triumph of French-Canadian 'isolationism' meant the sacrifice of the English-Canadian desire for international collective security.

The second group of anglophone historians considers that maintaining national unity was an impressive achievement, and it praises King for having developed an approach that effectively balanced majority rule and recognition of the minority voice.[17] The French-Canadian minority did not dominate policy, it says, but acted as a weight on the participationist English Canadians, although these historians admit that a strong imperialist impulse was more important than the smaller collective-security preoccupation among English Canadians.[18]

Both anglophone groups indicate that Quebec's voice was heard, making Canadian foreign policy more 'isolationist,' but focus on King rather than on Lapointe as being responsible. The collective-security group blames King for deciding to listen to Quebec's voice – for 'catering to the rigid isolationism of Quebec.'[19] In the words of C.P. Stacey, 'the policies of the government of Canada were essentially the personal policies of the man who held [the office of prime minister].'[20] The unity group also concentrates on King, praising him for his judgment. According to Granatstein, it was the prime minister who decided what Quebec would accept, although he does admit that King was aided by a second person, another unilingual anglophone: 'To Mackenzie King and to his Under Secretary of State for External Affairs, Dr. Skelton, Canadian duality was still too fragile [before 1939] to be subjugated to the strains that a forward [Canadian foreign] policy would entail, and the two men were probably correct if unadventurous.'[21] For anglophone historians, King did not need Lapointe's judgment or his prodding to incorporate the Quebec voice into his foreign policy.[22]

An element common to all groups is the impression that Lapointe shared the same views as King. Instead of being affected by their respective backgrounds, both men saw Canadian external affairs in the same light. According to Richard Veatch, 'Lapointe's point of view on foreign policy and League matters was virtually identical with that of King.'[23] If they differed, King would always have the final say, most have agreed. Neatby writes that 'King did not wait for a French-Canadian colleague to emerge. He selected the man who was to be his associate and then gave him the necessary status and influence ... only King could decide ... [and Lapointe] knew that a lieutenant was not a general.'[24] W.A. Matheson claims that King, the best-informed person in cabinet, was 'careful to preserve the veneer of consultation.'[25] Hillmer and Granatstein conclude that 'although he consulted people within a very narrow circle, Mackenzie King made the major Canadian foreign policy decisions alone.'[26]

What is striking about all references to Lapointe's role, particularly in Canadian foreign policy, is how vague they are. Whether Lapointe is considered a co–prime minister with great influence or a puppet with no influence, whether Quebec dominated Canadian policy or had absolutely no say, the affirmations are made in passing with little evidence to support them. Typical of this tendency is Esberey's comment that 'the relationship between King and his Quebec lieutenant – Ernest Lapointe – was probably the most important in King's political career but requires little in the way of analysis.' All that needs to be said is that Lapointe had the qualities that King sought: 'willingness to subordinate his personal preferences to King's view of political necessity.'[27] With no precise measure of Lapointe's influence, estimations have been vague and very much subject to the personal prejudices of historians. Authors have implied that in 1939 the new minister of finance, J.L. Ralston,[28] the postmaster general, Chubby Power,[29] or even the old senator Raoul Dandurand[30] had as much influence on King's foreign policy as Lapointe. Because the question is important, it continues to receive attention, passing generalizations, but little precision.

Authors occasionally refer in passing to Lapointe's enormous influence. In the 1960s Ramsay Cook wrote that, with vigorous leaders at Ottawa, 'something very near to a French-Canadian veto could be exercised within the federal cabinet, at least in matters that touched on French-Canadian affairs.' The veto had some notable failures (when Riel was hanged in 1885 and conscription imposed in 1917), but 'history says less about the cases where the veto succeeded. When the complete story of Canadian foreign policy in the inter-war years is revealed, the influence of a man like Ernest Lapointe will almost certainly appear enormous.'[31] But Cook was no more precise than writers claiming that Lapointe had no influence, leaving the door open for exaggerations. Even in the article and MA theses of the three authors who have chosen Lapointe as the subject of their work (Paul Bernier, Paul Bychok, and Elspeth Chisholm), references to Lapointe's influence remain vague. Bychok, who argues that Lapointe and King were co–prime ministers on all questions, agrees with other historians that both men 'shared a common vision of Canada, and viewed the role of political action in society in remarkably similar terms ... These complementary views of society and leadership extended harmoniously into the realm of foreign relations.'[32]

Of course, measuring influence is not easy. Referring to the King–Lapointe relationship, H.B. Neatby commented that 'no diagram or flowchart can illustrate this complex relationship in which the leader must lead but the lieutenant must influence.'[33] However, Lapointe's influence was significant enough that it deserves to be studied with greater precision than it has been. To begin with, the 'leader' did not always lead.

Measuring Influence

Amount: How Much Influence?

The works of the political scientist Vincent Lemieux provide some useful concepts to help specify Lapointe's influence on King's foreign policy. Lemieux explains that actors (individual or collective) participating in the making of decisions seek to ensure as much as possible that the decisions correspond with their personal choices. When they succeed, their voice is dominant. According to Lemieux, when identifying the dominance of an actor's voice, in relation to other parties to the process, three basic situations are possible: conjoint dominance, dominance, or conjoint non-dominance. Actor 'A' would have dominance over 'B' if a decision went in favour of the voice of 'A' and against that of 'B.' If the decision corresponded with both voices, there would be conjoint dominance, and if the decision corresponded with neither voice, there would be conjoint non-dominance.[34]

The way in which a decision is taken is fundamental for determining the dominance of the voice of an actor. For example, the prime minister's voice may be sufficient to determine a given policy, the support of the majority in cabinet may be required before the government adopts a policy, or cabinet unanimity may be necessary. In some cases, no decision may be reached. The threshold necessary for the acceptance of a decision by those involved plays therefore a decisive role in establishing the relations of dominance between actors on a given question. With enough information, it is possible to establish the dominance of an actor's voice on a given decision, even when not reached by a recorded vote, the fundamental consideration being the conformity of the decision with the actor's personal choice.[35] Estimating 'the dominance' of the voices of King and Lapointe can help us specify the role of each.

If Lapointe's voice was identical to King's, as historians often argue, a study of the relative influence of each would be unnecessary. Both would have conjoint dominance on all Canadian foreign-policy decisions. Or if King decided all questions, then Lapointe would have non-dominance, conjoint dominance, or conjoint non-dominance on all questions. But King and Lapointe rarely shared the same views on international questions, and at times – more often than historians have recognized – Lapointe's voice was clearly dominant over King's. In many cases King's government was able to minimize divisions between anglophones and francophones not because the prime minister was eager to listen to the minority voice but because Lapointe convinced him – at times forced him – to listen.

King, much more attached to the British Empire, was much less aware of French-Canadian public opinion than Lapointe. Typical of most anglophones of the time, King – despite occasional regrets –[36] spoke almost no French and knew little about francophone Quebec. An American journalist must have interviewed people who knew the prime minister when he wrote that 'Mackenzie King is thoroughly Scotch–English in temperament. He speaks but the poorest French and has little fondness for French-Canadians as such. But he is well aware of the need for unity.'[37] According to his secretary, J.W. Pickersgill, 'he had no affinity with the French culture, a sketchy and superficial knowledge of the language and all the Protestant intolerance of Catholicism.'[38] The Liberal MP and later minister Paul Martin agreed that 'King did not have a mind that brought him into easy intimacy with French-speaking people.'[39] King and Lapointe both sought unity and the re-election of the Liberal party, but this does not mean that any other differences were minor. King, a typical English Canadian, and Lapointe, a typical French Canadian, were as different as the two groups they represented.

Far from being harmonious, the King–Lapointe relationship was characterized by frequent disagreement. King does not mention Lapointe (and Quebec) in his diary often, suggesting that he was not as interested in the views of francophone Quebec as historians have assumed. Neatby and others acknowledge King's ignorance and dislike of francophone Quebec and conclude that he therefore decided to appoint a lieutenant in order to ensure that its voice was heard.[40] However, the voice that King had in mind was not what would have satisfied the minority. It was Lapointe, as francophone Quebec's representative, who seized his position of influence from a hesitant King.

Resources: How a Lieutenant Could Influence

How could a lieutenant's voice be dominant? The relationship between two actors, as we saw above, changes from one question to another and depends on the threshold required for the adoption of the decision. The prime minister may insist on his choice on certain questions or, more often, allow a free vote in cabinet or Parliament or a referendum on another. When the leader is not deciding a question on his own, the influence of others depends, to a large extent, on their resources.

Possession of the reliable support of a certain group, or having a particular and recognized expertise in certain areas, is a 'resource' that allows an actor to influence particular decisions. In the words of political scientist R. Dahl, an actor's 'domain' (the other actors influenced by him or her) and 'scope' (the matters on which he or she can influence them)[41] determine how great will be the actor's voice in a decision.

In addition to available resources, an actor's influence depends also on the skill with which he or she uses these resources and how many resources get used. An actor may have many resources (money, information, jobs, votes, and so on) but if he or she does not employ them judiciously, or decides not to employ them, his or her influence is less than it might have been.[42] Dahl also warns against falling into two common traps when measuring influence. First, power, or influence, is not necessarily equivalent to resources. Thus, arguing that 'money is influence' or that 'Quebec dominates the House of Commons because it elected a bloc of Liberal MPs' is insufficient.[43] The relationship between influence and the way in which one or more of the actors involved uses resources must be explained. The second trap involves describing power 'as if it were a single, solid, unbreakable lump [which] can be passed from one actor to another, but cannot be shared.'[44] Authors claiming that King had the final say on all questions because he was prime minister underestimate the influence of others.

The domain of Lapointe's influence varied during his career as minister, although, as this study shows, he consistently wielded his greatest influence on the francophone Quebec caucus. The size of this group, as well as its numbers compared to the anglophone caucus, and Lapointe's ability to mobilize it, proved crucial to his influence in cabinet.[45] Control of this group was Lapointe's most valuable resource. Chubby Power, a Quebec minister for much of the period, remarked that Lapointe read the Quebec population better than anyone and that he, not King, was considered by the Quebec caucus and population as leader of the Liberals in the province: 'The following was attracted by Lapointe, so the fact that [Quebec] remained Liberal for many, many years was due to Lapointe rather than to King himself.'[46] Lapointe, not King, had replaced Laurier in Quebec.[47]

By controlling this group, Lapointe held an invaluable card to be played at the cabinet table, particularly in decision-making about questions within his scope of influence: those involving francophone–anglophone relations. In King's political system each minister presented his region's concerns in cabinet; if a question divided the country's two major linguistic groups, King knew – and almost always sympathized most with – the views of anglophones. But, speaking no French and having almost no contact with French-Canadian culture, King could not judge what policies French Canadians would prefer or accept and did not consider this matter particularly important. He did need a lieutenant to present and defend their views, but he was not the one who realized this. If the minority voice was heard, it was due to Lapointe's strength, not to King's good will.

Lapointe also had access to other resources. He was a convincing speaker, aided by an impressive physical appearance. A journalist in 1929 wrote: 'Physically, Ernest Lapointe is perhaps the most gigantic man in politics in the British Empire. Standing six feet three inches in his stockings, with massive shoulders and head, and with an ample though not unbecoming girth, he is a veritable giant towering above his colleagues and gives an impression of great power.'[48] In fact, Lapointe was only six feet in his stockings, but to King, who 'suffered from chronic insecurity,' who saw himself as a 'little fat round man,' Lapointe probably appeared seven feet tall.[49] In addition, King was a poor speaker, and knew it, while Lapointe was an orator. In the words of Power: 'When he spoke he spoke not only with eloquence but with all the physical strength he could put into it, really he used to perspire so much that he was as wet as a rag when an important speech was finished.'[50] Lapointe's loyalty to King was another major resource though again difficult to quantify. He helped King win the Liberal leadership in 1919 and to survive an attempted 'coup' in 1925, and again, King knew it: 'But for him,' King wrote in his diary in 1941, 'I would never have been Prime Minister, nor would I have been able to hold office, as I had held it through the years.'[51]

King's owing Lapointe political favours does not mean that they were close friends, as some suggest.[52] King had neither French-Canadian nor political friends.[53] One author writes that 'Ernest' (pronounced in English) was the only minister whom King called by his first name; however, in his diary King usually referred to his lieutenant as 'Lapointe' or, at times, as 'Mr. Lapointe.'[54] King told a group of friends in 1945, 'Ernest Lapointe was one of my closest friends,' and then add with barely a perceptible pause, 'political friends, I mean.'[55] Lapointe's daughter remembered that the two men were not 'very intimate. They would not call on each other casually all the time.'[56] In fact, on several occasions Lapointe had recourse to the most confrontational of resources – his threat of resignation.

The 'Voices' of Lapointe and King

This study considers seventeen Canadian foreign-policy decisions, estimating the extent to which Lapointe influenced each decision and the resources he used to ensure his success. The presentation of each of the decisions is followed by a description of King's views, which suggests the policy that he would have adopted on his own, and a description of Lapointe's views, which indicates how he modified King's preferred policy. A look at public opinion reveals how much Lapointe was concerned to represent his people. Lapointe disagreed with King on many questions, particularly after 1926, but made sure that francophone Quebec's voice was heard and included in all decisions. Lapointe influenced all seventeen decisions – either with a dominant or, more often, a co-dominant voice – but the resources on which he relied varied greatly during three distinct periods of his career.

First, from 1921 to 1930 Lapointe established his influence at Ottawa, without completely consolidating his position as Quebec lieutenant (chapter 2). A large Quebec caucus and the fragility of King's position allowed him to play an important role in three decisions relating to the establishment of Canadian autonomy within the British Empire (chapter 3) – the Canadian reaction to the Chanak crisis, the signing of the Halibut Treaty, and Canadian support for the defining of dominion status at the Imperial Conference of 1926. He also influenced three issues at the League of Nations (chapter 4) – acceptance of Article X, acceptance of the optional clause, and the search for a seat on the League Council in 1927.

Second, from 1930 to 1938 Lapointe consolidated his position in 'shadow cabinet' and cabinet (chapter 5), although King was also stronger and the Quebec lieutenant resorted more often to his threat of resignation. In 1935 Canadian autonomy seemed assured, and Lapointe was more preoccupied with Canadian decisions concerning two explosive international events: the Ethiopian crisis and the Spanish Civil War (chapter 6); but as the threat of another world war increased, Canadian autonomy again came into question. The different visions of Lapointe and King were apparent during the Imperial Conference of 1937 and the Munich crisis of 1938 (chapter 7).

Third, from 1939 to 1941 Lapointe's position in Quebec was stronger, but, with the war on, King and anglophone members of cabinet were less likely to listen, and the minister of justice needed to rely on new resources – most notably, his ability to convince the Quebec population (chapter 8). The questions dividing anglophones and francophones were increasingly explosive, and Lapointe's voice became particularly valuable to King. In 1939 the Canadian government's reaction to the Nazi invasion of Czechoslovakia, to the Allied declaration of war on Germany, and to Duplessis's anti-war provincial election campaign showed how much King needed Lapointe to maintain some unity (chapter 9). After the fall of France in June 1940, four more decisions confirmed King's dependence: recognition of Pétain and/or of de Gaulle, reaction to subversive groups, application of conscription for the defence of Canada in 1940, and rejection of overseas conscription in 1941 (chapter 10).

To identify how and how much Lapointe's voice influenced these seventeen foreign-policy decisions is not easy. One major limitation surrounds the problem of representiveness. This study rests to a certain degree on the assumption that Lapointe represents Quebec's voice in Canadian foreign policy. Such a connection is difficult to prove definitively. In addition, Lapointe's influence on Canadian foreign policy may suggest to some a similar influence on other national questions. To prove this would require a much larger study, and the results would probably be disappointing. Lapointe rarely attempted to influence other matters — such as economic policy or distribution of patronage — unless they were of direct interest to francophone Quebec and risked dividing Canadians. His lack of influence on economic questions should not be seen as a weakness, nor should his strength on foreign policy be seen as a guarantee that he could have altered economic policy.

Furthermore, the foreign-policy questions to be studied were not necessarily the most important of the period. The issues that I selected were the ones that most preoccupied Lapointe during the period, because they were the ones that most preoccupied Quebec, and risked colliding the views of the 'two solitudes.' Lapointe rarely attempted to modify the U.S.–Canadian relationship, even on the tariff. The selection of the seventeen decisions is thus a significant limitation of the study, which is not a history of Canadian foreign policy but an analysis of a number of major decisions influenced by francophone Quebec, through Ernest Lapointe. If the questions in this study are not representative of Quebec's influence on all questions, they do nevertheless represent the influence that Quebec *could* have.

Another limitation of this study is the impracticability of identifying precisely the 'other voices' that influenced policy. Any foreign-policy decision had to take into consideration, to varying degrees, the opinions of business groups, religious leaders, the civil service, the intellectual community, and other more or less organized lobbies. Because the goal of this study is to determine Lapointe's influence, the only other voices that I consider in depth are those of King, of the anglophone caucus and population, and of the francophone caucus and population. Of course, measuring 'public opinion' would require a separate study, and all that I attempt here is an estimate based on newspapers, statements of MPs, and letters from the public.

It should be added that *a* public opinion does not exist; an entire nation will almost never share a monolithic *mentalité* on any question. This reality has been recognized when English-Canadian views of the period are presented, but French-Canadian opinion has often been seen as monolithic, usually conservative, clerico–nationalist dominated, and 'isolationist.' Recent studies have shown that French-Canadian socioeconomic views were much more complex and varied and suggest that the sort of liberalism represented most notably by Laurier and Lapointe, not conservative nationalism, was the major political ideology during the period from 1867 to 1940.[57] International affairs did interest and seem relevant to most French Canadians, who were greatly interested in dominion politics.[58]

This study shows that Lapointe, relying on his own strengths, succeeded in ensuring a Quebec voice in Canadian foreign policy from 1921 to 1941. To begin, chapter 1 describes how Lapointe had arrived at such an influential position in 1921. Introductory chapters 2, 5, and 8 set the context for each of the three parts of this study and, by presenting the political context at Ottawa – particularly the relative strengths of King and Lapointe – suggest how Lapointe was able to influence the prime minister on such questions. The seventeen decisions studied below refer to more general trends in Canadian foreign policy – autonomy from the empire (chapter 3) binding commitments to and vis-à-vis the League of Nations in the 1920s (chapter 4); Ottawa's reluctance to participate in international affairs (chapter 6) and hesitation to commit itself to military measures within the empire between 1930 and 1938 (chapter 7); the formulation and implementation of the no-conscription pact (chapter 9) and its modification after the fall of France (chapter 10).

1

Finding a Place to Stand

'Give me a place to stand and I shall move the earth,' Archimedes said. During his early life, Ernest Lapointe probably thought little about moving the earth, but gradually, without consciously seeking it, he acquired the foothold that would permit him to play a towering role in Canadian foreign policy.

A Catholic, French-Canadian World-View

Lapointe spent his formative years in a French-Canadian, Roman Catholic environment. He was born on 6 October 1876 and raised in the small village of St Éloi and studied at the neighbouring Séminaire de Rimouski and later at the Université Laval, where he received his law degree in 1898. His early life was remarkably devoid of the exposure to the English-Canadian culture and language so present in other French-Canadian leaders at Ottawa (such as Wilfrid Laurier, Louis St Laurent, and Pierre Elliott Trudeau). His upbringing, unmistakably rural, French, and Catholic, was thus more befitting a leader who would defend his people than one who, understanding both groups, would propose compromise solutions.

Similarly, William Lyon Mackenzie King's upbringing had been a poor preparation for a leader hoping to understand both groups. Born and raised in southwestern Ontario, King spent his formative years in an English-Canadian, Protestant environment. In the words of biographer H.B. Neatby, 'King presumably knew that there were French Canadians but that certainly created no bond of sympathy. He was a church-going Presbyterian ... brought up to distrust Roman Catholicism as authoritarian, dogmatic and priest-ridden, and he never overcame this prejudice.'[1]

To become leader of the Liberal party and then prime minister, King depended on the support of others more familiar with French Canada, others more respected by French Canadians, others with a background like Lapointe's.

Lapointe was aware that many of the most pressing issues of the late nineteenth century, when his political outlook was forming, pitted Catholics and Protestants, or francophones and anglophones, against each other – the Louis Riel affair of 1885, the Manitoba Schools question of the 1890s, and the country-wide plebiscite on prohibition of 1898 (when English-Canadian Protestants were much drier than French-Canadian Catholics). When Wilfrid Laurier became Liberal leader in 1887, and then the first French-Canadian prime minister in 1896, the polarization of Canadian politics intensified. During the federal election campaigns of 1896 and 1900, many English-Canadian newspapers emphasized the need to make French Canadians understand that Canada was an 'English country' and that English Canadians would not be 'dominated' by 'an inferior population' speaking a 'foreign language.' Many Catholic French Canadians were attracted by the argument of federal politician Israël Tarte, who suggested during the campaign of 1896 that French Canadians forget about being Liberal or Conservative and ask if it would not be an honour for their province if their country had a French-Canadian prime minister.[2] After receiving his degree in 1898, Lapointe returned to the Bas-St Laurent region to practise law in Rivière-du-Loup, where, probably influenced by such arguments, he became an active supporter of the Liberal party.

Two international incidents reveal how differently the two groups saw the world. In 1868, 135 French-speaking Catholic Pontifical Zouaves from Quebec volunteered to fight for the pope against the Garibaldians in Italy; very few Anglo-Protestants (who saw Garibaldi as a hero) were in the crowd of 30,000 that saw them off in Montreal. Conversely, when 7,368 Canadian volunteers went to fight for the British crown in the South African War from 1899 to 1902, only about 200 were French Canadians.[3]

In this context Lapointe, definitely identifying with the minority group, entered federal politics. In 1904, at the age of twenty-seven, he defeated W.A. LeBel for the Liberal nomination for the riding of Kamouraska, after the incumbent, H.G. Carroll, was appointed judge, and he won a by-election by acclamation in February 1904. He began a career that would take him into almost daily contact with a group about which he knew little. Interaction with these unknowns would at times be frustrating, at times confrontational. At the same time he married Emma Pratte.

Lapointe spent his first years at Ottawa adapting to the Canadian political reality. His views, and his approach to implementing them, slowly developed under the guidance of the Liberal leaders. He initially criticized the Quebec nationalists Armand Lavergne and Henri Bourassa for speaking English in the House of Commons;[4] however, he increasingly appreciated how difficult it would be for a unilingual francophone to defend his people. Under the guidance of Jacques Bureau, the Liberal MP from Trois-Rivières, he acquired English, becoming an increasingly effective speaker, while he learned from Laurier – who often emphasized that Canadian nationality was built on tolerance – the importance of compromise.[5] Laurier, the leader most responsible for having gained the support of Quebecers for Liberalism during the period, who always sought unity by emphasizing civil and religious liberties, tolerance, and compromise, remained a model for Lapointe throughout his career.

While Lapointe was a member of the Liberal caucus during the Laurier governments from 1904 to 1911, he had very little influence in the party.[6] Moreover, he does not appear to have been very interested in pursuing a long political career. In 1908, at the age of thirty-two, he hoped to be appointed judge; Laurier's reply reveals how small was his influence: 'Si j'ai bien compris ta lettre tu reconnais toi-même que tu es encore trop jeune pour aspirer à monter sur le banc, mais que si cependant le gouvernement croyait devoir passer par dessus ce défaut tu accepterais la position. Malheureusement tu n'es pas le seul qui consentirait ainsi à se laisser faire violence. Si j'écoute les désirs qui me viennent actuellement de tous côtés, il ne restera plus un seul avocat dans la députation de Québec.'[7] Possibly Lapointe had developed a distaste for the patronage side of politics – he often received demands, most of which had to be refused, leaving more people disappointed than pleased[8] – or possibly he despaired of ever acquiring any more influence. However, during the next ten years, he would gradually emerge as spokesman for an increasingly large portion of the Liberal caucus.

The election of 1911 would considerably affect Lapointe's position in Ottawa, and his views. The Quebec Liberal caucus had many leaders – notably Henri-Sévérin Béland, Jacques Bureau, and Rodolphe Lemieux – each supported by groups with varying interests, but for many French Canadians none of the Liberal leaders was a sufficiently strong defender of Quebec's interests. The approach of Bourassa and Lavergne was more appealing to them, and support for these Quebec nationalists rose rapidly. According to Chubby Power, a student at Laval at the time: 'Nearly all the young men who had not some tie or other with the government [either Laurier's Liberals at Ottawa or Gouin's Liberals at Quebec City] were inclined to follow the banner of Bourassa and particularly of Armand Lavergne.[9] To maintain support, Quebec Liberals, including Laurier, leaned in this direction. In 1911 the Liberals maintained thirty-eight of the sixty-five seats in the province, but the alliance between the Quebec nationalists and Sir Robert Borden's party led to a Conservative victory. As many Liberal seats were lost in 1911, space was created for Lapointe, increasingly appreciated, to move to the front benches, and by 1914 he was Laurier's chief political lieutenant and organizer for the Quebec City district and eastern Quebec.[10]

Reciprocity was a major issue during the campaign, but, as the question did not divide francophones and anglophones, Lapointe was less interested in it and much more absorbed in what he considered the main election issue – the naval question. In 1909 Laurier had proposed a plan for a Canadian navy, but the English-Canadian imperialists preferred to contribute directly to a common imperial navy. They claimed to favour a strong empire as a vehicle through which Canada would attain nationhood, although their 'nation' would have little room for francophones or Catholics.[11] At the same time, French-Canadian nationalists opposed any contribution to what would become an imperial navy in time of war. They claimed to be seeking their idea of a Canadian nation, although Laurier and many Liberals believed such nationalism to be based on anglophobia.[12]

On 5 December 1912 Borden introduced his Naval Aid Bill, which proposed to offer $35 million to Britain to build three ships for the Royal Navy. Although the Liberal-dominated Senate blocked the bill, Lapointe grew increasingly concerned that the minority's voice was not being heard at Ottawa. He believed that the principle for which he was fighting involved more than construction of a few boats: 'Le projet de loi que nous étudions actuellement,' he told Parliament, 'est peut-être le plus important qui ait été présenté à cette Chambre depuis la confédération.' If Borden's proposal were accepted, Lapointe warned, 'nous nous trouverons, par ce fait, à participer dans toutes les guerres de l'Angleterre, justes ou injustes.'[13] In 1914 Canada was at war not because of Borden's boat project but simply because Britain was at war. The lack of an adequate French-Canadian voice at Ottawa became increasingly apparent.

Not Necessarily Independence, But ...

The First World War and its by-products – conscription for service overseas, Union government, and socioeconomic upheaval – greatly affected the views of the young MP for Kamouraska. Canadian imperialists saw the war as Canada's struggle and labelled anyone who hesitated to support it a traitor. They hoped that Canada would have a voice in determining imperial policy but were willing to follow Britain whether this voice was heard or not: British interests were Canadian interests. In French Canada both Laurier and Bourassa accepted participation but, particularly for the latter, more for Canadian interests than for British or French interests.[14] Many French Canadians remained unconvinced that Canadian interests were involved and felt that Canada was at war only because Britain was at war.[15]

Lapointe accepted Canadian participation, emphasizing the defence of Canadian interests. 'Le devoir nous incombe,' he announced in 1916, 'de prendre toutes les mesures que peuvent nécessiter le maintien de l'honneur du Canada et la sauvegarde des intérêts les plus sacrés de la nation.' Canada – including Quebec – had been doing and would continue to do its part, Lapointe insisted, but he warned English-Canadian journalists that they, with their headlines equating a vote for Laurier with a vote for Germany, represented a far bigger obstacle to recruitment in Quebec than did Henri Bourassa. Lapointe was also critical of the government for not doing enough to ensure voluntary enlistment – especially in Quebec.[16]

In 1916 Laurier chose Lapointe to present to Parliament one of the most important motions of the period concerning francophone–anglophone relations. Four years earlier the Ontario government had passed Regulation 17, restricting the use of the French language in the province's schools and provoking considerable opposition throughout French Canada. Lapointe's motion proposed 'that this House, especially at this time of universal sacrifice and anxiety, when all energies should be concentrated on winning of the war, while fully recognizing the principle of provincial rights and the necessity of every child being given a thorough English education, respectfully suggest to the Legislative Assembly of Ontario the wisdom of making it clear that the privilege of the children of French parentage of being taught in their mother tongue be not interfered with.'[17] Five francophone Conservatives voted in favour of the resolution, while eleven western Liberals voted with the anglophone majority to defeat the motion. Many English Canadians could see no reason for anyone to speak French. O.D. Skelton, then a professor at Queen's University, probably represented the views of many English Canadians when he wrote that 'without the widest possible knowledge of English no common Canadian consciousness is conceivable ... This is and will be overwhelmingly an English-speaking country.' Thus, French

Canadians should learn English in provinces outside Quebec, but this did not mean that Anglo-Quebecers should learn French, Skelton concluded, because this would not help Canadian unity and would be of no advantage to the individual.[18] As presenter of this motion, Lapointe became increasingly recognized in Quebec as a defender of French Canadians.

The conscription crisis of 1917 marked the culmination of the tensions of the era, the crystallization of Lapointe's views, and the confirmation of his status as defender of francophone Quebec. When Borden's Conservatives proposed to apply conscription for military service overseas, Lapointe warned that the 'projet de loi ... le plus important de tous ceux dont la Chambre ait été saisie depuis l'établissement de la Confédération' was unacceptable to Quebec.[19] Opposition to conscription existed in all provinces, particularly among farmers, but Quebecers also possessed a vision of Canadian obligation to the British Empire very different from the English-Canadian view.[20] Lapointe told Parliament that only with the voluntary system could Canada contribute effectively to the war effort and ensure 'cet esprit de vraie liberté' so necessary for national unity, adding that if 'le Bas-Canada' had thought it possible that one day its citizens would be conscripted to fight for an imperial army it would never have entered the Confederation pact.[21]

When conscription for service overseas was adopted, it may have had some positive effect on the morale of the troops, but technically it added very little to the Canadian war effort and its effect on unity was disastrous. Laurier confided to Lapointe that he was concerned about the rising tensions. Everyone hates conscription, Lapointe replied, but the election has cleared the air, 'et la très grande majorité des citoyens paraît se résigner à subir ce qu'il est impossible d'éviter.'[22] He added that younger MPs had wanted to resist the measure strongly but had agreed that appearing intransigent would worsen the situation and help Bourassa. Remaining calm would lessen the risks of violence and of greater political complications.[23] At the end of March 1918, 'riots' did break out in Quebec City: after several days of disturbances the mostly English-speaking military was called in, opened fire, killed four civilians, and wounded many others.

It was after this incident, which intensified the attacks against Quebec by journalists in other provinces, that Lapointe turned up the heat. He rose in the House of Commons to deliver one of the most important speeches of his young career. The Liberal newspaper *Le Soleil* described it as one of the strongest presentations of French-Canadian sentiments ever presented in the House.[24] Lapointe was careful not to encourage the rioters: nothing can justify illegal violence, he insisted. However, he strongly attacked the Borden government and the anglophone press outside Quebec and seemed to imply that the increasing English-Canadian intolerance might force Quebec to leave Confederation to have a voice in international policy.[25] The historian Lionel Groulx even claims that 'dans une réunion intime ... Ernest Lapointe, indigné du sort fait au "grand chef," se serait même écrié, m'a-t-on dit: "Il ne nous reste plus qu'une chose à faire: nous rabattre sur nous-mêmes et aller notre propre chemin!"'[26] Lapointe sought unity, but he clearly did so through a firm defence of francophone Quebec's interests.

Lapointe criticized French-Canadian ministers who favoured conscription for clearly not representing the views of their constituents. He argued that Albert Sévigny and other nationalist 'jokers' in the Conservative cabinet had no influence in Quebec or in cabinet because they no longer had the confidence of the people.[27] To support his argument, he quoted Edmund Burke: 'Que les communes assemblées en parlement ne fassent qu'un seul et même tout avec les communes en général.'[28] It is ironic that he quoted Burke, because he would not have agreed with other of his comments, such as: 'Your representative owes you, not his industry only, but his judgment; and he betrays, instead of serving you, if he sacrifices it to your opinion.'[29] Lapointe would often refer selectively to this link between popular support and influence to criticize his opponents when they were in power or to legitimize his views when he was in power.[30]

The attitude of W.L. Mackenzie King was another element of the crisis that would prove to be important in later years. Candidate in a Toronto-area riding, King was not anxious to be seen with Laurier during the election campaign of 1917, and Laurier did not consider him the most loyal of his followers. King attempted to convince Laurier to change the Liberal position on the conscription bill; instead of promising to repeal the measure, King preferred promising not to implement it, unless necessary. In private, King's views were closer to those of the Union government than to those of Laurier, and he very probably considered joining it;[31] however, in public King continued to remain 'loyal' to Laurier, running as a Liberal candidate, while as much as possible favouring conscription. He recorded in his diary one of his conversations with Laurier: 'I asked if I took the position that I favoured conscription in principle, but not its application save in extreme necessity, other measures having failed, would he regard me as a follower of his and he said yes.'[32] King lost his seat but appeared to some to have remained loyal. Historians have recorded that Lapointe later saw King as a loyal Laurier Liberal because of the election campaign of 1917; however, because of this campaign it seems equally possible that Lapointe – in private – shared Laurier's suspicions of King.

Many other anglophones in the party joined Borden in a Union government for the election campaign of 1917. Quebec remained Liberal, English Canada favoured 'Union,' and the polarization between francophones and anglophones was complete. Ontario MP Newton Rowell's abandonment of the Liberal party, and his attacks on Laurier, created tensions, but Laurier confided to Lapointe and to King that for him the desertion of his senior colleague from the Maritimes, former minister of finance W.S. Fielding, with his attack against Quebec, was 'the unkindest cut of all.'[33]

The Union government confirmed most clearly what many francophones had believed: the dominion government was controlled by anglophone imperialists. The French-Canadian minority, which seemed to have no voice in the decision-making process, increasingly opposed the principle of coalition government and more and more favoured greater Canadian autonomy in the empire.[34] An MPP at Quebec City, the Liberal Joseph-Napoléon Francoeur, proposed a motion suggesting that if English Canadians considered French Canadians an obstacle to the development of the country it was time to end Confederation. This position remained far too marginal for Lapointe to support it – in public; however, the almost complete absence of government services in the French language during the period could only have encouraged these feelings. Within the Borden government between 1911 and 1917 the influence of French Canadians at Ottawa had been slight; with the Union government it reached an all-time low.[35]

Lapointe's vision of Canada was formed during a period of exceptional tension in Canadian history. The fundamental transformations of the socioeconomic structure of the country – urbanization and industrialization – exacerbated divisions between east and west, capital and labour. The most important conflict between labour and capital during the period was the Winnipeg General Strike of 1919, a symbol of increasing labour militancy and growing intolerance by labour's opponents. Lapointe was one of the few Liberals to express 'strong sympathies' for the workers of Winnipeg. Although he remained as opposed as the majority of his province to radical unionism, communism, and socialism, he believed that liberalism rather than force and censorship would be the most effective tool against the spread of socialism and strongly criticized the choice of Arthur Meighen as 'conciliator.'[36]

Lapointe almost instinctively supported the workers rather than capital, particularly when Catholic unions were involved. He hoped that both sides would work together: 'C'est une grave erreur,' he argued, 'd'opposer l'employé à l'employeur, le travail au capital et de parler entre eux de conflit d'intérêt.'[37] However, when there was conflict, Lapointe, coming from a small rural town, representing a region with very little industrialization, identified much more with the problems of the workers than with the group which he and King referred to as the 'big interests.'

Divisions between urban industrial interests and rural agricultural interests led to growing antagonism between east and west. The issue that best illustrated these tensions was the tariff. Business groups, increasingly dominant in central Canada, favoured a higher tariff to protect their manufactured products, while farmers, still numerous in all regions but dominant in the west, preferred a lower tariff to keep prices down – notably for manufactured goods – and to encourage the American government to lower tariffs so that they could export their products. Quebec was divided on the tariff question. The Montreal-based 'big-interest' group led by Sir Lomer Gouin, premier of Quebec from 1905 to 1920, and Louis-Alexandre Taschereau, Gouin's right-hand man from 1908 and premier from 1920 to 1936, favoured a higher tariff. Dandurand and Lemieux were the most prominent federal Liberals identified with this group, whose influence rested more on connections with the financial elite than on popular support. Closely associated with several large companies, Gouin had much in common with the English-Canadian business elite. Chubby Power remembered that Gouin said to him: 'I don't know why we ally ourselves with the western members, particularly those from Saskatchewan. They are nothing but bandits seeking to obtain subsidies from the federal government, and do not in any way help the economy of the country since they devote their attention only to one crop.'[38] He preferred subsidies for his corporate welfare bandits.

Lapointe, identified with the rural, agrarian (or labour) low-tariff wing of the Quebec caucus, did not enjoy a harmonious relationship with Gouin and Taschereau. In 1914 Lapointe called it a 'veritable affront' when Gouin and Taschereau considered naming an anglophone, instead of a local candidate, to the legislative council (upper house) for Lapointe's riding of Kamouraska. Taschereau insisted that 'nous n'avons pas affaire à M. Lapointe, nous avons ici notre député [provincial] et c'est lui que nous devons consulter.'[39] Lapointe clearly had no intention of making friends with Gouin and his group during the war when he sought an investigation of war profiteers: 'Les intérêts du Canada et de l'Angleterre paraissent avoir été mêlés avec les intérêts d'un petit groupe de financiers égoïstes.'[40]

Despite the many divisions in Canadian society, those that most preoccupied Lapointe throughout his early career were the conflicts between francophones and anglophones, particularly concerning questions related to Canada's role in the British Empire. He considered that these were the issues that most preoccupied francophone Quebec, and he saw his role as defending his people in the federal government. His power base thus lay outside two major francophone Quebec groups. He had very few connections with the larger business interests, and he was less nationalist than Bourassa and Lavergne, who considered that the Liberals were not adequate defenders of francophone rights. Lavergne explained to a Liberal secretary in Quebec City why he refused to be a Liberal candidate: 'Sur une question de la plus haute importance, clef de voûte de notre confédération – les droits imprescriptibles et constitutionnels de la langue française – la dernière convention libérale à Ottawa a gardé un silence ... prudent et de mauvais augure.'[41]

Between 1911 and 1919 Lapointe did not dominate a Quebec bloc, nor, as some argue, did Gouin's high-tariff big-interest group.[42] The Quebec caucus at Ottawa was divided on many questions. Lapointe's influence rose during the period, but he remained a long way from being recognized as Quebec lieutenant under Laurier. As late as 1917 an article in the Montreal *Gazette*, which Jacques Bureau brought to Lapointe's attention, remarked that the Liberal party was short of leaders in Quebec of national repute: 'Indeed, this defect is outstanding, and there is no promise of remedy in sight.'[43] Two years later, at the Liberal leadership convention in 1919, Lapointe would obtain the resource that would prove to be the most useful during his career, allowing him to exert considerable influence at Ottawa.

King-Maker

The Liberal party met in August 1919 to choose a successor to Laurier, who had died on 17 February. Sir Wilfrid's choice was not known, although King was convinced that the chief supported him.[44] More important, Ernest Lapointe was openly backing him, and this proved decisive.

The convention reflected the divisions in Canadian society – and in Quebec politics – during the immediate postwar period. Concerning the tariff, King was characteristically evasive; he later recorded in his diary that he decided to keep his 'sympathies with farmers, but adopt a middle course as between protection & free trade.'[45] On labour questions, King was perceived as being more open to unionized labour and social programs than Fielding, who found the modest reforms proposed by the party too radical.[46] King favoured the platform, resisted conservative elements in the party seeking to isolate labour 'radicals,' and recorded in his diary that this stand 'won me the labour men of the Convention.' The young candidate was sometimes very critical of the capitalist system when he was writing in his diary, as in April 1919: 'When one sees the enormous wealth controlled by a handful of capitalists, one cannot but feel that the system which permits this sort of control is absolutely wrong, unjust and indefensible; and that there will not be an end to social unrest until the transition is made to a joint control, with a restoration to the community of much that to-day is in private hands.'[47] Lapointe, considered a leader of the leftwing of the party, was also clearly in favour of implementing the program. In his speech to the convention he argued in favour of decreasing taxes on necessities for the poor and taxing 'further the superfluity of the rich.'[48]

Probably the most obvious division at the convention was between francophones and anglophones – or, to a large extent, between those who had remained 'loyal' to Laurier and those who had 'betrayed' him by joining the Union government. English-Canadian delegates were undoubtedly affected by the impression in their ridings that Quebec had not done its part during the war. Laurier, just before his death, had confided to Lapointe that he hesitated to force any by-election because 'le cri "down with Quebec" qui tend à s'apaiser est toujours là, et peut devenir dangereux.'[49] French-Canadian delegates were of course influenced by the increasingly united opposition in Quebec to the Union government, and because Fielding, one of the two leading candidates in the race, had joined the Union government King should have carried the Quebec delegates ... if they voted.

There was, however, a great deal of indecision in the Quebec delegation and no massive support for Mackenzie King. Chubby Power emphasized 'that there was never any strong sentiment in favour of King personally.' The delegation looked on him more as 'our vassal rather than our leader. We had put him there for a certain purpose.'[50] King's numerous references to Canada as an 'English-speaking' country did not increase his popularity in Quebec.[51] At a meeting during the convention, a motion was presented proposing that Quebecers abstain from voting.

Lapointe 'took charge' at this point, making a strong speech in support of King that rallied many of the undecided in the Quebec delegation and allowed King to edge out Fielding for the leadership on the third ballot, 476 votes to 438.

Most historians agree that the Quebec vote ensured King's victory. The west split between King and Fielding; Fielding had a small majority in the Maritimes and a big majority in Ontario, while Quebec supported King. Some speak of a solid Quebec bloc,[52] led by Lapointe. But the Quebec 'bloc' was not solidly behind Lapointe, and other historians argue more convincingly that about one-fifth of the Quebec delegation, led by Gouin, supported Fielding.[53] Nevertheless, given the narrow margin of victory, Quebec's support was vital to King, and it appears certain that Lapointe, with his intervention, tipped the balance in favour of the new leader. One observer commented that 'one may say with truth that Mr. Lapointe was the preponderant influence in the choice of Mr. Mackenzie King as Liberal leader.'[54] It would be more accurate to describe Lapointe's voice as being 'pivotal' rather than preponderant, but what was important for his career was that the new leader was convinced that he owed his nomination to Lapointe. It was after Lapointe's speech, King recorded in his diary, that 'the province almost solidly agreed to stand by me.'[55] King remembered the gesture throughout his career,[56] and he considered it appropriate in 1948, at his final Liberal convention as leader, that the first person he met was Lapointe's son Hugues, because he owed his nomination, and much else in his career, to Ernest Lapointe.[57]

King also realized that a small but powerful group led by Gouin opposed him. Ideologically Gouin was closer to Fielding, and he had not forgotten that Gouin had failed to fulfil a promise to the York North candidate (King) of a seat in Quebec after the 1917 election. He suspected Gouin's Montreal protectionist group of trying to control or overthrow him: 'I will not let the protectionists control,' he wrote in his diary. 'I don't trust [the big interests]. Wealth is out only for itself.' For many reasons, King clearly favoured the Lapointe–Bureau group over Gouin's and hesitated to encourage Gouin to enter dominion politics: 'It is clear the "big interests" want their hand in – as between Gouin and the big interests and Lapointe and the people, my alliance is with the latter.'[58]

Yet King could do little to help Lapointe. If Lapointe emerged as leader of the Quebec group, it was certainly not because King selected him. King was far from being solidly in control of the Liberal party in the years from 1919 to 1921, and complaints emerged about his leadership.

One Liberal remarked that when King was replying to the attacks of the former Liberal Newton Rowell and others, 'it seems to be the opinion among the Liberals at large that the new leader ... is not aggressive enough.'[59] Jacques Bureau told King not to worry about the press reports of conspiracy in Quebec: King was strong, 'and Lapointe is becoming a power. [Between the two of us] we can do something in the Province of Quebec.'[60] But King did worry: 'It is clear [the Gouin–Taschereau] group will be antagonistic,' he wrote in his diary. 'Much will now depend on Lapointe's strength.'[61] Lapointe's strength, not King's.

Lapointe's position in Quebec was aided by the exposure that he received during the convention and shortly afterward, when he decided to seek election in the riding of Quebec East. Lapointe gave the impression of being spontaneously drafted at a nomination meeting, but he had clearly decided in advance to seek election in the riding, vacant since Laurier's death. A by-election meant that the newspapers talked more about Lapointe, and he became increasingly known throughout his province. Le Soleil noted his 'prestige sans cesse grandissant' in parliamentary circles at Ottawa during the previous few years and suggested that 'si Lapointe n'était pas d'origine française, il serait le chef. Mais c'est le tour de l'autre côté.'[62] On 27 October 1919 he won the seat against a Labour candidate, further increasing his prestige;[63] in addition, the election proved a harbinger of things to come, symbolizing the passing of the torch in Quebec from Laurier to Lapointe.

King himself had wanted Quebec East. He had replaced his idol as leader of the party and would soon move into his house; sitting in Laurier's former seat would complete his succession: 'That I should rather have than all else,' he confided to his diary.[64] Some consider that King's initial desire to run in the francophone riding, until he became afraid of being identified too much with Quebec, shows his tolerance.[65] King's 'tolerance' would be more easily recognized as ignorance if he had been a unilingual francophone offering to represent a Toronto riding. He eventually saw that the seat was not as safe as he had thought, all other candidates fearing to confront the popular nationalist Armand Lavergne, and King even recommended that Lapointe not risk resigning his seat.[66] But King did not, would not, and could never replace Laurier in Quebec – this part of the succession would eventually fall on Lapointe's shoulders.

In the two years following his by-election victory Lapointe was increasingly recognized by the Quebec caucus and press as Quebec's voice in the federal Liberal party.[67] However, many could still refer throughout the period to Bureau, Gouin, or Lemieux as *le Chef*, or to the Quebec lieutenants at Ottawa.[68] Consequently, Lapointe cannot be considered to have consolidated his position as Quebec lieutenant before the election of December 1921.

The leading Liberals in the province were the leading Quebec politicians, despite the fact that the Union government remained in power. Francophone Quebec had no voice at all in this government, a defect that Meighen and Borden sought to fix as the election neared.[69] Liberal leaders in Quebec were approached, including Gouin, Lemieux, and Lapointe, who was the least sympathetic.[70] One Conservative also suggested appointing Lapointe to the Permanent Court of International Justice, to 'remove an opposition leader.'[71] But the Conservatives had no luck in attracting anyone to their sinking ship, least of all Lapointe, the Liberal leader with the most promising future.

Conclusions

Lapointe's background facilitated his gradual rise within the Quebec wing of the Liberal party. He grew up in an environment that encouraged the defence of francophone, Catholic rights, and as MP from 1904 to 1921 he was increasingly recognized by his people as one of their leading champions. Lapointe sought to represent Quebec when he spoke: 'La Chambre des communes est le seul lieu où puisse se faire entendre la voix de ma province.'[72] But there were limits: Lapointe's views made him much more popular with the left-wing, low-tariff, rural, agricultural elements in the party than with the big interests. Consequently, in caucus, where large corporations are often overrepresented, Lapointe was not the only, or even the leading, Liberal francophone lieutenant in 1921.

That Lapointe's socioeconomic views were compatible with King's was convenient for both leaders. Lapointe could support King's nomination, and later King could be of help to Lapointe. Both were influenced by Laurier's approach to politics, and either could have said: 'As you know, I am not doctrinaire, I am always ready to be practical on the tariff as well as on any other question.'[73] One rare criticism that King made of Laurier was that he thought Sir Wilfrid agnostic and wished that he had had more faith; Lapointe, however, he described as a good Christian.[74] Both considered themselves liberal, while accepting a certain degree of government intervention to ensure their position on the side of 'the people,' as opposed to the 'big interests.'[75] A rare criticism of Lapointe published in *Le Soleil* was one that could have been applied to King: 'Son caractère, jusqu'à ce jour, manquait peut-être de fermeté, et ses amis personnels lui reprochaient son indécision.'[76]

Lapointe had established himself by 1921 in a position that would allow him to exercise considerable influence on King in certain areas. He had risen by earning the respect of the Quebec caucus, not by being randomly selected and knighted by King, and his control over that caucus would be the key to his influence from 1921 to 1930. Lapointe did not owe King any favours; in fact, it would be more accurate to say that King was indebted to Lapointe.

PART I:
LAPOINTE'S RISE AND CANADIAN AUTONOMY,
1921–1929

2

Lapointe, Gouin, and King's Early Cabinets

The policies of the Union government during the war and the immediate aftermath had made it unpopular, for varying reasons, in many regions of Canada. The dominion election results of December 1921 confirmed the balkanization of Canadian politics. The Liberals won all sixty-five ridings in Quebec, as Meighen's Conservatives were unable to convince Quebecers to forget about the conscription crisis and let bygones be bygones.[1] In the Atlantic provinces the Maritime Rights movement was willing to trust the Liberals to defend eastern interests, but in the west the Progressive movement, voicing farmers' discontent, rejected both traditional parties and swept thirty-seven of the forty-three seats in the Prairie provinces.[2] After all the votes had been counted the Progressives had elected sixty-four MPs and the Conservatives fifty (almost all in Ontario and British Columbia); there were two Labour MPs and three independents; and the Liberals, with 116 seats, formed the first minority government at Ottawa since 1867. This context would determine the leadership style of William Lyon Mackenzie King.

King in Check

The new prime minister had no stronghold. He was not popular in his native Ontario, where he won the seat that he sought in only one of four general elections between 1911 and 1925. In addition, the Nova Scotian Fielding had received much more support from the Ontario delegation at the leadership convention of 1919 than had King, who admitted in his diary that he hesitated 'to speak in the name of a Province.'[3] King was forced to act as a conciliator between regional leaders, and the region on which he was most dependent was Quebec, where the Liberals had won

56 per cent of their seats. But he also hoped to avoid creating the appearance that Quebec dominated the party, in order to obtain backing in English Canada.[4] He needed the support of some Progressives to keep his minority government afloat, and he could not ignore Ontario, the most imperialist region, where the Liberals would need to make gains to win future majorities. The new, inexperienced prime minister would need the backing of as many of the leaders of these regional groups as possible.

King did not select the regional leaders. In Quebec, two had emerged: Gouin, representing the high-tariff, big-interest group centred in Montreal, and Lapointe, representing the low-tariff, agricultural group centred in Quebec. King clearly favoured the latter and in September 1921 promised Lapointe the portfolio of his choice. After the election, King reassured the member for Quebec East: 'I regarded him as nearest to me and would give him my confidence in full now and always. We would work out matters together. I regarded him as the real leader in Quebec, [sent for first, as promised]. Asked which portfolio he would like and said he could have it ... He said Justice would give him the prestige he needed in his province – He is worthy of Justice, is just and honourable at heart – a beautiful Christian character – he shall have it.'[5] However, Lapointe had not yet emerged as the Quebec leader, and King could not help him get his wish. When Gouin also sought Justice, King backtracked.

Gouin refused to accept Marine and Fisheries, and, on his suggestion, King 'began to urge Lapointe' to accept this less prominent post. The minister of justice would be responsible for legal questions and judicial appointments, while the minister of marine and fisheries would be responsible for fish and less important forms of patronage; Lapointe, obviously, was disappointed. Although it was a clear demotion, the prime minister was able to convince himself – if no one else – that this would help Lapointe's position in the province: 'If he was to lead in Quebec he must get good will of Montreal and be available for "outside" work. Justice would tend to isolate him, he said finally he would do anything for the sake of the party and to help me form a government – Gouin could have Justice.'[6] Lapointe might be just and worthy, but Gouin was just worth more.

King's support of Gouin, despite his seemingly overwhelming preference for Lapointe, was the result mainly of his fragile position as leader. However, King was also much closer to the 'big interests' than he would ever admit. Political scientist Reginald Whitaker has noted that men of wealth and social position were 'a source of profound ambivalence to

Mackenzie King, who alternately raised the darkest suspicions about the role of capitalism and then romantically idealized those capitalists who were his personal financial benefactors ... These contradictory impulses reflected the very profound contradiction between King's reformism and his conservativism.'[7] That Lapointe was not the leading Quebec lieutenant was again made clear when Gouin was seated next to King in cabinet.[8]

King aided Gouin more than Lapointe during the cabinet-selection process of 1921, without giving Gouin everything for which he asked. The Montreal group had major positions in cabinet, but Gouin had wanted Walter Mitchell at Finance, J.A. Robb and Lemieux as ministers, and himself as president of the Privy Council. Mitchell and Lemieux (the new Speaker) were excluded, while Gouin got Justice, Robb went to Trade and Commerce, and Raoul Dandurand became a minister without portfolio. Gouin complained that Lapointe's group was too powerful, as Jacques Bureau took over Customs and Excise and H.-S. Béland went to Re-establishment of Soldiers and Health, and King reassured Lapointe that he had resisted 'handing over Canada's future to the financial magnates of Montreal.'[9] However, he had handed over a fair chunk.

When King did refuse Gouin, he did so out of concern for his own position, not Lapointe's. For example, he did not name Gouin president of the Privy Council because he needed to keep that himself to increase his 'control and prestige in Council' as well as 'to avoid emphasis of Quebec control – it would be so regarded in other parts of Canada.' In addition, King was seeking the support of the low-tariff Progressives, who strongly opposed Gouin, a firm protectionist.[10]

When Gouin decided to leave politics, at the end of 1923, some authors suggest that King had squeezed him out, refusing to share power;[11] however, the leader of the Montreal group had considerably influenced Liberal policy. He had succeeded in convincing cabinet to accept higher tariffs than King and Lapointe desired and in preventing any serious talks of fusion with the Progressives.[12] Gouin's explanation – that he resigned because of poor health – seems much more probable. O.D. Skelton had noted in his diary during a conference just before the resignation that 'Sir Lomer is a very sick man; must give up soon.'[13] For whatever reason, Gouin did resign, and Lapointe became the leading Liberal in Quebec.

King, who had feared a coup led by the Montreal group in 1921, was perhaps too complacent after the departure of Gouin and the other leading high-tariff Liberal, W.S. Fielding. When Dandurand suggested names for King to consider as Quebec's lieutenant-governor – all members of the Montreal 'big interest' group – King decided to distance himself from this group: 'I think the time has come now to cut the Gordian knot to sever this connection completely and bring the Liberals and farmers together.'[14] Without the pressure from the 'big interests,' King felt greater freedom to take his 'own natural course'[15] – meaning lower tariffs and better relations with the Progressives. But the Liberal leader was not as solidly installed as he seemed to think.

The results of the October 1925 election revealed that the Liberal ship was sinking and sparked a mutiny. The party had fewer MPs than the Conservatives and, even with many of the Progressives coming into the party, depended on the two Labour members, A.A. Heaps and J.S. Woodsworth, to retain power. King, after losing his North York seat, found himself in a particularly vulnerable position, and at least one Toronto Liberal wished privately that 'he would drop out.'[16] Whether he remained leader depended largely on the Quebec MPs, who constituted 60 per cent of the Liberal caucus after the election. King had convinced himself that Quebecers strongly opposed his resignation and that he had 'won the hearts of the French Canadians' by staying loyal to Laurier – but he was also sure that Quebecers had forgotten about conscription. In reality, the Montreal group did not oppose his resignation, and if King were to survive he would need the support of Lapointe.[17]

Rumours had suggested that Premier Charles Dunning of Saskatchewan would become leader with Lapointe's support, that the two would become co-leaders, or that Lapointe would replace King. Journalist J.W. Dafoe, in a private letter, considered that 'there is no practicable alternative excepting Lapointe.'[18] Chubby Power remembered that many in the Quebec caucus 'thought it wouldn't do any harm' to replace King with Lapointe, but the Quebec lieutenant refused.[19] The position of the party remained extremely insecure, and Skelton advised King: 'The situation is going to be difficult in any case. It is possible that neither party can pull through, but it is clear that if any leader can snatch victory out of these difficulties he will win a prestige that will ensure power for twenty years.'[20] King's prestige grew, thanks to Lapointe's support.

Until the prime minister found a seat, someone would have to replace him in the House. Although Lapointe may have seemed the obvious choice, King's first thought was for Robb, the anglophone member of the Montreal group, aided by Lapointe. When the time came, in January 1926, King did name Lapointe interim leader, possibly in recognition of his loyalty. King seemed pleased to report that Lapointe had performed well in the House but took even greater pleasure in reporting Lapointe's problems, as he did after a close division when three Liberals were absent: 'I was not sorry Lapointe had had the anxiety he had, and has found the difficulty of leadership. It will give him a better understanding of my problem.'[21] King returned in March 1926 after winning a by-election, but his leadership remained fragile: Skelton remarked that he was 'very nervous and lacking in self-confidence.'[22]

With a shaky minority government – and many questioning its legitimacy – the prime minister had reason to worry. When a motion of censure relating to the administration of the Customs Department threatened to topple the government, King asked Governor General Lord Byng for a dissolution, which Byng refused. Byng called on Meighen, who took office and attempted to form a government, but, with no clear majority, the Conservative leader was soon forced to ask Byng for another election. The Liberals ran on the question of Canadian autonomy, and Dafoe remarked that King might win with the constitutional issue and 'make himself leader of the Liberal party which he has not yet become.' Clifford Sifton, a minister in Laurier's government, also remarked that there was 'no great faith in WLMK.'[23]

The scandal in the Customs Department did not seriously hurt the Liberals, mostly because the accusations were often exaggerated and appeared to focus disproportionately on Quebec. *Le Soleil* suggested that the branch of the department in Vancouver be looked at more closely, and the fact that one of the main Conservative prosecutors, H.H. Stevens, affirmed that Quebecers were less informed than other Canadians because of the preponderance of a unilingual press in the province made it easier for Lapointe to accuse the Conservatives of Quebec-bashing.[24] Even the 'straight-laced' Ernest Lapointe was accused of participating in 'a joy-ride' down the St Lawrence river on a government ship, much to the amusement of Chubby Power. The hard-drinking Power assured one audience 'that if it was that kind of a party ... Bureau would not have invited Ernest Lapointe to take part in it. I would have been his special guest.' Lapointe was less amused and insisted on a public inquiry to clear his name.[25]

In public, King condemned the Customs probe as 'nothing but an attack upon the province of Quebec,'[26] but in his diary his attitude was different. He was 'glad our Quebec friends' faced the pressure in Parliament alone because they had prevented action and had a different mentality on such questions. Some threatened to 'oust' King before they would accept his suggestion to 'sacrifice' the minister, Georges Boivin, and King concluded that the French-Canadian willingness to do anything for one of their number was a chivalrous attitude but, 'from the point of view of morality[,] open to question.' He promised himself never to have another French-Canadian minister at Customs. King's morality also seems to be open to question, as he was prepared to sacrifice a man he considered 'innocent' to provide Parliament with a victim 'to save the Government from defeat.'[27] After the Liberals were returned with a majority in 1926, King was more convinced than ever of his popularity in French Canada;[28] however, the prime minister needed Lapointe.

The Importance of Being Ernest Lapointe

Conservatives had predicted Lapointe's decline in 1924, but as he ensured King's place as Liberal leader, for the second time in seven years, he solidified his own position as leader of the still-large Quebec caucus.[29] After Gouin's resignation he became responsible for filling Quebec cabinet and Senate positions at Ottawa. In 1924 he ensured the appointment of P.J.A. Cardin against the opposition of Dandurand; in 1925 he favoured Lucien Cannon over King's objections, vetoed another King choice, and refused to allow King to drop Bureau from the cabinet and the Senate.[30] When Lucien Cannon entered cabinet, King believed that Lapointe had possibly offered him a position on the Supreme Court, but King added in his diary: 'What the understanding maybe between Lapointe and Cannon I do not know; this is just a surmise.'[31] Lapointe's influence on such questions was also suggested when King preferred to name to the Senate a French-Canadian friend of a party supporter who had donated $10,000 to the prime minister's personal fund but his Quebec lieutenant insisted successfully on naming Napoléon K. Laflamme – a move that King considered risky 'but one our French Canadian friends know most about.'[32]

Lapointe's influence extended, to a lesser extent, beyond Quebec. He had a say in the appointments of French Canadians of other provinces. For example, Franco-Ontarians, insisting that it was their turn for a Senate appointment, solicited his help often between 1922 and 1926. When an Irish Catholic was named on 23 December 1926, the pressure increased. King noted in his diary on 9 January 1928 that French-Canadian colleagues were insisting on a francophone senator from Ontario and were 'rather extreme in threatening not to go into Ontario to work if we didn't appoint one.' The next day, King wrote that he 'decided for Dr.

[Lacasse] because Cardin and Lapointe and Cannon favoured him.'[33] Lapointe also became increasingly responsible for many other appointments, allowing him to consolidate further his position as leader of the Quebec caucus, but it was a responsibility that he never enjoyed.[34]

The Montreal group that remained lacked enough influence to obtain for Gouin his long-sought Senate seat. When Dandurand asked King in cabinet about Gouin's seat, Lapointe replied that there was no rush. King was not only strongly favourable to appointing Gouin to the Senate, but he had even promised to do so; however, he left the decision to Lapointe.[35] Gouin wrote of his disappointment in his diary: 'King m'est favorable, Lapointe reste le gros petit homme qu'il fut et restera toujours. Grand bien lui fasse! Je demande à mes fils de ne pas oublier que deux ou trois jaloux sans crinière, temporairement aux avant-postes ne constituent pas le parti libéral, auquel j'ai donné ma vie.'[36] Lapointe did approve Gouin's appointment as lieutenant-governor of Quebec in 1928.

Although Lapointe had clearly emerged as leader of the Quebec wing of the party, his leadership remained fragile. The Montreal group had not disappeared, and King continued to be of little help. He appointed Béland to the Senate despite the opposition of Lapointe and supported the minister of public works, James H. King, by approving a public-works project in Quebec against Lapointe's wishes: 'It is a painful situation, as Lapointe needs all the help possible, but I must support the Minister who has the responsibility.'[37] King complained that Lapointe was too hesitant concerning the appointment of Lemieux to the Senate, and, when King discovered that Walter Mitchell was apparently involved in corrupt dealings, he thought that 'Lapointe should know all and take the responsibility.' King concluded: 'We are without strength in Quebec. Lapointe has no organizing capacity and is not in touch with the province. We will fare badly there [in an election].'[38] However, Lapointe realized that he risked dividing his still-fragile support if he strongly supported or opposed Lemieux and Mitchell, members of Gouin's group.

Lapointe's influence, and its limits, are apparent in 1929, when King faced increasing pressure by the United States to build a St Lawrence Seaway and the possibility of T.A. Crerar's joining the cabinet at Railways and Canals. King would not act until Lapointe returned from Europe: 'I got word Lapointe would not be back till 22nd of December which puts off conference re. St. Lawrence. A great pity and may cost us heavily with U.S. ... Lapointe should be here now, or at least leave a free hand to all who are. As to Crerar we may lose him if a decision is not speedily reached.'[39] King did not feel that he had a free hand on these questions without Lapointe's permission. Both matters involved Quebec, the province most opposed to the Seaway and most affected by Crerar's nomination, which would mean a westerner replacing a Quebec minister (J.A. Robb). Lapointe insisted successfully that King wait before appointing Crerar to Railways,[40] but the prime minister did not need Lapointe's approval on all decisions. Even on these two questions Lapointe did not have a veto because English-Canadian interests were also involved. In fact, Crerar did come in at Railways and Canals without Quebec's receiving immediate compensation. Lapointe accepted the fact that an appointment to replace Robb would be made later and that 'aucun Premier Ministre ne peut sembler avoir la main forcée quand il s'agit de choisir ses collègues.'[41] On other questions he would insist that his voice be dominant.

A possible limit to Lapointe's influence was his fragile health, which would affect him throughout his career. King first heard of this problem in 1922. He recorded in his diary: 'I was shocked to have Bureau tell me that Ernest Lapointe is a very sick man, looks like one not likely to live long according to Lemieux. This will be a very serious loss to us in Quebec, and it puts a terrible load on my shoulders.' Lapointe did live and continued to be troubled by health problems, particularly in 1926.[42] These problems, however, never seriously affected his command over the Liberal caucus from Quebec.

In addition, Lapointe continued to have little influence with the provincial Liberals led by Taschereau and the Quebec nationalists. Armand Lavergne criticized Lapointe, as Lapointe had criticized him twenty years earlier, for speaking English in the House of Commons.[43] Lapointe's relations were, however, better with Henri Bourassa. Because Lapointe hoped to reconcile these groups and maintain as large a base of support as possible for himself and for his party, both groups influenced his liberalism, encouraging him to take an increasingly strong stance to guarantee provincial autonomy. From his first year as minister he promised that none would be a more ardent defender. During the 1920s he gradually convinced Quebecers that he could and would look after their interests at Ottawa.[44]

Lapointe's liberalism, like Laurier's, was shaped to a great extent by the desire to ensure unity. For both men this meant encouraging tolerance and compromise: 'Those who are entrusted with public functions,' Lapointe announced in 1928, 'are trustees, not for one class, not for one section of the country, but for the whole people of the country at large, and it is their duty to find what are the causes of divergence of opinions and even of interests, and try to find, if possible, the concessions which it may be desirable to give or obtain. Some members have said that they are sick of the word compromise. Mr. Speaker, compromise has been the policy upon which this country was built.'[45] Lapointe's search for unity through compromise characterized his career, although as he was Quebec lieutenant to an anglophone prime minister his idea of compromise was not the same as Laurier's.

French-Canadian Concerns

Questions that risked dividing francophones and anglophones were clearly Lapointe's priority. With most Canadians of British origin (about 55 per cent of the population in 1921) seeing their country as a homogeneous English-speaking nation of the British Empire, and most Canadians of French origin (about 30 per cent of the population) perceiving Canada as a bilingual association of two nations, the two visions often collided. While Lapointe fought for the extension of francophone rights, King was convinced that he exaggerated the risks posed by unilingual government services.[46] For example, the government had accepted, during the Confederation jubilee celebrations of 1927, the issue of some bilingual stamps. But King did not want bilingualism to become a habit: 'We have made a mistake in permitting them beyond the special issue for the Diamond Jubilee' he told Dandurand in 1929, adding that 'I looked to him to influence Veniot, Lapointe and Cardin.' King felt that it was a 'mistake politically to press this bilingual business too far.' A year later, after losing power to the Conservatives, King consoled himself with the thought that the minister responsible for issuing the bilingual stamps, Pierre-Jean Veniot, would find out that 'new ministers will give short shrift to the bilingual stamps. I hope they end them.'[47] Lapointe's struggle to become bilingual and use both languages in the House of Commons impressed Bourassa – as an example to anglophones – but probably not King.[48] Arthur Meighen was one of the very few anglophones who attempted to learn French, and his efforts were applauded by francophone MPs, but not by King, who condemned Meighen's 'intellectual arrogancy – for the French I am told was poor.'[49]

Because he sought unity, important economic questions – which did not divide anglophones and francophones – rarely attracted Lapointe's attention. He admitted to Parliament in 1924 that 'les questions de commerce n'ont pas le don de provoquer de fanatisme chez moi, les mots "protection" et "libre-échange" ne sont pas, pour moi, les mots de combat qu'ils semblent être pour certains de mes amis favorables ou hostiles à ces régimes économiques.'[50] When he intervened in debate on tariff policy he insisted that he sought to further the interests of the entire population, not those of certain classes.[51] On one occasion he did argue in favour of the imperial trade preference, announcing that the trade barriers of the United States – Canada's natural partner – made a British alliance preferable, and he was generally inclined more often to free trade than to protection but was always ready to compromise on these questions.[52]

The economic issues of most interest to Lapointe concerned the larger transformations in the economy. Rapid industrialization and urbanization led to dominion–provincial disagreements over jurisdiction (and to greater dependence on U.S. direct investment in Canada, which rose from $1.6 million in 1918 to $4.7 million in 1930, alarming French-Canadian nationalist groups).[53] Many of the debates concerning the appropriate role for the state shared two common denominators: they divided francophones and anglophones, and they came under the Department of Justice. The position adopted by Lapointe in these debates demonstrates effectively that he was much more a Quebec lieutenant, defending francophone views, than a minister of justice, defending federal jurisdiction.

In the late 1920s the Quebec lieutenant, with Bourassa, insisted on guarantees concerning the control of bilingual, Catholic separate school lands during the negotiations for the transfer of the Prairie provinces' natural resources from dominion to provincial responsibility.[54] King was convinced that Lapointe exaggerated the potential risks: he repeated throughout that Lapointe was 'creating a crisis,' was 'terrified of Bourassa,' and only made his job more difficult.[55] King's account of one meeting reveals much about how he conducted cabinet meetings: 'Lapointe I fear may draw us into a school question. Dunning [spokesman for the west on this issue] is not standing out against him as he should.'[56] Ultimately, the prime minister followed the advice of Lapointe, and agreements were signed without any serious problems in Alberta or Quebec.

When francophone Quebec opposed the extension of Ottawa's role in social programs, Lapointe, arguing that such matters came under provincial jurisdiction, opposed unemployment insurance and old age pensions. Under pressure from Labour MPs, the Quebec lieutenant did accept, in cooperation with the provinces, a modest federal pension program (which was defeated in the Senate).[57]

Lapointe also used provincial jurisdiction to justify his cautious approach to 'women's issues.' He announced his support for overturning the court ruling of April 1928 declaring women ineligible for the Senate because they were not 'persons' and confided privately to Thérèse Casgrain that he favoured granting women the right to vote. But, with Quebec being the last province to adopt such a policy, he insisted that Ottawa should not discuss this question, which came under provincial jurisdiction.[58] After hesitating to take a clear stand on the bills facilitating divorce, which sharply divided Catholic MPs from others, he came out strongly against divorce. Not only was divorce a matter for the provinces, it was also 'detrimental to the public good: instead of making it easier,' he argued, 'we should endeavour to suppress it.'[59]

These views greatly influenced King, who during the discussion in 1930 of a divorce bill presented by J.S. Woodsworth was surprised that Lapointe opposed the debate: 'It is astonishing how afraid the Catholics are of their Church,' King wrote. Lapointe confided to King that if a Quebec MP did not oppose the bill he would not dare be a candidate again. 'Hardly conceivable,' King felt, but he admitted that this stance influenced him and he decided not to cast his favourable vote, which would have broken the eighty-seven–eighty-seven tie. Instead, it was the Speaker, Lemieux, who broke the tie with his 'no' vote.[60] King followed Lapointe's advice closely concerning divorce, as he had on whether or not to accept an invitation from a Catholic delegation, not because it involved the justice department but because it risked dividing francophones and anglophones.[61]

Lapointe again defended provincial autonomy in 1927. A dominion–provincial conference was called to discuss the increasing expenses of the provinces, immigration, Senate reform, and – Lapointe's priority – a formula for amending the constitution by Canadians. Premier G.H. Ferguson of Ontario and Taschereau saw no reason to reform the Senate but did agree to dominion subsidies to the Maritime provinces in return for their support to help defeat a proposed formula for amending the constitution that Lapointe was advocating.[62] Taschereau feared for provincial rights, arguing that Quebec 'unanimously' agreed with him, an affirmation that Lapointe questioned.[63] Whether Ottawa needed provincial consent to implement Lapointe's constitutional amending formula was unclear, but Lapointe announced that for him – especially concerning the provinces that signed the original Confederation pact – it was necessary: 'Le pouvoir fédéral est l'enfant des provinces; il n'en est pas le père.' He added prophetically that Ottawa's imposing its will would not solve the problem harmoniously.[64] When asked by Ferguson if he represented the views of the government, Lapointe replied: 'In a way I do.' Although King had been less eager to have Ottawa's hands tied,[65] an important precedent had been established.

The minister did not have the final say on all justice issues, which were often decided by a cabinet vote.[66] However, for any question involving Quebec or that risked dividing Canadians, Lapointe's voice, as Quebec lieutenant, would be much more influential – and often dominant – in cabinet. He prevented consideration in cabinet in 1928 of the St Lawrence Seaway project, insisting that Quebec was not yet ready for it. He also played a leading role in the discussions to determine jurisdiction over the increasingly significant area of hydroelectric power.[67]

In international affairs the crucial questions dividing francophones and anglophones involved imperial relations, and the prime minister's views were not always clear. Certainly Mackenzie King opposed a common imperial foreign policy in the first half of the 1920s. He wrote in his diary that 'one feels that Canada has everything to lose and nothing to gain by merging its identity in an imperialistic programme which will lead to the control of its affairs by a people who regard themselves as superior, but who merit only equality of status and nothing more.' He was thus closer to the autonomist position than to the imperialist position of someone like Fielding, whom he considered a 'colonial ... out of joint with our times.' But he certainly did not seek to cut all links with the empire and considered the autonomist J. Ewart 'too extreme,' in his desire for separation from Britain.[68] Ewart believed that King had no clearcut views of nationalism and imperialism,[69] and the prime minister was certainly much more favourable than the autonomists, led by Lapointe, to the maintenance of close contacts with Britain.

An incident in 1928 illustrates how attached King was to the empire. Cabinet was considering the building of two Canadian destroyers, and King was surprised that 'Lapointe and others had become largely committed' to their construction in Canada. King feared the 'danger of corruption in Quebec etc.,' had assumed that they would be built in England, and thought that Lapointe had agreed. When he was silent, King wrote, 'I confess I felt hurt.' Isolated in cabinet, King announced that if cabinet insisted on building the ships in Canada it would be without his consent, and he stormed out to see the governor general, who agreed that creating jobs in England rather than in Canada was a good idea. King proudly recorded that the governor general saw that 'I was really trying to help the motherland.'[70] This was not the motivation that fuelled Lapointe's actions.

Throughout the period from 1921 to 1929 the Quebec lieutenant was keenly aware that francophones eagerly sought greater autonomy from the empire. Quebec newspapers focused on the issue, most notably during the dominion election campaign of 1926, when King remarked that the constitutional question in Quebec 'appears to be superior to all the others.'[71] Meighen attempted to shed his obsequious colonial image by suggesting in a speech at Hamilton, Ontario, that an election be called before any troops could be sent to any war overseas. Lapointe replied that he hoped that Meighen was not attempting to please Quebec by promising another divisive referendum in time of war.[72] Despite such occasional interventions, English Canadians were generally less interested in Canadian autonomy.

As ties were loosening with London, they were strengthening with Washington. On some questions both trends coexisted, such as the signing of the Halibut Treaty, the establishment of the first Canadian legation abroad, and certain issues in the League of Nations. Lapointe was interested in these matters, but less so in uniquely Canadian–American relations. The latter dimension was important – particularly the Canadian reply to American tariffs and the Canadian policy concerning the export of liquor after the United States went dry –[73] but did not present a great risk to francophone-anglophone relations.

Conclusion

During the period from 1921 to 1929, King was not in a solid position and needed to rely on the support of regional and factional leaders. At the start of the period he had been seeking the support of the Progressive T.A. Crerar and wrote in his diary that 'if the three of us [Crerar, Lapointe, and King] ever get together on the one platform we will be able to sweep the country.'[74] At the end of the period the three were united on the Liberal platform, Crerar and Lapointe representing their regions in a political system in which King, still not solidly installed as leader in 1929, acted as conciliator.[75]

Lapointe was able to establish a place to stand for himself to wield influence by accumulating a variety of resources. First, he was a convincing speaker: 'Vous avez vraiment le tempérament du parlementaire,' Dandurand told him; 'J'admire votre flegme.' King often remarked that Lapointe had made an effective speech – that 'he has a very happy way of expressing himself.'[76] Second, he had proved his loyalty to King. When Lapointe returned to the House after an absence, King remarked that it was good to have him back: 'It is indeed a fortunate thing that I have so true and able a colleague from the Province of Quebec.'[77] Third, and most important of all, Lapointe had a solid base of support, which included most of the Quebec caucus. In 1921 he shared this invaluable resource with Gouin; but its size allowed both men to enjoy considerable weight in the decision-making process. After 1926 the Liberal caucus was slightly smaller, but Lapointe had greater control. The Quebec nationalists threatened his position as voice of Quebec, but he was able to convince most of his people that he was a sufficiently strong defender of francophone-Catholic rights.

The areas that interested Quebec – and risked dividing francophones and anglophones – interested Lapointe. The guiding star of all his actions, he claimed, was the effect that they would have on unity; his principal objective was to remove, without animosity, all relics of colonialism.[78] As Parliament rarely discussed such matters, and others in cabinet showed little interest, to a large extent King, representing the anglophones who sought slightly more autonomy in the future, and Lapointe, representing the francophones who sought considerably more autonomy immediately, decided Canadian foreign policy during the period.

3

Autonomy in the Empire:
A Sure-Fire Reliable

Between 1917 and 1921 the Conservative-Union government had hoped that Canada would have a voice in a common imperial foreign policy. However, the First World War and subsequent conferences revealed the technical difficulties in such an arrangement, as well as British hesitation to implement such a policy. Probably the Conservatives would have changed Canada's course, but it was the Liberal party that won in 1921, abandoned the common imperial foreign policy, and governed up to the declaration of dominion equality in 1926.[1] Some historians acclaim Canada's progression from a colony to a nation, others condemn the betrayal of Britain and regret Canadian vulnerability to American influence; some praise or blame the prime minister, while others argue that his freedom of action was very limited. Common to most interpretations is the assumption that W.L. Mackenzie King, more than any other individual in Canadian politics, was responsible for advances in this direction.[2] Certainly King agreed, up to 1923, with Ernest Lapointe, most francophones, and English-Canadian autonomists that Canadians should seek more their own interests rather than British Empire interests.[3] But after the Imperial Conference of 1923, King seemed satisfied, and further advances towards Canadian autonomy were greatly influenced by the prodding of Lapointe.

Canada and the Chanak Crisis: Firmly Noncommittal

Less than a year after the election of December 1921, and less than three years after the war to end all wars, the Liberal government was forced to decide whether or not it would accede to another British request for troops. The Turkish nationalists, led by Mustapha Kemal Pasha, had recently overthrown the sultan and repudiated the terms of the Treaty of Sèvres of 1920. Advancing Turkish soldiers threatened the British garrison at Chanak. In mid-September 1922 the British government, led by David Lloyd George, decided to intervene, and Winston Churchill, the colonial secretary, asked the dominions if they 'would desire to be represented by a contingent.'[4]

When King first heard – from a journalist – of Churchill's request he replied that he would have to meet cabinet before making a statement: Canada's is not 'a one man government,' he added.[5] The Liberal government's reply to London, typical of its policy on questions involving military commitments to the empire during the interwar years, went on 18 September: 'It is the view of the Government that public opinion in Canada would demand authorization on the part of Parliament as a necessary preliminary to the despatch of a contingent to participate in the conflict of the Near East. We will welcome the fullest possible information in order to decide upon the advisability of summoning Parliament.'[6] Two days later Lloyd George sought a statement that 'Canada will stand by the empire in the event of terms of Armistice being broken,' but Canada remained noncommittal, insisting that its Parliament would decide policy.[7]

Most historians have agreed that King's policy during the Chanak crisis 'was all his own work.' There is much truth in this, as the policy of no commitments in advance was formulated and announced by the prime minister. However, when historians imply that Lapointe shared King's views or that, if he was consulted at all, he was willing to accept whatever King decided, they underestimate the cleavage between the two men.[8] Lapointe did not share King's views. Although the crisis fizzled without incident, the split between the two, which would widen during future crises, was present.

King was annoyed at Churchill's request and the way in which it was delivered. He suspected that it was either an 'imperial game, to test out centralization vs. autonomy as regards European wars' or an election manoeuvre. King believed that Canadians opposed the sending of troops and attempted to use the issue of 'Canada vs. imperialism, the people vs. the jingoes' to bring Crerar and the Progressives into the government and thus lessen the impression of Quebec domination. Thus Ottawa would seek more information, and any decision to go to war would be made by Parliament.[9] King did not mention what information would satisfy him that a Canadian contingent was necessary, but clearly he was somewhere between 'Ready, aye ready' and 'Never, nay never.' Lapointe's voice was also somewhere between these two extremes, but much closer to the latter.

At the time of the crisis Lapointe was attending a session of the League of Nations Assembly in Geneva with the most imperialist member of the cabinet, W.S. Fielding. King sought their opinions, and on 18 September Fielding wired: 'We heartily approve attitude British government respecting Constantinople. Would willingly have some statement made on behalf of our Government indicating readiness to participate if necessary, but send troops abroad at present without parliamentary authority very undesirable. Cannot something be said that will serve the purpose without actual sending of contingent.'[10] Because Fielding and Lapointe – the two extremes of the cabinet – were both expressing their views, it is impossible to determine Lapointe's stance from this telegram.

That Fielding, the head of the Canadian delegation, exaggerated Lapointe's 'hearty' approval of the British position is suggested by a message that Lapointe sent to King the following day: 'Regarding our official cable, I was glad my colleague agreed to two essential conditions, necessity and consent of Parliament. Be governed by Canadian public opinion. Imperial authorities should not have made such a request. French newspapers and part of the English press very critical. Would advise delaying answer and being non-committal. Doubtful if France will join and seems certain Italy will not.'[11] Lapointe makes no mention of a promise to send troops or of the need to seek more information; in addition, he is much more critical of the British attitude than Fielding. The next day Lapointe sent another telegram to King, announcing that 'appeal to Dominion deemed not judicious everywhere. Press strongly hostile to war. Seems untrue that France and Italy have agreed. British Government likely changing its attitude.'[12] Lapointe did not have the same views as Fielding, and yet both seemed agreed as to what the Canadian reply should be.

After King's statement, Fielding again wired, expressing the views of Lapointe and himself: 'Lapointe concurs entirely in your action. In the main I concur, but if I had been with you I would have advised the making of a more emphatic statement of our willingness to co-operate in case of actual war.'[13] Fortunately for King, actual war never came, and most Canadians, even those with views as divergent as those of Fielding and Lapointe, seemed to approve of King's stance, leading the prime minister to believe the Canadian position 'justified beyond our dreams.'[14] But public opinion approved the policy for varying reasons, and Canadian unity on this decision was a fragile illusion.

The English-Canadian 'imperialists,' led by Meighen, were 'Ready, aye ready,' to stand by Britain. The number of English Canadians caught up in the emotional movement to support the empire was considerable enough to be of great concern to King. He wrote in his diary: 'I am sure the people of Canada are against participation in this European war. However the issue is serious [and] it will arouse jingoism and with jingoism passion, which combined with the prejudice against me on account of conscription and war feeling still lingering, will mean a heavy and difficult role for me.' Two days later he added that 'if we judge by the voices that are heard through the press and in resolutions, the other forces are silent. It is amazing how readily the country will yield to jingoism.' He remained convinced that most Liberals and Progressives opposed the idea of committing Canada in advance to participate in Britain's war. However, King noted a desire to satisfy 'jingo sentiment' even in the Liberal cabinet: '[Solicitor General] D.D. Mackenzie was for recognition of principle that when Britain is at war we are at war, which others agreed to, with premise that it is for us to determine our part in the conflict. He was for approving British position and stand. [Minister of the Interior Charles] Stewart [of] Alberta was for getting in some word of approving "attitude," sound the British note to satisfy Jingo sentiment somewhat, if that could be arranged.'[15] Had war broken out, English Canadians would have been even more inclined to support British policy.

Francophone's opinions appear similar to those of anglophones who hesitated to follow British policy. Both groups favoured greater Canadian autonomy when questions of war and peace remained academic; however, francophones not only sought the right to remain neutral, they intended to exercise this right. They did not agree that when Britain is at war Canada is at war. Had war broken out at Chanak, francophones would have strongly opposed Canadian participation, as indicated by comments of the Saint-Jean Baptiste Society, of Henri Bourassa in *Le Devoir*, and by writers in *Le Droit* and *Le Soleil*. Most francophones argued not only that Canada should not help Britain but even that Britain was wrong.[16]

King sought to follow anglophone opinion, and Lapointe, francophone. A policy of no commitments proved acceptable to both Lapointe, who later described it as a decision not to send soldiers,[17] and to King, who sought more information on the situation. Lapointe, who had announced before the Chanak affair that 'notre politique sera à base canadienne toujours et partout. Notre pays est le Canada,' was recognized by many francophones as the autonomist influence on King.[18] After the crisis, Lapointe announced that Chanak had established that it would be Parliament that would decide whether the country would participate in wars affecting other parts of the empire.[19] Lapointe was also more eager than King to emphasize that Ottawa would not be bound by the British signature on the Lausanne treaty of July 1923 with Turkey: Canada would not be responsible for negotiations in which it took no part or for treaties not ratified by Parliament.[20] King agreed, and he was glad when Britain did not invite the dominions to sign the Treaty of Lausanne, but he preferred to avoid conflict with the mother country and did not draw attention to Canada's position. King resented the 'jingoes,' and the fact that some British officials expected the dominions to back them up on everything, but he remained more open to the possibility of aiding the empire.[21]

During the crisis Lapointe did not directly push King to act; the British request was so insulting to dominion autonomy that it offended the visions of empire of both Lapointe and King. King could thus reply knowing that many English Canadians and almost all French Canadians would approve a no-commitment policy. Had war erupted, the differences between the two men would have emerged; but it did not. The voices of both King and Lapointe thus corresponded with Canadian policy.

The Halibut Treaty

In addition to deciding on war and peace, signing treaties was another mark of dominion autonomy. Canada had been negotiating its own commercial treaties since 1907, but the British ambassador to the country concerned had always signed for the empire. Many in London still agreed with Lord Ripon's doctrine enunciated in 1895: 'To give the colonies the power of negotiating treaties for themselves without reference to Her Majesty's Government would be to give them an international status as separate and sovereign states, and would be equivalent to breaking up the Empire into a number of independent states.'[22] In the early 1920s the British government was more receptive to considering greater autonomy and seemed ready to consider the possibility of granting permission for a dominion to sign treaties – if the dominion insisted. In 1923 the Canadian minister of marine and fisheries and King decided to insist on signing an international treaty with the United States – concerning conservation of halibut stock – without the signature of the British ambassador to the United States, Sir Auckland Geddes.

Lapointe was determined to sign alone for Canada and did, on 2 March 1923 in Washington, DC, with American Secretary of State Charles Evans Hughes signing for the United States. Ottawa had delayed telling the British of its plans, anticipating opposition, and indeed Geddes wanted to sign the treaty with Lapointe. Two weeks before the ceremony, he asked Ottawa 'whether Mr. Lapointe will sign treaty with me.' King replied that 'my ministers are of the opinion that as respects Canada, signature of the treaty by Mr. Lapointe alone will be sufficient and that it will not be necessary for you to sign as well.' Geddes continued to object, but London acquiesced.[23]

According to historian R.M. Dawson, when Lapointe went to sign the document the atmosphere was tense, and he was glad that the Americans broke the silence, but Dawson appears to exaggerate when he claims that the British embassy resented the gesture and omitted the courtesies of meeting and communicating with Lapointe.[24] Lapointe told the story to his family, possibly as a joke, that he was alone in a taxi, urging the driver to hurry to arrive before the British.[25] The story that Meighen presented in Parliament – that Lapointe was impolite, and even 'elbowed' the British representative – also seems to have been intended as a joke.[26]

Although Lapointe formally signed the document, most historians who refer to the treaty have argued that King was solely responsible for insisting that Canada sign alone.[27] Stacey points out that the Conservatives also had considered signing a treaty in 1919 with the United States but did not push when their idea met resistance in Britain's Foreign Office. It was not until 1923 that King, less concerned with British resistance, seized the moment. Stacey adds that King preferred to make his stance on halibut rather than on renegotiation in 1922 of the Rush–Bagot Treaty of 1817, limiting naval armaments on the Great Lakes, because the Halibut Treaty seemed to affect only Canadian and American interests.[28] However, British interests could be found – by anyone who sought them – just as easily in the halibut issue.[29]

King definitely preferred that Canadian representatives sign international treaties, without having to add the signature of any British representative. However, as with the Union government in 1919, King was not eager to establish the precedent against British resistance. In the summer of 1922, when King had visited Washington, DC, to discuss renegotiation of the Rush-Bagot Treaty, Secretary of State Hughes proposed a draft treaty. King sent the proposal to London, with the following note: 'As for the method of signature of the proposed Treaty our view is that, having regard to the character and implications of the document, it would be appropriate that the full powers should be issued to Canadian subjects of His Majesty.'[30] The British did not answer the references to the signing of the treaty, and King did not insist; in fact, the treaty was never signed. King had not insisted that Fielding sign treaties in Europe without the British representatives, and if he did so vis-à-vis Lapointe and the Halibut Treaty it was largely because the minister of marine and fisheries (Lapointe) was even more determined.

Lapointe had fought for establishment of the precedent even before he became a minister. He wondered, in April 1921, why Canada did not sign treaties on its own: 'Pourquoi toujours passer par le "Bureau des Affaires Etrangères de Londres"?' And when he became a minister he sought to establish a precedent.[31] A week before the signing of the Halibut Treaty, King wrote that 'Geddes is determined to figure in the transaction, we [King and Lapointe] see no need for that.' But the person who would have to insist was Lapointe, not King. The prime minister wrote in his diary that he hoped that Lapointe would sign alone: 'I hope so, I hope he will be firm, though would not be surprised if he yielded to Geddes under pressure.'[32] The Conservatives had yielded in 1919, as King had in 1922, but Lapointe was more determined than King realized.

In English Canada there was opposition. Meighen, of course, opposed the precedent, later calling it a useless, indelicate gesture harmful to the empire.[33] Even some Liberal ministers were opposed. Fielding, who had recently signed economic treaties in the name of King's government with France and Italy, was the minister most favourable to continuing with the former procedure. Concerning the treaty with Italy he told the House that 'whatever others may have said, it appeared to me that the name of the distinguished Principal Secretary of State for Foreign Affairs, Lord Curzon of Kedleston, rather added to the weight of this document, and I was glad to have it there.'[34] The signing of the Halibut Treaty, however, aroused little emotion in English Canada.

In Quebec the press was very much interested in the precedent for Canadian autonomy. The title of Le Soleil's front page article on Lapointe's trip to Washington was 'L'Autonomie,' and the signing was referred to as Lapointe's act.[35] During the parliamentary debate on the question, an editorialist praised the role of Lapointe and his considerable influence in advancing Canadian interests.[36] It would have been hard to find any francophone who opposed the precedent. In cabinet Dandurand asked Fielding why British government representatives signed treaties without their ambassador but Canadian government representatives required such aid: 'Pourquoi cette difference si ce n'est qu'il voyait en nous des "colonials" toujours en tutelle.'[37]

The prime minister, more influenced by English-Canadian pressure, approached the matter with more caution than the Quebec lieutenant. After Lapointe had signed the treaty, he and the prime minister exchanged private congratulatory telegrams,[38] but King played down the importance of the episode in Parliament. He noted that Canada had signed the Treaty of Versailles and other treaties in its own name, and he emphasized that such acts would ensure the strength and durability of the empire, not end it.[39] Lapointe, representing Quebec, was more willing to admit, and even stretch, the meaning of the precedent. Canada had signed Versailles, but this was an act of Canadian courtesy with no judicial significance, according to Lapointe, because Canada was already bound by Britain's signature.[40] The Quebec lieutenant, using arguments more political than legal, placed little emphasis on the unity of the empire: 'Nous sommes l'une des nations de l'univers et les Canadiens n'ont pas à en rougir,' he insisted.[41]

Lapointe's role in pushing King was recognized at the time: 'The battle of the halibut had been won by Mr. Lapointe,' according to one observer.[42] Meighen, in a private letter to Robert Borden (who approved of the signing), 'did not like the exclusion of the British ambassador at the hands of Messrs. King and Lapointe.'[43] In the House, the leader of the opposition made clear that he held Lapointe at least as responsible as King for the action. He reminded the prime minister that Fielding had approved of the participation of the British ambassador during negotiations and the signing of treaties, but that Lapointe did not, and that the government approved this attitude.[44] The instigator he identifies as Lapointe, who would soon sign other international treaties.[45]

The difference between King and Lapointe on this issue was not enormous and should not be exaggerated. Canadian policy regarding signing of the Halibut Treaty clearly corresponds with the views of both men. Certainly King would not have asked W.S. Fielding to sign. A British observer remarked in 1926 that Fielding had the French treaty signed also by the British ambassador, for he would have done it no other way, while the fishing agreement was signed by Lapointe, 'a more recent minister,' from the generation seeking new status.[46] King was from the same generation and favoured the precedent; however, he was not so eager to press the issue when met by British resistance. As the relationship between Britain and the dominions evolved, the differing views of the two would become increasingly apparent.

Defining Dominion Status at the Imperial Conference of 1926

The relationship between London and the dominions in 1926 was not the same as it had been in 1921, but exactly how much it had changed was unclear. Some dominion prime ministers preferred to clarify the situation, and defining this new relationship became the principal objective of the Imperial Conference of 1926. Establishing the role and responsibilities of the dominions was particularly important concerning questions of war and peace: were they committed to participate in British wars, or did they have the right to decide their own policies – including the right to remain neutral in a major war involving Britain?

The Balfour Declaration that emerged from the conference defined the dominions as follows: 'They are autonomous Communities within the British Empire, equal in status, in no way subordinate one to another in any aspect of their domestic or external affairs, though united by a common allegiance to the Crown, and freely associated as members of the British Commonwealth of Nations.' The definition formally recognized equality between the dominions and Britain and, despite the protests of some Conservative imperialists that the definition changed nothing, the word 'commonwealth' began to replace the word 'empire.'[47]

Historians have focused on the role played by King at the conference. Acting as mediator between the dominions pushing for independence (South Africa and the Irish Free State) and those resisting (Australia and New Zealand), King convinced Prime Minister Hertzog of South Africa not to insist on including the word 'independent' in the declaration. According to Thompson and Seager, 'King was nervous about the term "independent," for it violated his concept of the Commonwealth and threatened to have political repercussions among English Canadians who felt attached to the Empire.'[48] How he attempted to persuade the Australian and New Zealand delegates to modify their position is less clear, yet historians give the impression that King, representing the Canadian point of view, preferred a middle road, or greater autonomy.[49]

King might have been expected to lead the charge towards a clear definition of Canadian–British relations. After opposing Canadian participation at Chanak in 1922, he had led the attacks against the idea of a common imperial foreign policy at the Imperial Conference of 1923.[50] The journalist J.W. Dafoe considered that this conference in 1923 'was the decisive moment [for dominion autonomy] and that in 1926 it was simply a case of mopping up the situation';[51] however, King saw little to mop up in 1926. He had never intended to end all imperial cooperation – even in questions of war. He had told the conference in 1923 that 'if a great and clear call of duty comes,' as in 1914, Canada would be at Britain's side: 'Our attitude is not one of unconditional isolation,' he added, 'nor is it one of unconditional intervention.'[52] Consequently, apart from his wish to limit the powers of the governor general,[53] King was not interested in seeking further autonomy in 1926 and showed very little interest in the conference. Just before the meetings, O.D. Skelton complained that King 'has not yet read through the agenda. It requires a tremendous belief in one's star or one's secretary to go into an Empire Conference in such shape.'[54]

King's vision of empire is best seen by comparing the influence of O.D. Skelton as it was in 1923 and in 1926. At his first conference, King had followed closely the suggestions of adviser Skelton. But after becoming undersecretary of state at External Affairs, in March 1925, Skelton's influence was much less obvious at the conference in 1926 when his recommendations differed from what the prime minister wanted to hear. King increasingly considered Skelton too anti-British. Skelton recorded in his diary: 'I defend ultimate independence, which he [King] opposes,'[55] while King remarked in his diary that Skelton 'is at heart against the British Empire, which I am not. I believe in the larger whole, with complete independence of the parts united by cooperation in all common ends.'[56] This is what King believed that most Canadians wanted in 1926, and Skelton – who had no resource other than his technical expertise to use against King when the two disagreed, and depended on the prime minister for his job – could do little to alter King's policy. Certainly historians who claim that Skelton was King's most, or only, influential adviser have exaggerated his role.[57]

The main pressure in the 1926 Canadian delegation for a more autonomist definition of the dominions came neither from King nor from Skelton but rather from Lapointe, who had clearly and consistently opposed commitments for Canadian participation in any British war.[58] At the conference of 1923 French Canadians were represented by Sir Lomer Gouin, who, according to Skelton, was much less eager for autonomy than Lapointe.[59] One indication of this difference was Lapointe's campaign to abolish the granting of titles.[60] At the conference of 1926, when he presided over the committee on treaty procedures and participated in committees on dominion appeals to the Privy Council and on the Locarno guarantees, Lapointe sided much more than King with the group pushing for independence.

Lapointe had the weight of the francophone population behind his views, and he knew that francophones sought a clearly defined independent status. Just before the conference, Henri Bourassa, speaking on the Locarno treaties, had appeared to King as 'most agreeable and far from anti-British. He said he had declared a truce on independence so long as the imperialists kept the truce on avoiding their extreme measures.'[61] But the Quebec lieutenant knew the views of Bourassa, who encouraged him to be firm in his quest for greater autonomy: 'Je suis plus persuadé que jamais qu'en faisant bloc avec les Irlandais et Afrikanders vous pouvez faire ce que vous voulez à la conférence. Mais ne laissez pas glisser la lame entre l'arbre et l'écorce.'[62] After the conference, Bourassa acknowledged Lapointe's importance: 'Dans cette marche vers le vrai progrès ... nul, parmi nos hommes publics, n'a exercé une action plus efficace que celle du Ministre de la Justice.'[63] *Le Soleil* consistently opposed a common imperial foreign policy and presented Lapointe as the 'guide' for King in the Canadian fight against entangling alliances. The prime minister had spoken at Quebec, when leaving for the conference, of 'maintaining' Canadian autonomy.[64]

Skelton fully appreciated Lapointe's role and relied on his influence to keep King on track. On one occasion during the conference when King participated without Lapointe in a private committee of prime ministers only, Skelton feared the worst. When Lord Balfour sought to turn the declaration of equality demand 'into a pledge of one Empire and one Crown interdependence,' Skelton remarked to his wife, 'He pretty well carried W.L.M.K. with him. I wish Lapointe were on that committee.'[65] On other occasions Skelton complained that King spent too much time at 'dinners [and] portrait sittings' and not enough time on conference questions; he concluded that with Hertzog 'ready to go off on unexpected tangents ... the Irish and Mr. Lapointe are our only sure-fire reliables.'[66] According to D.B. MacRae, who covered the conference for the *Manitoba Free Press*, 'Lapointe and Skelton seemed to be on the right track but King was side-stepping,' more interested in social obligations.[67]

The difference between the views of King and those of Lapointe concerning dominion status – in practical terms, as opposed to the more abstract declaration – was illustrated during the discussion of the Locarno treaties. Lapointe had argued before the conference that the dominions were not bound by Britain's signature on the treaties.[68] At the conference he again made a strong speech against Canada's signing them: the benefits resulting from the additional obligations in a European field, he explained, 'while of interest to us as to all the world, [are] not our primary concern.'[69] Concerning the possibility of a war involving one part of the empire and not others, Lapointe specified: 'If we do not sign the question remains as it was, to be settled as occasion arises in the light of the conditions and needs of that day, and in full regard of our obligations as a member of the British Commonwealth and of the League of Nations.'[70] But after Lapointe spoke, King, while opposing automatic commitments, was much more willing to offer a clear assurance, as he did in 1923, that Canada would help Britain in any major war.[71]

That Lapointe had pushed the Canadian position further towards autonomy than King would have on his own is also suggested by the reaction of both men after the conference. On the one hand, Lapointe was eager to draw attention to the statement of dominion equality and to the interpretation that Canada would not be committed to respect the Locarno treaties, arguing that the country, though influenced by League and empire obligations, was master of its destiny. Much had changed at the gathering, Lapointe insisted.[72] However, he had argued even before the conference that Canada was not bound by the Locarno treaties. On the other hand, King was markedly less eager to draw attention to the Canadian position concerning the Locarno treaties and the Balfour Declaration.[73] When W.T. Cosgrave and D. Fitzgerald from the Irish delegation visited Ottawa, King noted privately that they were 'so outspoken on the subject of status, I almost feared our Tory friends think Lapointe and I have gone too far in trying to help the Irish.'[74]

In addition, after the declaration of dominion equality, Lapointe was much more determined to ensure that the principle was put into practice. In 1927 he attended the technical Conference on the Limitation of Naval Armaments in Geneva. He reported to Skelton that he had persuaded the British representative to specify in his statement to the conference that he was speaking only for Britain.[75] More important, Lapointe led the Canadian delegation to the conference in 1929 that sought to translate into constitutional form the equality principles established in 1926. In the words of Skelton, it wished to consider 'how far it is possible to remove every remaining vestige of Imperial legislative supremacy, save for the present the power of the British Parliament to amend the Canadian Constitution.' Lapointe insisted that Parliament in Ottawa wait for the consent of all provinces before seeking this power.[76] There would be no compromise: it was 'better not to touch the matter at all,' Skelton told King, 'than attempt to maintain the dominance of the United Kingdom in half the field and thus increase irritation and agitation.'[77] Although King showed little interest, Lapointe emphasized to the conference the need to clarify the situation so that the 'Parliament of Canada will have as full and complete authority as the Parliament at Westminster.'[78] He did not add, as King would have, that if Britain were involved in a major war Canada would be there. According to Skelton, when the British representatives hesitated to accept the decentralization, Lapointe, pacific hitherto, 'put the fear of the Lord' into two British representatives.[79] For years afterward the British remembered the role of Lapointe, who, one constitutional authority considered, 'was really leading' the conference of 1929.[80] Dandurand, during a campaign speech in 1930, recognized the role played by Lapointe – not King – in the implementation of the principles of 1926.[81] Lapointe also led the charge to establish legations abroad – an 'essential mark' of Canadian sovereignty.[82]

King was clearly less eager than Lapointe to push for greater dominion autonomy from Britain at the Imperial Conference of 1926 and afterward. Without the Irish and South African leaders, and King's acquiescence, Lapointe would not have had the success that he did. But the prime minister took no initiative during the campaign to define dominion status clearly, and it was Ernest Lapointe who propelled Canadian policy in this direction.

Conclusion

Lapointe clearly and consistently sought greater Canadian autonomy from Britain throughout the 1920s. During the Chanak crisis he opposed the sending of Canadian troops to help Britain and insisted firmly that Canada sign the Halibut Treaty without the British ambassador. Precedents were established. A clear definition of dominion equality was also needed to formalize what had been accomplished by the precedents, and Lapointe fought hard for this during the Imperial Conference of 1926. The prime minister was much more in favour of maintaining a strong connection with the mother country and, particularly after 1923, less insistent when seeking greater Canadian autonomy. Yet, despite their differences, King and Lapointe advocated very similar policies that corresponded with the three decisions, and they thus shared co-dominant voices.

Their different views of empire would cause greater problems in later years, but during the 1920s King accepted greater autonomy and Lapointe tolerated what remained of the British connection. The editor of London's *Empire Mail* wrote Lapointe with a new year wish for 1929: 'With your staunch imperialism, you will, I know, join me in the fervent desire that the coming year will knit still more closely the ties that bind our great

Empire together.'[83] Lapointe wrote at the bottom: 'Pas de réponse à faire!' King would not have been as sure that the comment was ironic; he opposed a common imperial foreign policy, resented imperialist bullies, but was much more hesitant in pushing for autonomy. French Canadians and English-Canadian autonomists counted on Lapointe to stiffen King's spine against the imperialists on the road to Canadian autonomy.

4

Autonomy and the League

To demonstrate Canada's evolving status to its people, and to the world, Ernest Lapointe and William Lyon Mackenzie King hoped that Canada would play a major role at Geneva, where the League of Nations met, as a fully autonomous member. The search for recognition of Canadian status became one of the main themes of Ottawa's participation at the League during the 1920s. At the same time, and equally important, Canada wanted to avoid all commitments to international collective security, which risked limiting its sovereignty. King and Lapointe, like all Canadian leaders during the 1920s, faced a dilemma – reconciling an important role at Geneva with the desire to avoid commitments would not be easy. Lapointe, more eager to advance Canadian status and autonomy than King, pushed the prime minister towards a greater role at Geneva, without himself being any more eager to accept commitments to apply the coercive sanctions of the League.

Article X: The Coercive Heart of the Covenant

Article X of the League Covenant symbolized the commitment of all members to participate in coercive activity against an aggressor. The principal objective of the League was to prevent war, and most countries agreed at the Paris Peace Conference in 1919 that military and economic sanctions had to be available to ensure this objective. Article X, described by U.S. President Woodrow Wilson as the 'heart of the Covenant,' specified: 'The Members of the League undertake to respect and preserve as against external aggression the territorial integrity and existing political independence of all Members of the League. In case of any such aggression or in case of any threat or danger of such aggression the

Council shall advise upon the means by which this obligation shall be fulfilled.'[1]

Many North Americans considered the article unfair. War in North America, where, Canadian speakers at the League often repeated, their nation shared a 3,000-mile undefended border and 100 years of peace with the United States, seemed improbable.[2] Why should North Americans accept the same commitments as Europeans, many asked. Lapointe and others argued that if dislike of Article X had prevented the United States from joining the League, deleting or modifying it would encourage that country to accept membership and increase the chances of successful collective security.[3] Canadians opposed the article when it was being discussed in 1919, and their Union government attempted to delete it at the first two League assemblies in 1920 and 1921.[4] When the Liberals took over at the Third Assembly in September 1922, they changed tactics, seeking an amendment to the article. Lapointe proposed to add that if ever Article X were applied, the League Council would take into account 'the political and geographical circumstances of each state' and that 'no Member shall be under the obligation to engage in any act of war without the consent of its Parliament, Legislature or other representative body.'[5] The French delegation, clearly supported by most countries,[6] continued to oppose any modification of Article X, and the question was held over for consideration by the Fourth Assembly in 1923. Unanimity was necessary for the formal adoption of the Lapointe's motion, but as there was only one vote case against it in 1923, the Canadian interpretation was accepted in practice: 'We have finally succeeded,' Gouin informed King.[7]

Historians focus on King when describing Canadian policy and the decision to oppose Article X in 1922 and 1923. Stacey credits King with the carefully balanced choice of delegates to the League's Third Assembly: 'Fielding, English-speaking and a conservative in his views on external policy; Lapointe, French-speaking and an autonomist. The mix bears what was to be the characteristic mark of King.'[8] But the prime minister had little choice: Lapointe and other French-Canadian MPs – not King, or Gouin – had strongly criticized the absence of francophones from the delegations in 1920 and 1921.[9] If the Canadian delegation of 1922 had not included a French Canadian, Lapointe would have reconsidered his support of King, which was not unconditional. Fielding was the most appropriate choice to ensure that the cries of Quebec domination were muted. But Lapointe not only affected the choice of delegates, he also contributed much more to the Canadian policy than some authors have realized. James Eayrs suggests that when Lapointe, as the Canadian representative at Geneva, sought to delete Article X, he had 'no great zeal for the cause.'[10] In fact, Lapointe proved the most zealous of King's ministers in the Canadian fight against Article X.

King opposed the article. He saw the League more as a think tank to inform public opinion than as a military organization to intervene in conflicts. He believed that the 'most effective sanction whether in international or in industrial disputes is [the] force of informed and focused public opinion.'[11] For King, the function of government, and of the League, was to provide 'machinery for getting at the facts and formulating an intelligent public opinion,'[12] not applying coercive measures. King announced in the House in 1920 that 'the supremacy of Parliament should be maintained at all cost,' adding two days later that the League should limit its activity to publicizing aggression.[13] However, the prime minister was not greatly interested by the League. His criticisms of Article X were less frequent and less forceful than Lapointe's, and his appointment of Fielding – a minister apparently favourable to Article X – seems to suggest a desire to have a counter-balance to Lapointe's strong opposition.

Lapointe's views were clear. He had stated them in the House before he was selected to represent Canada: 'The representatives of Canada moved that Article X be stricken from the Covenant of the League. I am pleased that they did so. No action was taken on that motion, which was postponed; but I hope that whoever represents Canada at the next meeting of the Assembly will see that the motion ... is proceeded with and that Article X shall be eliminated from the covenant.'[14] The impression that Lapointe had no great zeal for the attempt to delete Article X originated from a message of Fielding's to King: 'Mr. Lapointe and myself would have been quite content if we had not been called upon to do anything about it. However, it was there and we had to deal with it in some shape.'[15] But in the same message Fielding also told the prime minister that Lapointe 'spoke very forcefully' against the article, and the Quebec lieutenant earned a reputation for being strongly opposed to coercive measures. He was also known as one of the most effective of all Canadians at Geneva in the 1920s.[16]

In French Canada there was very little support for Canadian participation in the coercive measures of the League. Some *Le Soleil* editorials did indicate a certain support for the League, and even for coercive measures to help France, as long as Canadians would not be committed to enforcing these measures. Most editorials voiced strong opposition to coercive measures, linking them with British imperialism, and French Canadians in the House also opposed the article.[17] Lapointe hoped to convince French Canadians that the League was important, particularly as an effective means to further Canadian autonomy, and when he joined the Canadian delegation in 1922 the Liberal *Le Soleil* was already more impressed by the 'auguste assemblée' than it had been when members of the Union government represented Canada.[18]

Most English Canadians were as opposed as French Canadians to Article X and to any commitment that risked involving Canada in international conflict. However, English Canadians, as a group, were not as interested as French Canadians in using the League to further Canadian status. Imperialists such as Meighen preferred greater emphasis on relations in the empire, and thus had little interest in the League.[19] There were more genuine supporters of the League in English Canada than in French Canada, but they remained so marginal, and had such diverse visions of the League, that they never influenced Ottawa's policy.[20]

Canadian leaders' visions for the League reflected the views of the population. Lapointe, more than King, hoped that autonomy would be advanced by membership at Geneva. He later confided to the Canadian advisory officer at Geneva, W.A. Riddell, that everything gained at the League was important on the road to independence, which was his primary aim.[21] Lapointe thus hoped to ensure that the requirements of this membership were as uncontroversial as possible.[22] He realized that with League membership came responsibility, and clear limits to Canadian sovereignty. He pretended that Canada accepted the limits: 'L'entrée d'un État dans la Société restreint la souveraineté de cet État, soit au point de vue de la limitation des armements, soit au point de vue du droit de faire la guerre.'[23] However, as long as Article X remained, Canada agreed not only to act peacefully but also to help meet aggression against any League member – by military force if necessary – and Lapointe knew that this obligation threatened support for the League in Quebec. Lapointe was also more concerned than King about French views, as suggested during the debate over Germany's admission to the League.[24] This consideration perhaps tempered his opposition to Article X, which France strongly supported, or, more probably, required him to use greater diplomatic skills.

The difference between King and Lapointe concerning the Canadian attacks against Article X was not great, but the latter man was consistently more insistent. When King outlined the agenda of the delegates selected to represent Canada at the Assembly of 1922, he told Fielding that his trip to Europe had four objectives: to adjust unsettled accounts with Britain, to conduct negotiations with France concerning a commercial treaty, and to consider other commercial deals, and 'to this programme there is added ... a share of the duty ... of representing Canada in the Assembly of the League.'[25] Lapointe wrote King that he hoped that Fielding 'would be able to remain with us at Geneva as long as possible.'[26] While at the Third Assembly, Lapointe fought against Article X and also helped craft the Canadian response to another proposal to strengthen coercive measures at the League – the Treaty of Mutual Guarantee. After Ottawa had replied evasively, the League asked for a clearer statement, and Lapointe recommended to King that Canada oppose military guarantees: 'I do not think that our people would be prepared to ratify any agreement binding Canada to help other nations, under our present circumstances.'[27] Ottawa's second reply announced more clearly that the government 'does not see its way to a participation in the Treaty of Mutual Guarantee.'[28]

Certainly Lapointe played an active role in the Canadian opposition to the coercive measures contained in Article X. However, because he was continuing the fight of other Canadian delegates – a struggle that King favoured – his influence should not be exaggerated. Had his voice, and the French-Canadian voice, been silent, Canadian policy would have evolved in the same direction, though with less insistence. It would also have been similar if implemented exclusively by Lapointe. What the Liberal reaction to Article X illustrates is that King and Lapointe did not have the same interest, or the same intentions, for the League.[29] These differences remained throughout the 1920s, surfacing with greater consequence on later issues.

An Alternative to Coercion: The Optional Clause

When Lapointe and King opposed Article X they argued that coercion could not ensure peace. Both claimed to favour a conciliatory role for the League, and their public statements implied that they would support other attempts to replace the excessively binding Article X. When the Protocol for the Pacific Settlement of International Disputes, or Geneva Protocol, was introduced at the Assembly of 1924, it contained three elements: compulsory arbitration of all disputes not settled peacefully, military measures on a regional basis, and the convening of a disarmament conference. Despite apparent initial support, the protocol never came into effect. Canada again opposed the coercive element; however, the idea of compulsory arbitration by the Permanent Court of International Justice – the so-called optional clause, whereby a country could agree in advance to accept the jurisdiction of the court in all cases or with specific exceptions – seemed to correspond with Canada's view of the League's role, and Ottawa indicated support for this element.

The Canadian reply to the Geneva Protocol was greatly influenced by British policy-makers. Ottawa announced on 9 March 1925 that, even though Canada would not accept additional commitments to enforce economic or military sanctions, it did continue to support the League's work of 'conciliation, cooperation, and publicity,' it would participate in a disarmament conference, and it would be interested in signing the optional clause.[30] Britain's Labour government had helped sponsor the Geneva Protocol, but when the Conservatives led by Stanley Baldwin came to power in 1924, they withdrew British support for all elements of the proposal and suggested – to ensure that the empire had a 'single policy' – that Canada not proceed with its intention of signing the optional clause.[31] Instead of being eager to demonstrate Canadian independence from Britain on the international stage, King hesitated when faced with British opposition. He agreed to postpone acceptance of the optional clause until an imperial conference had discussed the question and had come up with a common imperial policy: 'It is highly desirable that similar attitudes should be adopted.'[32] Four years later, in January 1929, King finally told Britain that Canada intended to sign even without Whitehall, but again Baldwin asked King to wait.[33] King did wait ... until the Labour party returned to power a few months later and Britain became supportive of the 'Canadian' decision.

Authors have noted that Canadian initiatives at Geneva in support of non-coercive measures were rare.[34] According to Veatch, Canada's contribution to the League's conciliatory functions 'was not substantial,' and if it threatened to sign the optional clause in 1929 it did so because 'King, with his strong interest in Canadian independence in foreign policy matters, could hardly have found comfortable' the position of seeming to have abandoned the policy of accepting the clause because of British objections.[35] Stacey also implies that the autonomist King was uncomfortable with the coordinated policy suggested by the British;[36] however, it seems probable that King was much less worried about creating this impression than Lapointe and Dandurand.

King personally had no objection to the optional clause. It clearly corresponded with his vision of the League as a machine for conciliation, cooperation, and publicity. However, he was more interested in maintaining friendly relations with Britain than in supporting any policy at Geneva. Maintaining friendly relations did not mean that he was uninterested in greater Canadian autonomy on the international stage. For example, King was pleased to sign the Kellogg–Briand Pact of 1928 outlawing war, particularly because the invitation to sign had come directly from the United States to Canada.[37] Canadian status was advanced, and cordial relations were maintained with Britain. Had Britain opposed this treaty – or the procedure for inviting Canada – King would certainly have been less comfortable with the precedent. When confronted with a clear British request not to sign the optional clause, King conceded. Cabinet expressed the desire that Canada keep a separate identity from Britain,[38] but King consulted – and was very hesitant to oppose – Britain's decision-makers. Another example confirms this split between King and his cabinet. When the British government cancelled its trade agreement with the Soviet Union, King wrote in his diary that 'as soon as I read it I felt we should follow suit.' If Canada did nothing, he feared that it would seem as if Canada were siding with 'Russia against Britain'; however, he found cabinet 'most insistent' that Ottawa avoid the impression of following Britain.[39]

Lapointe seems to have had two reasons for supporting the optional clause. First, he very much favoured the League's being a non-binding organization for peace. He realized that some organization was necessary and argued in 1927 that no matter how much a country desires peace, if its neighbours seek war there will be war, and if it is a big war the whole world will be affected; then everyone had an obligation to cooperate.[40] He considered the League the best hope for world peace and often praised it in public, particularly its role in encouraging disarmament.[41] He was also as convinced as King that the best way to ensure peace was to encourage enlightened public opinion and remove the causes of wars.[42] Second – and the factor that separated his views from King's – he wanted Canada to demonstrate independence from Britain.

French Canadians were generally more supportive of the optional clause than English Canadians. Dandurand – from May 1921, when the court was being organized – had supported this institution and had criticized the Union government for not accepting it. He again pushed King to accept the optional clause while the Geneva Protocol was being rejected.[43] King, of course, had to keep in mind the reaction of English Canadians. Skelton and autonomists would like an independent Canadian policy, but other more imperialist anglophones would be less pleased with King – a consideration, particularly during the period of the 'King–Byng affair' and two elections (in 1925 and 1926). Thus, although the optional clause seemed unobjectionable to most English Canadians, King was not anxious that Canada accept it without Britain's also doing so.[44]

Lapointe's voice was undoubtedly one of the loudest in cabinet pushing King towards Canadian acceptance of the clause. While the prime minister hesitated to differ from British policy, his Quebec lieutenant emphasized the differences – and at times exaggerated them. In a published speech in 1927 he stated: 'Le Canada refusa de ratifier le Protocole de Genève et affirma une fois de plus son droit de prendre ses propres décisions et de déterminer sa propre ligne de conduite. Il est vrai que la Grande Bretagne refusa aussi de ratifier le Protocole, mais ses raisons furent entièrement différentes des nôtres. En effet, la Grande Bretagne déclina d'accepter une politique d'arbitrage, alors que le Canada déclara expressément son approbation du principe de l'arbitrage. Le discours de M. le sénateur Dandurand et celui de sir Austen Chamberlain à la récente assemblée de la Société des Nations ont démontré que cette différence d'opinion sur la question d'arbitrage existe encore.'[45] This statement was deliberately misleading: Britain and Canada differed on ratifying one element of the protocol – the optional clause – and there was no reason why Canada could not accept this clause while refusing the military aspect of the protocol. Lapointe would have favoured this course, as he made clear at the Imperial Conference of 1926, and was clearly one of the voices pushing King in this direction.[46]

In addition to Canada's showing interest in signing the optional clause, its only other initiative at Geneva was a proposal aimed at protection of minority rights in eastern Europe. King took no interest in the matter, and Dandurand, who played the key role, clearly preferred not to coordinate Canadian and British policy, even though such action would have helped the cause.[47] Lapointe had taken a similar attitude concerning requests to help a Canadian in a British prison charged with a murder that took place during the war: 'Je ne veux pas faire de démarches officielles auprès du Gouvernement [anglais],' he consistently repeated. He had brought up the matter informally with the British government but emphasized that he would not want Britain to interfere in Canadian cases.[48] The minister of justice undoubtedly encouraged Dandurand's independent attitude during the minority-rights initiative.

Exactly how Ottawa's decisions were taken concerning the Geneva Protocol is difficult to determine. Parliament was not consulted before Canada made its initial decision to reject the protocol (while expressing interest in the optional clause), which seems to have been taken at Laurier House. On 2 February 1925, King invited to dinner a group of eleven including Dandurand, Ewart, Lapointe, and Skelton. The consensus that emerged was that Canada should not participate, both because the United States was not a member of the League and because of the opposition in all parts of Canada to collective security measures. Concerning the decision to announce the Canadian interest in signing the optional clause, as expressed in a statement of 9 March 1925, the two Quebec ministers were clearly the force pushing King, who later asked Dandurand: 'Who drafted that document anyway?'[49] If the prime minister decided to bring up the question again in 1929 he was almost certainly acting under pressure from them.[50]

Lapointe's influence is apparent in his pushing King to suggest Canadian acceptance of the optional clause, but King's is also strong. Lapointe hoped to use the League to promote Canadian status, and he supported Canadian adherence to the binding arbitration of the Permanent Court of International Justice, with or – even better – without Britain's doing so. The prime minister was not interested enough in the League or in demonstrations of an independent policy to insist on Canadian acceptance of the optional clause. The Canadian policy reflected a compromise between the two visions. The different views of the two men were to collide in 1927, on an issue that precluded compromise.

A Seat on the League Council

Desire for more independent status was shown by many Canadian actions at Geneva during the 1920s. When Dandurand was elected in 1925 as president of the League Assembly, Skelton was interested primarily in the choice of a dominion representative as 'a very notable recognition of the distinct status of the Dominions in the League.'[51] Lapointe certainly favoured this initiative, which, since it entailed no commitment at all, did not arouse King's suspicion. The concern with status, as opposed to substance, was also apparent when King visited Geneva in 1928. One constructive element of the trip, according to Skelton, was that the League Assembly selected King as one of the six vice-presidents, 'an honour usually reserved for the Great Powers.'[52] In Canadian relations with the International Labour Organization (ILO), a branch of the League, Lapointe and Robert Borden both fought to ensure that Canada would be classed among the eight most industrialized members of the ILO, allowing it one of the eight permanent seats in the twelve-seat administrative council, but Canadians were less anxious to contribute concretely to the success of the ILO.[53]

A more important question was whether Canada should seek a seat on the League Council in 1927. Canadian election to one of the non-permanent seats would imply not only ceremonial status but also major responsibilities at Geneva during the three-year term. Canada did present its candidacy and, with the support of Britain, did become the first dominion to sit on the Council. Its election as an independent member of the Council helped clarify its status not only for other League members but also for some British statesmen. The British foreign secretary, Austen Chamberlain, had insisted that he spoke for the entire empire at the League, until Canada was elected to the Council.[54]

H.B. Neatby has argued that King has been unfairly criticized for his inaction during the period. As evidence he points to the prime minister's bold decision, ahead of 'all' Canadians, to seek a seat for this country on the League Council.[55] But Neatby and most historians agree that King opposed the move and reluctantly accepted it only when Lapointe insisted.[56] This Canadian initiative provides the clearest demonstration of the 1920s to disprove the dominant impression that King determined Canadian League and foreign policy completely on his own.[57]

The prime minister had continued to show little interest in the League. When he led the Canadian delegation in 1928 he commented that he was reluctant to do any speaking: 'It all looks like lecturing European countries and I have really no message.'[58] He felt that the League cost too much, that Dandurand spent too much time at Geneva, and that giving up his summer at Kingsmere was a great sacrifice.[59] But why was he against the idea of a Canadian representative on the Council?

King strongly opposed the concept in June, hoping to avoid European matters that might oppose Britain and France, 'with the consequent political reverberations in Canada.'[60] He reported in his diary that he had told Dandurand: 'We are just as wise not to get too far into European politics [and entanglements]. It would mean French-Canadian representation and Canada's siding on the League against England possibly, which would raise a major political issue here. – If not likely to differ with England then no need for separate representation. Better avoid mistakes.'[61]

He was clearly concerned with the fact that Canada would be represented by a francophone and feared a pro-France bias. Skelton noted in his diary that Dandurand naturally took this slight rather personally, being the probable candidate as Council representative;[62] however, Skelton shared King's fear. He had asked Dandurand's opinion on Germany's admission to the Council in 1926, 'tho fearing somewhat Dandurand's pro-French leanings.'[63] In cabinet King did not mention this point, basing his opposition to a seat on the inconvenience caused by the absence of ministers, the danger of European entanglements, and the possibility of a question dividing French and English Canadians. Lapointe also would have hesitated for similar reasons, but a final consideration of King's was the one that distinguished the prime minister's views from Lapointe's: 'Canada's status,' King told cabinet, 'is well established now.'[64]

Lapointe was not satisfied that Canada had achieved appropriate status, and he insisted that it seek a seat on the League Council. He wired King from Geneva that its election would be a 'natural step and crowning point of our policy. We owe it to Canadian prestige and development. Am not afraid of any dangerous aspect, quite the contrary. Let Canada again lead the Dominions.'[65] Dandurand later claimed that it had been his advice that led Lapointe to send this telegram to King on 12 August 1927. However, Lapointe had wired Skelton a month earlier, urging Canadian candidacy 'to advertise Dominion status to international world.'[66] Britain recognized the dominions as equal, and Canada, with a seat at the League, was clearly 'maître de ses destinées,' according to Lapointe.[67]

Rumilly argued that French-Canadian editorial opinion in Le Devoir and Le Soleil was unanimous in the 1920s: it was bettèr for the peace of Canada for this country to stay out of European affairs.[68] However, editorials in Le Soleil had placed great emphasis on the election in 1925 of Dandurand as president, showing 'l'autonomie dont jouit le Dominion,' and one editorialist affirmed that Dandurand's election would show to French readers of Maria Chapdelaine that the 'coin reculé décrit n'est pas plus le Canada que la Brière n'est la France.' Some, including Dandurand, also favoured the initiative of 1927 as a means to increase Canadian sovereignty: one editorialist announced that thanks to Lapointe's efforts (not King's), 'on ne pourra plus jamais dire: "Quand l'Angleterre est en guerre, le Canada est en guerre".'[69]

English-Canadian imperialists saw no reason to demonstrate autonomy from Britain. Even as strong an autonomist as Skelton had doubts and initially opposed the idea, 'particularly on account of European entanglements, [and a] lack of persons to send,' but he agreed that some domin-

ion should be appointed, and as he knew that the British would oppose
the election of the Irish – his preferred choice – he eventually accepted
the initiative.[70] Skelton later confided to Lapointe, in a letter attached to
a copy of a report to King, that 'I still have my doubts as to what we are
doing in this galley, but once we are in it we will have to try and meet our
full responsibilities. I hope very much that you will find it possible to
attend some meeting of the Council soon.'[71]

A seat on the Council, Lapointe was convinced, would advance Canadian autonomy, and he fought strongly for it. As he was leaving a meeting, Lapointe told King, who recorded the conversation in his diary, 'It
was the only time or thing on which we had differed. I said I would not
differ with him and he was free to cable, though I thought he should
meet council first, he said council would do my wish, not his. I said well
go ahead.' King added that he felt it a mistake 'unduly pressing own
individual status as a nation, and inviting differences; but a cleavage with
Lapointe on a matter on which he feels deeply would be more unfortunate in the long run.'[72] Lapointe told W.A. Riddell, who was representing
Canada at Geneva in 1927, that he had threatened to resign at the time.
When explaining to Riddell why final authorization to seek election had
been delayed, Lapointe complained that King 'kept putting me off and
putting me off ... I got tired of it ... I told him that we'd always stood
together on the same platform and I'd always backed him up but if he
wouldn't consent to Canada running for a seat on the Council I would
not stand or sit on the same platform with him again.'[73]

The question remains whether Lapointe was exercising a deliberative
voice in King's sphere or a dominant voice in his own sphere. Lapointe
and King had notably different views on many questions, but this decision in 1927 led to their first serious disagreement and Lapointe's first
threat to resign. Lapointe had been satisfied that King was moving in the
right direction, though not always as fast as Lapointe would have liked,
towards Canadian autonomy. The occasion in 1927 was too good an
opportunity for Lapointe to let pass, and he insisted that King act. Clearly
King had the final say, or at least Lapointe felt that he needed the prime
minister's permission. However, the decision corresponds not with King's
views but with Lapointe's, showing his dominant voice on this matter.
Theoretically King was free to refuse, but, as he appreciated, refusing
Lapointe's demand would have been unfortunate, not because the two
were friends – King was more calculating than that – but because the
leader of the Quebec caucus had become too important.

Conclusion

During this period from 1921 to 1929 Lapointe pushed the prime minister in the direction of independence from Britain faster and further than King would have gone on his own. At Geneva both men hoped to avoid commitments, but Lapointe, more interested in Canada's status, was more willing to see it play an active role. He was able to impose a dominant voice over the prime minister's on the decision to seek a seat on the Council because of at least three factors: King's weakness, cabinet's lack of interest in foreign policy, and Lapointe's position in the Quebec caucus, which on the issue of autonomy from Britain did form a bloc. He did not exaggerate the use of this resource, realizing that many anglophones were concerned about 'Quebec domination' and believed, like one Toronto newspaper in 1925, that Lapointe, rather than King, was 'calling the shots on all important matters.'[74] Though not dominant, Lapointe did influence other policies at Geneva by sharing a co-dominant voice with King in the decisions to oppose Article X strongly and to support the optional clause.

On the long march towards Canadian autonomy, King is often seen as 'leading the pack.' This was certainly how the prime minister presented his role in his diary, where he was never shy about distributing credit to himself. He wrote in December 1926 that 'the Imperial Conference has helped to give me a place in history,' and in 1928, with Canada's having legations abroad and a seat on the League Council, he was 'convinced the period of my administration will live in this particular as an epoch in the history of Canada that was formative and memorable.' In 1930 he noted that 'Lapointe made an excellent speech on the question of status, – a subject I should have made my own, and on which I will speak more frequently later on. I am inclined to let others get credit for much for which I have a rightful claim, just as one sees continuously Baldwin and Lafontaine given the credit for much that was due to Mackenzie and Papineau.'[75] King had contributed to the advancement of Canadian autonomy in the 1920s largely because of pressure from Lapointe, and, despite his intention to speak more frequently on the subject, it was pressure from Lapointe that would continue to move him in this direction in the 1930s.

PART II:
A NEW ROLE IN AN UNCERTAIN WORLD,
1930–1938

5

A Stronger Voice and Popular Support

In the period from 1920 to 1929 William Lyon Mackenzie King had been a new, inexperienced leader dependent on the help of regional leaders. Ernest Lapointe had proved most helpful to the prime minister, and the influence of each man grew throughout the decade. In 1930 this relationship changed. That year the Liberals lost decisively to R.B. Bennett's Conservatives, and King was much less impressed with Lapointe. Even when the Liberals returned to power in 1935, King now solidly installed as leader, remained hesitant to accept the advice of Lapointe, or anyone else. Consequently, in the period from 1930 to 1938, Lapointe would need to re-establish himself in the decision-making structure of the party.

The Fall and Conditional Rise of King

King had accepted credit for the position of the party before the election of July 1930. 'I think I can claim credit for the tactics,' he wrote in his diary, referring to the pre-election budget debate strategy, 'for excepting Lapointe, I have been pretty much alone in some of the stages that have brought us to where we are.'[1] After the defeat, in which the Conservatives had won 137 seats, the Liberals ninety-one and other parties seventeen, he began looking for people to blame. Although the Liberals won a majority of ridings in Quebec, they had been reduced from sixty to forty seats, and this loss seemed the most disappointing to King: 'The result is a great surprise ... Quebec was not as good as expected, we lost many seats there,' he commented in his diary when he received the first results. He criticized Lapointe, blaming the loss of Quebec seats on Ottawa's slow reaction to demands for tariffs on New Zealand butter and on a certain overconfidence among the Quebec leaders.[2]

During the campaign Lapointe had seemed to some out of touch with his electors. When he returned from his European trip at the end of 1929 he was told by Oscar Drouin, a Liberal from his riding, that although international affairs should not be neglected, it was time to re-establish contact with the voters of Quebec East and the region.[3] Chubby Power commented that 'the authority and prestige of Lapointe in this campaign was lower than it was before or afterwards and there was a consequent deterioration in the strength of his leadership in the Quebec district.'[4] Lapointe had suggested to King that the gains made at the 1926 Imperial Conference be used as a main issue against the more imperialist Tories and during his own speeches focused on autonomy and on the Balfour Declaration, which fascinated some intellectuals but did not inspire the general public. Faced with a dissolving economy, Quebecers were interested less in international affairs and more in tariffs on New Zealand butter and in putting bread on their tables.[5]

Being out of touch with the electors is a serious problem for any politician. For Lapointe, whose influence in cabinet depended so greatly on his ability to act as the middle man between King and the population of Quebec, the problem could be fatal. After the election King often criticized his Quebec lieutenant: 'Lapointe is as flat as a pancake,' he complained to his diary after one parliamentary sitting.[6] On another occasion, in November 1932, he complained: 'Lapointe I do not think was quite as loyal as usual, in not giving better support' to King's position concerning economic treaties, which he doubted any members had read. Two days later he added that Lapointe was 'inclined to be resentful when I said I was going to speak on it, and left his seat while I was discussing it.' King complained that Lapointe did not support his speech on the upcoming imperial trade conference, or his opposition to increased tariffs, or his fight for unemployment relief, and concluded: 'Lapointe, alas, is more taken with social life than anything.'[7] Lapointe's ability to influence King was in jeopardy.

By the time the Liberals returned to power in 1935, winning 55 seats in Quebec and 173 seats overall, Lapointe had regained his popular support. During the election campaign of 1935 he visited his riding more often and talked less about international affairs.[8] He wrote a series of articles in Le Soleil, twice a week during the campaign, devoted almost entirely to economic matters and the new role for the state. He emphasized several themes, including liberalism (which he argued was not a laissez-faire attitude), the balance between individual liberty and state intervention (notably concerning tariffs), and the 'New Deal' social laws of R.B. Bennett (which he called hypocritical and unconstitutional). Canada's most important international question during the election – its reaction to the Ethiopian crisis – he almost ignored.[9] Quebec voted Liberal, but when King was returned as prime minister he was not as dependent on Lapointe's support.

Sixteen years after the convention of 1919, and with a new majority in Parliament, King was solidly installed as Liberal leader. King's system remained, and he continued to depend on each regional leader to represent his area; however, he was more confident as leader and sought greater control. He told his diary, 'I drive my colleagues at the loose rein purposely so as to have moral attitude of watching what is going on, and of bringing things into line the right way at the right moment.'[10] The size of the Quebec caucus also made King increasingly hesitant to follow the advice of his Quebec lieutenant. Although Lapointe's control over this sizeable bloc of seats was unchallenged in 1935, the group was relatively smaller than it had been during the 1920s, when it had accounted for very close to half of the parliamentary caucus. In 1935 it remained large, but its fifty-five members – one fewer than the Ontario group – accounted for less than one-third of the 173 Liberal MPs. But the greatest limit to Quebec's influence continued to be the impression in English Canada that the province somehow dominated government.

In 1930 King had not been completely sorry to lose so many seats in the province: 'The religious cry of Quebec domination cannot longer be raised,' and he was 'glad Quebec bloc is broken.' Now, in 1935, Quebec had 31 per cent of the government seats – a reasonably representative amount – but still too much for King: 'As a party we will have to carry the load of Fr[ench] and C[atholic] domination, and I am afraid our friends F[rench] and R[oman] C[atholic] won't help us in meeting the situation.' King again had little respect for the francophone Quebec mentality: 'The men from that province view things very differently from ourselves. They have no consciences in some things,' King wrote, referring to discussions during the Beauharnois scandal.[11]

The extent to which King was concerned about the impression of Quebec domination, and the degree to which his anxiety affected Lapointe's influence, were suggested during cabinet selection in 1935. Lapointe asked to be appointed minister of external affairs, to replace King. The prime minister was too fearful of the appearance of Quebec domination for that: he believed 'that English speaking Canada would not welcome his having control of External Affairs, during a European war that increasingly seemed imminent.' King asked the anglophones in cabinet if they thought that Lapointe could handle External Affairs (if war broke out in Europe), and all agreed that this was not wise, as did Skelton.[12] However, King was not as strong, nor Lapointe as weak, as this incident may suggest. The Quebec lieutenant possibly considered his request as a personal promotion for himself rather than for his province. When he asked for personal favours – such as being named to the bench or to the Senate – he never insisted. In addition, Lapointe knew from experience that he could considerably influence External Affairs from his position at Justice.

During the disposition of cabinet positions, King seemed to oppose all other French-Canadian possibilities. He was convinced that Lapointe suggested Cardin and Rinfret because he did not want to oppose the Quebec members; he 'is very weak when it comes to resisting the forces that are likely to create trouble. With him it is "who the boys want."' King opposed both men, as well as Power, and looked to others for support in cabinet: 'I told Dunning that he must support me against Lapointe, where Lapointe would be yielding. It was, however, all as I expected. Before we had gone very far, both Dandurand and Dunning were finding it would be impossible to do what I wanted to do with respect to both Cardin and Rinfret.'[13]

King also preferred to replace Dandurand as Speaker of the Senate, but here again Lapointe had his way. King did not even try to suggest his choices for Quebec Senate seats during this period, considering it 'useless to oppose French colleagues. They know their problems and apparently this is the only way they can effectively meet them.'[14] That Lapointe saw his role as Quebec lieutenant more than as French-Canadian lieutenant is suggested by the fact that he was not present when King met with the French-Canadian ministers outside Quebec, Joseph-Énoil Michaud and Pierre-Jean Veniot, and did not insist on a cabinet seat for the Franco-Ontarian Lionel Chevrier. This is particularly surprising as he was present when King met with the more important ministers outside Quebec: T.A. Crerar, C.A. Dunning, W.D. Euler, J.G. Gardiner, and J.L. Ralston.[15] As in the 1920s, he did not seek economic positions for any of his Quebec colleagues.

Lapointe did not go to External Affairs, but he was recognized by the Quebec caucus as having a bigger voice than King in Quebec politics. Power commented on his 'overwhelming prestige' in the province: 'As time went on Lapointe grew enormously in stature and prestige [and] became so completely the representative of the Liberal party in Quebec that for many years King counted little in the political life of the province ... It was to Lapointe that we looked for leadership, for generalship, and for anything relating to either policy or tactics in Quebec political life.'[16] King was aware of these views. He recorded in his diary in 1932: 'Power had made it clear that it was Ernest who they cared about in Quebec and who had the following there [Power added that he did not like King]. One could have no more loyal colleague than Lapointe, nor a better one politically.'[17] If External Affairs questions interested Quebec, Lapointe would be able to influence King, but it would not be easy for him to do so.

New Resources in the New Cabinet

After the election of 1930, Lapointe had become much more conscious of his need to represent the people of Quebec, in order to re-establish his influence on King. Bennett's Conservative government had helped, as francophones did not have significant influence in it. Solicitor General Maurice Dupré, considered more popular in 1934 than the other francophone Conservative ministers Arthur Sauvé and Alfred Duranleau, was nowhere near as effective a defender of Quebec's interests as Lapointe had been.[18] After 1935 the Liberal daily *Le Soleil* of course claimed that all Quebecers followed and trusted Lapointe, and even the director of the more nationalist *Le Devoir*, Georges Pelletier, told Lapointe in 1938 that he hoped that rumours of his impending retirement were false because French Canadians needed him. Lapointe, who worried about the rise of nationalism in Quebec, thanked Pelletier for the letter: 'Je serais bien heureux si elle représentait les idées de tous tes collaborateurs et de la province en général.'[19]

Lapointe continued to stress the need for the government to have the support of the Canadian population. The moment the government no longer speaks for the country, he remarked in 1934 referring to the Conservatives, it no longer had any reason to stay in power.[20] How Lapointe estimated public opinion is unclear, as party members made little direct input into the decision-making process.[21] One occasion when he solidified his role as defender of the people was during the fight to allow Quebec City to municipalize electrical power in 1931. The city took on Lapointe to defend the popular project against the large companies that opposed it; Quebec Power hired Louis St Laurent. This debate magnified divisions within the Liberal party – Taschereau and the more conservative friends of big business against Lapointe and the defenders of the public interest. It was the conservative element that became the target of

Maurice Duplessis and the nationalists.[22] Lapointe also acted as president of a committee studying the electrical situation in the province in 1934 – public ownership, rates, and rural access.[23]

Lapointe improved his position with the Quebec provincial Liberals during the period. Although he showed little interest in party organization, Lapointe, according to Power, helped substantially in Taschereau's re-election as premier in 1931,[24] and his relations were increasingly cordial with Lomer Gouin's successor. Lapointe's position in the party was further solidified when Adélard Godbout, born and raised in Lapointe's home town of St Éloi, replaced Taschereau in 1936, with the support of Lapointe. At the provincial Liberal convention in June 1938, Lapointe played an important role, encouraging adoption of several new policies in the Liberal program – an agricultural credit, improved consultation with labour, and the vote for women. Thérèse Casgrain acknowledged in her memoirs that Ernest Lapointe's presence certainly helped her cause.[25]

A respected and influential figure among Quebec provincial Liberals, Lapointe was equally esteemed by the rival party Action Libérale Nationale (ALN). This splinter group, led by Paul Gouin, left Taschereau's provincial Liberals in 1934, advocating a more interventionist program. The ALN opposed Taschereau's conservative tendencies but remained fans of Lapointe, who followed closely the development of the new party.[26] As Chubby Power and Paul Martin mention, Lapointe's interest in the ALN was motivated less by an attraction to its left-wing program than by the hope of reuniting the party.[27] Because he found himself in the unique position of being sought by both groups as leader, his role minimized the loss of Liberal support, for which Godbout thanked him.[28]

Lapointe continued to be responsible for many patronage appointments, which helped solidify his influence at Ottawa.[29] The type of patronage was changing as the state grew, and government relations with business evolved. The new opportunities might have given Lapointe greater influence had he abused the situation. Such abuse might also have lessened the confidence that the Quebec population and King had in his disinterested loyalty, and he remained hesitant to accord personal favours to individuals. When a Liberal offered 'thousands' to the party in exchange for a Senate seat, Lapointe remarked: 'Quelle mentalité pourrie.' Liberal MP Wilfrid Lacroix demanded that a dominion arsenal be moved to Valcartier and then denounced the disgusting patronage when he did not receive as many patronage positions for supporters as he had hoped.[30] Lapointe knew that he disappointed more people than he could satisfy and did not enjoy this aspect of his role as minister:

'Beaucoup de gens semblent oublier qu'un ministre doit être un serviteur du pays mais non le commissionnaire de chaque individu de son comté. Le bureau d'un ministre n'est pas un bureau de placement.'[31]

Other resources are more difficult to quantify but should not be forgotten. Lapointe remained a persuasive and popular speaker. Unlike Meighen, he did not seek to ridicule or humiliate his opponents, and he was liked and respected by members from all parties.[32] J.W. Pickersgill, a member of the prime minister's staff, remembered that whenever Lapointe – 'almost certainly the most popular member of Parliament' – filled in for King as prime minister, the atmosphere in the office was more relaxed; however, Pickersgill added that King had the pressure of being responsible for the final decision.[33] King, who had not forgotten Lapointe's loyalty and who remained insecure concerning his own 'worn and haggard appearance,' poor speaking ability, and ignorance of the French language, was undoubtedly pleased to have Lapointe at his side. He admired Lapointe's kindness, and during the abdication crisis in 1936 King 'was delighted' that he and Lapointe 'appeared together as we did and the more we can do this over the radio the better it will be for our government.'[34]

King at times criticized his Quebec lieutenant. Referring to a debate on redistribution of seats in the Commons, the prime minister complained that Lapointe was 'straddling the fence'; a month later King said that Lapointe 'threw out the sponge completely,' and Quebec gained little as Lapointe seemed played out. 'I wonder what he would do if he had had my job.'[35] Those familiar with Lapointe, Chubby Power remembered, knew that despite his 'seeming lack of decision ... he was, when those decisions had been reached, a man of strong character and almost obstinate in his intention to abide by them.'[36] The prime minister, despite occasional criticisms, was glad to have Lapointe on his side.

Lapointe's health remained a possible limit to his ability to influence the prime minister. He was ill after the 1930 campaign and told King, as late as July 1935, that he would not run again.[37] He did run and again exhausted himself during the campaign of 1935.[38] His wife wrote to King that she was worried about her husband, that he was terribly nervous and did not have the endurance that he had had a few years earlier.[39] In March 1936 King noted: 'Lapointe is far from well and needs a change. He is losing his nerve in many directions and says that he is also finding it impossible to make up his mind on anything, and feels more like crying than anything else. This is all evidence of a threatened nervous breakdown.' In August 1936, upset with Duplessis's win in the Quebec provincial election, Lapointe again informed King that he would not seek re-election and that if Quebecers had lost confidence in him to look after their concerns he would resign.[40] This incident reveals that Lapointe's poor health, rather than being a limit to his influence, became a valuable new resource to influence King, as it added credibility to his threats of resignation.

A more significant restraint on Lapointe's influence was increasing support in Quebec for the French-Canadian nationalists. Some nationalist leaders, most notably Lionel Groulx, referred to the authority of the Roman Catholic Church to bolster their political ideas – an approach that Henri Bourassa and Lapointe agreed was 'monstrous.'[41] Lapointe would have to be careful not to aid this movement by taking stances too far ahead of public opinion. He would have to offer sufficiently nationalistic leadership to maintain his support and prevent the channelling of this movement into a single party. This threat became greater in 1936 when Maurice Duplessis led his Union Nationale to power in the province.

The 'nationalist movement' took many forms during the interwar period, and Lapointe's Liberalism was undoubtedly affected by his desire to maintain the support of as many nationalist-leaning Quebecers as possible. This meant strongly opposing 'communism.' For example, a peaceful trek by unemployment relief camp strikers from Vancouver to Ottawa in 1935 was interrupted in Regina with excessive force by the Bennett government. The Liberals did not object, because Lapointe, as King wrote in his diary, 'was fearful that in Quebec the impression might be fostered, which the Tories were seeking to foster, that we were sympathetic with communism. On the whole, it seemed preferable to let Woodsworth introduce the subject.'[42] Many English Canadians, including Skelton, also supported Bennett.[43] Lapointe's silence, when compared with his strong defence of the Winnipeg strikers in 1919 against the Union government's actions, suggests how much he was affected by Quebec public opinion.

Francophones, more influenced by the Catholic church, were generally much more willing to restrict the freedom of suspected communists than were anglophones. This did not mean that there existed general support for fascism in Quebec, as some anglophones assumed.[44] There were indeed fascist parties in Canada, and the Quebecer Adrien Arcand, who wrote to remind Lapointe of the 'communist danger,'[45] was perhaps the best known of their leaders; however, Lapointe assured worried anglophones in 1938 that Arcand's party included fifteen to twenty-five adherents, not 75,000 as reported, and that there would be no revolution in Quebec.[46] To call Quebecers 'fascist' because they were anti-communist, or because they admired the work of Mussolini, would mean that 'fascism' was very popular in English-speaking Canada.[47] Referring to how Mussolini had cleaned up his country by controlling the communists, King wrote in his diary that 'one becomes filled with admiration' and that 'it seems to me the people are truly governing themselves under his direction.'[48] Winston Churchill also admired the fascists.[49] Toronto's *Mail and Empire* preferred 'Fascism to the Moscow-bred program of the CCF' and referred to Arcand as 'the brilliant young French Canadian.'[50] If francophones were not more fascist than anglophones between the wars, they do appear to have more strongly favoured radical measures against 'communism.'

French-Canadian Concerns

Other questions continued to divide francophones and anglophones, and these deeply interested Lapointe. As government services in English expanded, the need for access to these services for francophones became increasingly obvious. In 1936 a study estimated that French Canadians, about 30 per cent of the country's population, made up only 16 per cent of the public service and received only 11 per cent of the payroll.[51] King and Skelton could not understand the increasing regionalism and disunity in Canada in 1937: they had done all that they could to restore prosperity, and such regionalism they felt irrational and unjustified.[52] Lapointe was quicker to see how a unilingual civil service could fan the flames of French-Canadian nationalism.

One policy that Lapointe fought for was bilingual notes and coins. He received about seventy-five letters favouring bilingual money from francophones and two from anglophones. Three anglophones opposed, one arguing that the 'French' in Canada did nothing but complain.[53] When in opposition Lapointe had proposed this measure, but the Conservatives defeated the motion.[54] Anglophone Conservatives in 1933 had accused Lapointe of creating disunity by angering anglophones with requests for bilingual money, and in 1936 one Conservative MP condemned the 'militant minority' for seeking to impose its will on the 'passive majority' who, twenty-five years earlier, would have revolted.[55] King, and Dunning, also feared arousing English-Canadian hostility, but Lapointe insisted, strongly supported by French Canadians.[56]

Francophones also hoped for a more equitable presence of their language in governmental services. A *Le Soleil* editorial suggested that anglophones, 'les moins doués des hommes pour l'étude des langues,' which they saw as a calculated fault, to encourage use of English, should try harder to acquire some French, as Lapointe had learned English, if they sincerely sought to maintain a national identity.[57] Few radio services were available in French, and even those that existed provoked a letter-writing campaign to protest against the 'unnecessary and even annoying' use of a 'foreign language' on Canadian radio.[58] In a province where the majority spoke French, Ottawa provided the following services: government listings in the Quebec City phonebook in English only, agricultural services in English only, unilingual anglophones sent to settle a strike in Trois-Rivières, Canadian Pacific telegraph forms in English only, access to the Civil Service Commission through one telephone answered by a unilingual anglophone, and at least one Quebec census officer refusing to write even one word in French.[59] Lapointe devoted much time to seeking remedies for each situation.

Finding a job in the civil service was difficult for a French Canadian – first, because the entry exam was often in English, but also because anglophones hired their friends. Lapointe complained to King about the absence of French Canadians in senior posts. He sent King a study that estimated the number of French Canadians occupying higher posts in the civil service at eleven of eighty-four, or fewer than half of the twenty-four to which their population entitled them.[60] Lapointe intervened often with colleagues,[61] including the prime minister, who was informed that it was 'essential' for him to translate a radio address.[62] King remained hesitant on such matters and complained that the only senior francophone member in the unilingual Department of External Affairs, Laurent Beaudry, had become 'obsessed and fanatical' in 1937 with demands for equality of languages.[63]

Such concerns absorbed much of Lapointe's time, but he did not always get the recognition for his efforts that he felt he deserved. As he accepted the praise for his successes, he also received the blame for the much more frequent failures. When criticized by colleagues from Quebec for the insufficient number of francophone nominations, he replied that his efforts should be supported and that criticisms hurt his bargaining position, and he hinted at resigning: 'Je vous dis en toute sincérité que si j'abandonne la vie publique dans un avenir plus ou moins rapproché, cette attitude de ceux sur qui j'ai droit de compter pour me défendre quand nos adversaires nous frappent sera le grand mobile de ma décision.'[64] Some Quebec MPs replied that they realized that the situation was not his fault and hoped that he would stay.[65] Lapointe thus used his threat of resignation not only on King but also on the Quebec caucus.

Canadians were very much concerned with the changing role of the state in the economy during this period, but Lapointe continued to show little interest in the economy unless his riding was concerned directly.[66] He began the decade opposed to increasing state intervention, which he believed many francophone Quebecers equated with decreased individual freedom or communism. A law to organize agricultural markets met opposition in Quebec, and Lapointe strongly opposed 'coopération obligatoire' as an anti-democratic idea from Russia, Italy, and Germany that eliminated producers' freedom of action.[67] By 1938 he began cautiously advocating greater intervention: 'The old individualism is gradually giving way to the idea of necessary co-operation, co-operation between groups, between classes, between all citizens.'[68]

Lapointe took greater interest in economic issues that also concerned his Department of Justice, particularly when they risked dividing francophones and anglophones. Bennett's New Deal, presented in January 1935, proposed several interventionist reforms, all opposed by Lapointe on the grounds that they interfered with provincial jurisdiction. As a Liberal hoping to give the impression of siding with the people he favoured these reforms; as Quebec lieutenant he would gain more support by defending provincial rights against Bennett's 'centralisation' or 'fascism.'[69] When he became minister he referred most of the legislation to the courts, without threatening his popular following by offering any serious alternative.[70] Lapointe again invoked his refusal to interfere in provincial jurisdiction to explain why he did nothing to support laws in favour of insurance for the unemployed, a minimum wage, and a forty-hour work week – legislation that he claimed to favour.[71]

Many other matters involved the increasingly complex question of federal–provincial jurisdiction. Duplessis hoped to present himself as defender of provincial rights much more than Taschereau had, and Lapointe did not wish to increase Duplessis's support by insisting on policies that might have been unpopular in Quebec, such as seeking power to amend the British North America (BNA) Act, 1867, in Canada and to abolish appeals to the Privy Council in London: the dominion is the child of the provinces, not the father, he repeated.[72] At the Dominion–Provincial Conference of 1935, when he chaired the committee on constitutional questions, he repeated that the constitution was not eternal and should be updated to protect minority rights, but only with the agreement of the provinces.[73] King at times understood Lapointe's position and agreed that provincial consent was necessary[74] but more often complained that Lapointe was too cautious. For example, King wrote in his diary that when Lapointe objected to a program to implement state medicine 'on score of jurisdiction, I said BNA Act could be changed if need be,' outlining the effect on illness and the importance of the party's standing on the side of the poor.[75] But King's complaint went no further than his diary.

Lapointe also objected initially to the appointment of a royal commission to investigate financial relations of the provinces and the dominion,[76] which became the Rowell-Sirois Commission. Lapointe later felt that many in Quebec did not understand the mandate, which he said was not to decrease the autonomy of the provinces but to ensure their survival. Because René Chaloult and many Quebec nationalists argued that Ottawa should stay out of the unemployment programs while Quebec and other provincial governments insisted that Ottawa intervene, a commission became necessary to clarify such matters.[77]

Lapointe's concern to follow rather than lead his electorate was again apparent during two issues involving the rights of workers. In the first, his defence of provincial rights eclipsed his desire to guarantee unions the right to organize. The minister of justice argued that workers must unite, and he could not understand why some employers opposed this process, as unions provided the best means to uphold capitalism against the detested communism.[78] However, in Parliament Lapointe opposed Woodsworth's motion of 31 January 1938 seeking to guarantee to labour the right to organize, arguing that this fell within provincial jurisdiction, involving property and civil rights (unless he included it in the Criminal Code, which he opposed).[79] In the second issue, during the 1937 strike at the General Motors plant in Oshawa, the Ontario government linked the union, which belonged to the U.S.-based Congress of Industrial Organizations (CIO), with international communism, and Lapointe claimed to support this interpretation. Whether he sincerely believed that the strikers were led by communists is difficult to determine; however, any other stance would have placed him in a delicate position with the Catholic unions and anti-communists in Quebec.[80]

King was disappointed with Lapointe, feeling that his sympathies were against the workers, that he was blinded by Duplessis, but that he would soon 'come around':

I was astonished in finding Lapointe ready to use every means to prevent a C.I.O. getting any recognition in Canada or allowing representatives of the organization to come from the United States ... Lapointe would try to have purely Canadian Unions formed and no representative of organized labour come from across the border. I pointed out that this was a battle forty years ago ... To think of turning back the hands of clock to that extent, was ridiculous ... Members of the cabinet were all opposed to Lapointe's view which I think is simply begotten of the fear being aroused through the intolerant attitude of political unions in his own Province. He will come around all right to seeing the right of labour to defend itself in a most effective way.[81]

The Quebec lieutenant was also very probably influenced by the views of his province during the debate over deportations of individuals without trial, a policy that King opposed in 1931 but accepted in March 1933 and during the Vancouver riot of 19 June 1937, when police stormed a post office protest. Ottawa's attitude – that the riot was a provincial problem – left premiers to solve labour unrest in the absence of any effective dominion response, even though all labour groups except Quebec's Confédération des travailleurs catholiques du Canada (CTCC) sought a greater dominion role.[82]

However, the issue that best illustrates the extent to which Lapointe was willing to subordinate his personal convictions in order to represent the views of the majority in his province was Ottawa's reply to Duplessis's Padlock Law. Quebec's Act Respecting Communist Propaganda, 1937, epitomized the anti-communist hysteria of the period. The 'Padlock Law' allowed Duplessis, as attorney general, to order a house used for 'propagating communism' to be locked up for a year and to order the destruction of any documents 'tending to propagate communism or bolshevism.' It offered no definition of communism: 'Any definition would prevent the application of the Law,' Duplessis reasoned, adding that 'Communism can be felt.'[83] Woodsworth complained that the law, adopted 24 March 1937, had been applied arbitrarily over fifty times between 9 November 1937 and 27 January 1938 and led the charge calling for Ottawa to disallow it.[84] The dominion government had one year, from the date on which it received notice of the provincial law, in July 1937, to announce that the law would be disallowed or referred to the courts.

The King government decided in July 1938 not to confront Duplessis on this issue. Lapointe noted, when he announced the government's decision, that there was considerable opposition to the Padlock Law, but mostly outside Quebec.[85] He explained unconvincingly that Ottawa's recent disallowance of legislation introduced by William Aberhart's Social Credit government in Alberta was very different because the Alberta laws were deliberate 'attempts to interfere with the operation of Dominion laws,' while it was the constitutional validity of the Padlock Law that was in doubt.[86] But the minister of justice refused to refer it to the courts for an opinion, leaving individuals the responsibility to contest it in court. The law remained until most of it was finally ruled unconstitutional in 1957. Some suggest that Lapointe decided not to disallow the law because he saw communism as a serious threat to Catholic society;[87] however, Lapointe personally did not fear communism and did not believe the law to be necessary.[88] He did have his own opinions, but he also had a role to play at Ottawa as voice of Quebec, defender of the views of his province.

As Quebec lieutenant, Lapointe could not let the dominion government overrule a provincial law – affecting only Quebec – that Quebecers overwhelmingly supported. Questions of law, and even principle, took a back seat to politics during Lapointe's deliberations.[89] King, confirming how lost he would have been without the guidance of Lapointe in Quebec politics, clearly favoured following anglophone opinion and disallowing the act,[90] convinced that most Quebecers would support liberal policies if effectively presented, by himself. After Lapointe decided not to disallow the law, King complained that in cabinet 'all would have been prepared to disallow it had it not been that it was clear that Lapointe would not go that far ... In the circumstances we were prepared to accept what really should not, in the name of Liberalism, be tolerated for one moment.' King added that he 'personally would be quite prepared to fight a Federal battle on the issue, strongly denouncing the legislation of the Quebec government.'[91]

On matters involving his Department of Justice, Lapointe had the final word when they concerned francophone–anglophone relations, but not on all questions. At times King would leave decisions to Lapointe, as he did in 1937 concerning the case of A. Jarvis, a man jailed but widely considered innocent by people demanding a new trial.[92] At other times the prime minister or cabinet decided, as when a penitentiary commission was reduced from five to three members.[93] When the decision was Lapointe's, King often complained that he could not understand Lapointe's 'anti-liberal attitude,' believing that he was too much influenced by officials in his department and by the mood of the francophone population.[94] Lapointe's interpretation of French-Canadian attitudes also continued to affect foreign policy.

When R.B. Bennett became prime minister in 1930 most Canadians probably expected a more imperialist foreign policy. However, during the Bennett years, to 1935, there was a definite continuity in Canadian foreign policy. Despite his complaints that he was ignored, Skelton maintained a certain influence, and the drift away from the commitments of empire continued.[95] The Statute of Westminster of 1931 confirmed Canadian autonomy – the final stage of the evolution led by previous Liberal governments, Lapointe argued. Imperial free trade proved impractical, and the Ottawa Trade Conference of 1932 left unpleasant feelings. Canadian legations abroad were maintained, and Canada was no more committed to participate in British wars under the Conservatives than it had been under the Liberals.[96] There was no revolution in Canadian foreign policy, but Quebec's voice was less present.

When King returned to power in 1935 he had to deal with some divisive issues, and Lapointe followed his actions closely. The international economic depression led to greater acceptance of calls for more controls from fascist and socialist groups, and in Europe these two ideologies collided, most noticeably in the Spanish Civil War. The world took sides, Canadians were divided, and Lapointe sought to minimize the divisions. One possible reaction was encouraging greater world order through collective security, and this option reached a decisive point with the Ethiopian crisis of 1935. Autonomy in the empire had evolved, but Lapointe continued to seek more legations (Skelton's priority in early 1938 was for one in South Africa, Ireland, or Argentina, but Lapointe most favoured Belgium, which became the Canadian priority)[97] and to avoid commitments: the Imperial Conference of 1937 and the Munich crisis would test how autonomous the dominions could remain.

The U.S. position continued to be a major consideration in Canadian decisions on these questions. President Franklin Roosevelt promised that his country would not stand idly by if Canada were attacked.[98] However, this declaration did not indicate any evolution towards collective security. The Americans stayed away from Geneva – an absence that Canada continued to use to justify its own imperfect commitment to collective security. The United States was committed to defending itself, and, in its view, this included the Western Hemisphere.[99] Roosevelt had assured King earlier that the United States would declare war on Japan if it attacked British Columbia, but not if it attacked Australia.[100] The prospect of the American protector replacing the British was less frightening to French Canadians, who seemed more open than English Canadians to the idea of participating in a Pan-American Union.[101]

The most vital relations with the United States continued to be commercial, and one of King's first acts after returning to office in 1935 was to conclude a trade treaty – which Bennett had been negotiating for three years – with the southern neighbour. Skelton remarked privately that he was glad that the deal would prevent the United Kingdom from thinking that 'we had no place to go and gouging us accordingly.'[102] King wired Lapointe after signing the agreement so both could share the historic moment, the crowning of Laurier's work: 'For over a quarter of a century, we have been associated together in working out those Liberal policies with respect to international trade and international goodwill which have today found such noble expression in the relations alike of individuals and nations.'[103] Lapointe replied that the deal justified the work of Laurier, 'l'homme qui a été pour nous deux l'étoile qui nous a guidés dans la vie publique du Canada.'[104]

Conclusion

During this second period of Lapointe's career, King had become firmly placed as leader, and the decision-making structure at Ottawa had changed. Lapointe could no longer rely on King's weakness to permit him to influence policy, but he had also become stronger. He consolidated his support in caucus and the party, becoming a regional leader with definite powers; however, these powers were so different from King's that he should not be considered a co–prime minister. Each man had his own sphere of influence: on matters concerning only Quebec, King accepted the fact that Lapointe had a greater voice; on those involving Quebec and English Canada that risked dividing the two solitudes, Lapointe would have to convince King to listen.

Lapointe could impose his voice with such resources as his influence over the Quebec caucus, his loyalty, and his speaking skills. In addition, he increasingly gained the confidence of the Quebec population in the fact that he would look after its interests. Consequently, if he did not move too far ahead of public opinion, he was increasingly valuable to King as a potential moulder of public opinion. The possibility for an individual to alter public opinion should not be exaggerated: General M.A. Pope, reflecting on the period twenty years after, remarked that 'over the years one has constantly heard the view that it is the business of the politician to lead and to form public opinion. So far as I can judge a public man can mould the opinion of his countrymen to but a minor extent, say, some five or perhaps ten percent; greater change is brought about solely by the hammer blows of events. Consequently, political action is in large measure dependent on an ability correctly to gauge public opinion.'[105] Lapointe could assess sentiment in Quebec as well as anyone, and, within limits, he could encourage it towards a certain direction; but King, unaware of the mood in Quebec, was convinced that Lapointe did not lead Quebecers enough, and during this period confrontations involving issues of foreign policy were more frequent, as we see in chapters 6 and 7.

6

The League, Lapointe, King, and Chaos

During the later 1920s Lapointe had pushed King towards a policy of greater autonomy in the empire. To this end, Lapointe had also encouraged him to accept active Canadian participation at Geneva. In the 1930s the situation was different: the Statute of Westminster of 1931 seemed to ensure autonomy from Britain. Consequently, Lapointe did not have the same interest in the League of Nations, which was no longer needed to establish Canadian status. For example, when the high commissioner for refugees resigned, Skelton opposed the idea of promoting the election of a Canadian to succeed him, unless Canada were willing to accept more refugees, and King agreed.[1] Both men had also opposed Canada's seeking a seat on the Council in 1927, until Lapointe had insisted; but in 1935, instead of pushing King to accept initiatives, Lapointe became as anxious to avoid coercive measures in the League as in the empire.

The Fall of 1935: The Ethiopian Crisis

The League's collective security measures, untried during the 1920s, met their first serious test during the Manchurian crisis of 1931. Japan was quickly identified as the aggressor by most observers, including Prime Minister R.B. Bennett and O.D. Skelton at External Affairs. However, the League could not agree to sanctions, Manchuria was abandoned, and Japan went unpunished.[2] Hopes for the success of the non-coercive measures of the League also suffered a serious blow with the failure of the Disarmament Conference of the early 1930s.[3] The League's reputation was in serious jeopardy, and when Italy threatened to invade Ethiopia in 1935 many observers considered that this test would be decisive. The international response would determine, according to one commentator, whether this is a world of law or of force, 'whether the world begins to work its way slowly upwards towards the sunshine, or whether it slips down towards the dark ages.'[4]

There appeared to be agreement at Geneva that strong measures should be adopted if the Italian invasion occurred. In September 1935 both Britain and France – whose support was essential for the success of sanctions against Italy – pledged themselves to respect the League Covenant if Mussolini attacked Ethiopia. Unimpressed, the Italian dictator defiantly invaded the northeast African country on 4 October 1935, and the League began to consider the application of sanctions against the obvious aggressor. In Canada, Bennett hesitated to approve military force but, influenced by Britain's position, did favour economic sanctions. He instructed the head of the Canadian delegation, G.H. Ferguson, to support Britain's call for economic sanctions on 14 September and on 10 October, over Skelton's opposition. Skelton accused Bennett of abandoning the policy of Canadian opposition to sanctions 'merely because Britain has changed,' while Bennett reminded Skelton that Canada had accepted definite responsibilities as a League member.[5] A month earlier Bennett had called Skelton and Loring Christie, a counsellor in the Department of External Affairs, 'welshers,' for trying to avoid League commitments accepted by Canada.[6]

However, after losing the election of 14 October to King's Liberals, Bennett no longer determined Canada's policy. Who did decide its stand on economic sanctions against Italy was less clear during the two weeks that followed. The Canadian advisory officer, W.A. Riddell, who had replaced G.H. Ferguson as the ranking Canadian delegate at Geneva, took advantage of the confusion to apply his own policy, suggesting that oil be included in the list of items denied to the aggressor.[7] Riddell's proposals to add 'oil, coal, iron and steel' to the list were presented during a meeting of the League's Special Committee of Eighteen on 2 November 1935. The inclusion of oil would add considerable weight, and danger, to the League's sanctions, and Canada became known as one of the countries most firmly behind its stand against Italy. The new Canadian government was not at all comfortable with such a prominent position and warned Riddell not to take any more initiatives.

Throughout November 1935 the debate dragged on at Geneva, and the international press repeatedly referred to 'the Canadian proposal.' On 26 November, Skelton, in the United States with King, wrote Ottawa to remind Riddell not 'to act at his own discretion or pull any more of Mr. Anthony Eden's chestnuts out of the fire.'[8] Lapointe, as acting secretary of state at External Affairs, was not satisfied and wrote Skelton and King that further action was necessary. King agreed and instructed Lapointe to 'arrange to be interviewed' and to state: first, that Ottawa's position as stated on 29 October (when it supported the economic sanctions under consideration at that time) had not changed; second, that Riddell's initiative 'represented only his opinion as member of the committee'; and third, that Canada would continue with others 'to consider changes in situation as they arose.'[9]

Lapointe's statement for publication on 2 December 1935 effectively repudiated Riddell's proposal. Lapointe's wording was similar, though not identical, to what King had proposed: 'The suggestion which has appeared in the press from time to time, that the Canadian Government has taken the initiative in the extension of the embargo upon exportation of key commodities to Italy, and particularly in the placing of a ban upon shipments of coal, oil, iron and steel, is due to a misunderstanding. The Canadian Government has not and does not propose to take the initiative in any such action; and the opinion which was expressed by the Canadian member of the Committee – and which has led to the reference to the proposal as a Canadian proposal – represented only his personal opinion, and his views as a member of the Committee, and not the views of the Canadian Government.'[10] Canada's contribution towards effective sanctions at the League was not only ended, it was reversed. The European press interpreted Lapointe's statement as meaning that Canada would oppose oil sanctions.[11] Soon afterward the French and British were also retreating from their position of strong sanctions, and the Italian invasion was complete. Canada was not responsible for, but did contribute to, the failure of the crucial test for the League.

Most authors who have studied the repudiation of Riddell's initiative have focused on King's role. Of course Lapointe announced the decision, and Riddell was convinced that Lapointe had been responsible for it, but most argue that King shared his Quebec lieutenant's views and as prime minister was responsible for the decision.[12] Veatch describes the exchange of letters between Ottawa and Georgia (where King and Skelton were at the time) and concludes that Riddell's impression that Lapointe and Beaudry bore the main responsibility for repudiating his action 'is clearly not correct. While they raised the question with King, the decision to publicly repudiate Riddell, the way in which it should be done, and the essential content of the statement were all determined by King and Skelton.'[13] Veatch adds that it was King's 'distrust of sanctions and of

Canadian initiatives in world affairs' that made him act.[14] Stacey writes that 'it is not surprising that a government as dependent on Quebec as King's should shy away from the bold sanctionist policies of Ferguson and Riddell.'[15] The impression that most writers leave is that King could read French-Canadian opinion clearly, even without Lapointe's assistance.

The prime minister did have to approve the policy; however, a look at the views of each man throughout the crisis – from August to December – indicates that King was not as uncomfortable as Lapointe about the Canadian position and acted only when pushed by his Quebec lieutenant. Just before the Italian invasion of Ethiopia and during the early stages of the crisis, King strongly supported the League. He even suggested that Canada should lead others in applying coercive measures. In 1934 he announced that economic sanctions against an aggressor would ensure world peace, if all countries were united in their application: 'May I ask my fellow Liberals if there is any reason why, in a matter of so great importance to the world, Canada should wait for any other nation to take the lead? This country should definitely declare not only that it will give no succor to any nation which wantonly disturbs the world's peace, but that it will provide neither arms nor foodstuffs nor credits to such a nation.'[16] 'I confess,' King wrote in his diary in October 1935, concerning the Ethiopian crisis, 'I feel it Canada's duty to stand four square behind the League of Nations. It is another fight of Force vs. Reason. The Brute vs. man. Dictatorship vs. Democracy.'[17]

It was no coincidence that this was also the period when Britain was expressing strong support for the League: King remained more a supporter of Britain than a supporter of the League. He wrote privately that he was 'truly glad the League of Nations is standing for collective security as she is. Britain has never been finer in her whole action for mankind than within this past year and the effort she has made to preserve the peace of Europe.'[18]

Lapointe had also been a strong supporter of the League just before the crisis. He was president of the League of Nations Society in Canada in 1934 and often praised Geneva's work in public.[19] He even claimed in 1935 to support collective security; however, his vision of it required that all countries of the world participate (particularly the United States), and even then it was not clear that he supported the involvement of Canadian soldiers in such activities.[20] He ruled out any form of compulsory cooperation: 'Freedom does not exclude cooperation, on the contrary, it invites it ... [but] compulsory cooperation is a terminological

hypocrisy.'[21] Thus Lapointe's support had been not for a strong organization able to coerce members to cooperate but for a League based on
educating public opinion and conciliation. Not only would there be no
advance commitments to apply force, there would be no force: he argued that there has never been and never will be a war to end all wars,
that war would be eliminated not by war but by the will of the people.[22]

The pressure coming from English Canada was not sufficient to affect
King's views on the question of whether to repudiate Riddell. Anglophones
were divided. Some isolationists such as Skelton opposed Riddell's initiative, linking it with British imperialism,[23] but their voice had not been
sufficiently strong to make King act. Nor were the voices of those supporting Riddell – a very few advocates of collective security and many
more people loyal to British policy – sufficiently strong to influence
King. After Ottawa repudiated Riddell, half the anglophone press supported the policy, and half opposed it.[24] A handful of critics complained
that the League had been undermined, while most had little confidence
in collective security and condemned Ottawa for not standing by Britain.[25] J.H. Fisher of the *Toronto Evening Telegram* argued that Ottawa's
'non cooperation policy as dictated from Quebec' was anti-British and
anti-League. The most controversial reaction was a cartoon of a priest
whispering instructions to Lapointe under the title 'His master's voice.'
Lapointe complained bitterly in Parliament about this caricature and
about comments that he had heard in Toronto and read in *Saturday
Night* magazine, to the effect that because he was Catholic and French
Canadian he was the last person to make such an announcement; his
opponents immediately interpreted it as a disavowal of Britain.[26]

There was much clearer pressure to repudiate Riddell's action coming
from French Canada. In 1934 and 1935 *Le Soleil* at times encouraged the
League to stand firm against aggressors – without Canadian troops. However, most editorials opposed the League's actions, believing that Britain
had too much influence in Geneva and fearing that Canada would be
dragged into a war by high-ranking Britons making policy there.[27] Consequently, there was strong opposition to Riddell's statement in the
francophone press and population and support for the repudiation of
Riddell. One letter thanked Lapointe for reminding Riddell 'que celui-ci
n'était pas le porte-parole de l'Angleterre, mais du Canada.'[28] Chubby
Power credited Lapointe with the statement of 2 December and believed
'that Lapointe, in acting as he did, rendered good service to the nation.'
Power specified that 'it would have been far more difficult, when the

great testing time came over the question of participation in the European war of 1939, for a government so imperialistically and internationally minded to carry Quebec with it.'[29]

Even if King had appreciated the depth of French-Canadian opposition to Riddell's action, he was eager to avoid the impression that Quebec dominated Canadian policy. For example, when Lapointe had asked for a statement repudiating Riddell, he had also asked: 'Would Prime Minister consider sending Dandurand to next meeting of League Committee with special instructions to survey situation and prevent further commitment. He is in Paris.' Skelton immediately replied: 'Prime Minister thinks would be most unwise to send person named.'[30] According to Veatch, 'King's reaction to being represented by a cabinet minister notably sympathetic to the League was blunt.'[31] However, King's concern was more with Dandurand's ethnicity. King wrote in his diary: 'With the European situation what it is, it is better for our French Canadian members to appear in it as little as possible.'[32]

King and Lapointe had sent conflicting signals during the election campaign of 1935. Lapointe sought permission to announce that no Canadian troops would be sent to Ethiopia, but King, strongly favouring economic sanctions against Italy and hesitant even to rule out military sanctions, refused. 'Lapointe rang me up today to have my approval of his saying Canada would not send her men to Abyssinia,' King wrote in his diary. 'I told him this was all right so long as we were not obligated thereto under our adherence to the League of Nations. We must continue to support the League.'[33] During the campaign, King, and Bennett, remained noncommittal, announcing their intention to avoid conflicts where no Canadian interests are involved, thus leaving the door open to the possibility of participation. But Lapointe went much further than his leader, announcing: 'In my opinion no interest in Ethiopia, of any nature whatever, is worth the life of a single Canadian citizen. No consideration could justify Canada's participation in such a war and I am unalterably opposed to it.'[34]

After the Liberal victory and Riddell's initiative, the fundamental difference in the views of King and Lapointe remained. In fact, King justified his refusal to grant Lapointe's desire to take over External Affairs by arguing that Lapointe 'has not stood up for the League of Nations as I think he should have.' On 19 October, during a meeting with Lapointe and Minister of Agriculture J.G. Gardiner, King spoke of his concern that cabinet would split if war broke out over the Ethiopian situation:

'Lapointe immediately said there would be no going into war by Canada,' but King again refused to commit himself. He replied: 'That was well enough to say, but we had in this room itself a divided view on that point; that Gardiner himself thought we ought to go into war, so that was what we may expect – a division of opinion, over which the party may be split wide open.'[35]

When a statement of Canada's position had to be sent to the League, Lapointe threatened 'that he would resign at once' if the government decided for military sanctions.[36] Confronted with this threat, King now, for the first time, agreed to commit himself against military – but not against economic – sanctions. In the statement to Geneva, dated 29 October 1935, King wrote: 'The Canadian Government will take the necessary steps to secure the effective application of the economic sanctions against Italy proposed by the Coordination Committee. The Canadian Government at the same time desires to make it clear that it does not recognize any commitment binding Canada to adopt military sanctions, and that no such commitment could be made without the prior approval of the Canadian Parliament. It is also to be understood that the Government's course in approving economic sanctions in this instance is not to be regarded as necessarily establishing a precedent for future action.'[37] King also began emphasizing national unity: 'Our own domestic situation must be considered first, and what will serve to keep Canada united.' King referred in his diary to the statement's 'going, perhaps, a little more in the way of caution and reservation than the majority of the cabinet would have liked, but which Lapointe regarded as most important.'[38]

After Riddell's initiative of 2 November, Lapointe was undoubtedly more uncomfortable than King with references to the Canadian proposal. King was angered by Riddell's unauthorized initiative and reminded the Canadian advisory officer that he was acting for 'the Government of Canada and not for any other government, delegation or committee.'[39] But, because he remained open to the idea of economic sanctions, he did not feel it necessary to repudiate Riddell until Lapointe suggested action. It was only after Lapointe had insisted on some action that the prime minister wrote in his diary that he had decided 'that we should not delay in making it known, through an interview with the press by Lapointe, that the resolution was not one of which our Government had any knowledge, nor with respect to which Riddell had authority from the Government; that it was a Committee resolution brought forward by Riddell himself.'[40] In addition, Lapointe clearly went further than King would have in suggesting that Ottawa opposed an oil sanction. The event strained relations between the two men, according to one contemporary.[41] In a press conference on 6 December, King stated that his government opposed the unauthorized initiative, not the proposal.[42]

King's views became increasingly synchronized with Lapointe's and more critical of British and League policy. On 11 December he continued to favour the oil sanction, which Lapointe still opposed, until the British and French announced proposals to appease Italy. The prime minister at this point began arguing that even economic sanctions could cause war: 'I agree with Lapointe that the League of Nations, as an agency for world peace, cannot contemplate action which necessarily means war.' King's support for any action by the League rapidly disappeared during December 1935, when he criticized the British and French for their indecisiveness and for sacrificing Ethiopia.[43] He was now on Lapointe's side in cabinet.

In February 1936 King recorded that during a cabinet meeting, some members favoured oil sanctions: 'I was outspoken about our doing nothing which would encourage an act that might set Europe aflame – Lapointe and [Ian] Mackenzie were strongly with me. I think they all began to realize something of the seriousness of world conditions today and the folly of regarding the League as other than papier mâché ... We should be out of the European situation altogether.'[44] King even implied that he had always opposed sanctions and that 'his' repudiation of Riddell had helped prevent a European war.[45] In June 1936, King continued to attack the League in Parliament. 'Collective bluffing cannot bring collective security,' he announced, adding that Canadian governments had always opposed military sanctions and even that economic sanctions lead to war.[46] He himself headed the Canadian delegation to Geneva the following year to make clear the Canadian position that 'emphasis should be placed upon conciliation rather than coercion.'[47]

Lapointe's influence on the decision to repudiate Riddell's initiative was important. His views of sanctions were very different from King's during the autumn of 1935: he announced in public, during the election campaign, that Canada would not participate in military sanctions, and he wrote the statement released on 2 December in a manner that implied that Ottawa opposed oil sanctions. However, these views were not Canadian policy until King adopted them. The prime minister became increasingly opposed to sanctions at Geneva after 2 December 1935. Perhaps he was influenced by events, but it was also the strong pressure coming from Lapointe, particularly his threat of resignation, that made him aware of the danger to unity and of the need to include Quebec's voice in Canadian policy.

Divergent Views of Spain

During the 1930s traditional economic liberalism was questioned in many Western countries. The nineteenth-century illusion that absence of regulation meant equal opportunity and individual liberty was challenged by the reality of an unequal industrialization that did not always reward the most deserving. Innovation and hard work were often no match for big capital, monopolistic corruption, and immoral exploitation. Many individuals considered that the state had to play a new role to ensure equality and liberty, without intervening excessively and destroying the liberty that it sought to preserve. Finding the optimal role for the state was complicated by the fact that economic alternatives were confounded with non-economic considerations. The Soviet Union's experience with 'communism' encouraged prejudice against any state intervention. In reaction, many voices throughout the Western world insisted that, to ensure liberty, 'communism' must be destroyed and 'order' restored; consequently, there was surprising admiration for the economic programs of fascist leaders in the 1920s and 1930s. As Canadian minister of justice, Lapointe would have to be sufficiently severe with 'subversives' to please anti-communists without alienating civil libertarians; as Quebec lieutenant seeking to consolidate his popular support, he would have to guide King.

When the Liberals returned to power in 1935 Lapointe appeared vulnerable to attacks accusing him of being too tolerant towards communists. During the election campaign he had joined those Liberals who were calling for repeal of the repressive Section 98 of the Criminal Code. This law, introduced by the Union government in 1919, effectively declared the Communist party an unlawful association and placed the burden of proof to the contrary on the accused. The Canadian fascists, R.B. Bennett, and many francophones complained to Lapointe that the measure was necessary to control the communists.[48] Section 98 was indeed repealed, and, although communists were refused access to Canadian radio stations, the minister of justice was suspected of not being sufficiently aggressive in the war against communism.[49] After their return to power the Liberals had also removed the embargo of February 1931 on the USSR, and Lapointe told King that this move would be highly unpopular in Quebec but that he 'would face and fight' the pressure.[50] The

Quebec lieutenant would have to be careful not to encourage the impression that Ottawa was 'soft' on communism.

Spain became the centre of international attention in 1936, particularly for the Communist and fascist parties that had taken root throughout Europe and the world. In February the Popular Front, a coalition of left-wing groups favouring greater state intervention, obtained the majority of seats in the Spanish Parliament. A republic had replaced the Spanish monarchy in 1931, and during the election of 1936 the left coalition won a majority of seats, even though the right and centre groups had won a majority of the votes. Only fourteen of the 600 members in the Cortes were Communist, but right-wing 'Nationalist' rebels led by General Francisco Franco decided that the 'communist' Parliament was unacceptable and, on 18 July 1936, attempted to overthrow the 'Loyalist' Republican government.[51]

Germany and Italy massively supported Franco's fascists and referred to the clash between communism and order; the Soviet Union supported the Republican government and spoke of a battle between democracy and fascism. Officially, most Western countries adopted a policy of nonintervention, although individual citizens from many of these countries did fight for democracy with the Republican government, including 1,239 Canadian volunteers.[52] These volunteers, the Mackenzie–Papineau Battalion, presented a dilemma for the dominion government. Of the 1,239 Canadians who volunteered, only thirty-six were francophone Quebecers, and the Catholic church everywhere strongly opposed the Republican government. There was much pressure on Lapointe from Quebec to ensure that all Canadians remained neutral and did not help the Spanish 'communists.'[53]

The Liberal government's reply to the war was to pass, with little debate in Parliament, the Foreign Enlistment Act in early 1937. This law specified that any Canadian volunteering for either side would be imprisoned for two years, although the only side on which Canadians were enlisting was the Loyalist. It also forbade sale of equipment or munitions to either side, although supplies shipped from Canada were reaching Franco through Morocco.[54] Ottawa's intervention clearly had the effect of discouraging aid to the Republican government. Lapointe admitted that 'dans une certaine mesure ... le bill comporte un empiètement sur la liberté, mais c'est pour le bien du pays.'[55] The legislation infringed on the rights of those who sought to volunteer (mostly anglophones), and the minister of justice, possibly in an attempt to defend the act in English Canada, emphasized the similarities with the British neutrality act.[56]

It may have deterred some from volunteering in Spain, but it was not applied to the Canadian veterans on their return, after the fall of Barcelona to Franco's troops ended the war in February 1939.[57]

Many historians again focus on King when describing the formulation of the Canadian reaction to the Spanish Civil War. According to Thompson and Seager, 'Mackenzie King at once recognized that Spain ... provided a cause for the potential domestic conflict he so dreaded.'[58] There was indeed potential for disunity in what some francophone historians describe as the struggle between Catholic rebels and the communist government.[59] However, King considered that Lapointe exaggerated the possibility of domestic conflict, and other historians have acknowledged that Lapointe, more than King, influenced the Canadian policy.[60]

King saw little reason to favour either side in the civil war. He was not one of the English Canadians with great sympathy for the Republican government, which he believed was controlled by Moscow. King was particularly upset because Canadians fighting for this side named themselves the Mackenzie–Papineau Battalion (he described the group as the 'W.L. Mackenzie Company'). His grandfather would have fought communists, King believed.[61] At the same time, King saw no reason to help Franco's rebels and resented accusations that his government's policy favoured the fascist group. He wrote to an American friend: 'I am at a loss to understand how you or anyone else could be of the opinion that my sympathies in the Spanish Civil War have been with Franco and the rebels.'[62] Because it corresponded with British policy and did not arouse significant opposition in English Canada, King accepted the Foreign Enlistment Act; however, he remained relatively uninterested in the conflict and in any Canadian reaction.

Some anglophones pressed Ottawa to support the Republican government and the Canadians fighting for democracy in Spain, but such pressure was not great.[63] The greatest pressure, which came mostly from francophone Quebec, encouraged the government to support the Nationalists or at least to ensure that Canada did nothing to help the Republicans.[64] The intense Catholic antipathy towards communism was not strong enough to inspire francophones to join Franco's army, but it did inspire considerable sympathy among them for the Nationalists. Duplessis sought political points when he accused Ottawa of siding with the Loyalists by providing passports for Canadians fighting in Spain and by allowing the recruitment of communists in Quebec.[65]

The pressure coming from Quebec was again interpreted through the voice of Lapointe at Ottawa, and again King was sure that his Quebec

lieutenant exaggerated. For example, Lapointe strongly opposed a request, supported by King and the anglophones in cabinet, to allow four
Spanish Republican speakers to tour the country. He warned King that
there would be a strong, even violent reaction to them in Montreal. King
could not understand why 'Lapointe seemed to think that if they were
allowed to come into Canada at all, it might only lead to secession of the
Province of Quebec from the rest of the Dominion.' King added in his
diary that he feared acting like the dictators and that such action would
lead to worse abuses: 'I would rather go out of office and out of life itself,
if need be, fighting to maintain the liberties we have and which have
been bought so dearly, than to be a party to losing them through fear
and prejudice however strong. Lapointe's fear of the Cardinal and
Duplessis amounts to absolute terror. No one can convince me that if he,
himself, and a few others would begin to expound the doctrines of Liberalism to the younger generation of Quebec, it would not take long to
free them from clerical or political intolerance.' An incident in October
1936, when students from Loyola College and the Université de Montréal
clashed with students from McGill University over the freedom of speech
to be allowed Republican speakers, helped persuade King to agree that
the four Spanish speakers should not be allowed near Quebec when they
sought admission to Canada in December 1936.[66]

The prime minister continued to believe that Lapointe overestimated
possible nationalist reactions in the province and that he was too fearful
of the church.[67] He wrote in his diary that Lapointe was too timid with
Duplessis, that he should assert himself. King remarked that Duplessis
was provoking Lapointe and that in cabinet 'Power was quite outspoken
as to the need of Lapointe, Cardin and Rinfret, as Federal Ministers,
taking a stronger and firmer hand in the forthcoming Provincial Liberal
Convention at Quebec, than they had proposed to do. Lapointe is rather
timid in the matter ... I am inclined to think, however, that Power is
right, and that they will have to assert themselves as I have no doubt they
will, when the time comes.'[68] Lapointe, not King, would know when the
time had come.

Lapointe's voice corresponds closely with Canadian policy towards the
Spanish Civil War. Reacting to issues involving communism was a delicate task for any leader of the period, and the debate over section 98 and
Quebec's Padlock Law had considerably affected Ottawa's response to
international questions involving communism and fascism during the
1930s, most notably concerning the war in Spain. The opinions of
Quebec's francophones, stronger than many anglophones such as King

realized, had to be present in Ottawa's policy. Concerning the relatively minor question of admitting the Loyalist speakers, Lapointe pushed King further than King would have gone in limiting their freedom of speech, but he could not convince King to keep them out of the country. More important, as minister of justice Lapointe played a significant role in formulating and applying the Foreign Enlistment Act, and, as voice of Quebec, he was particularly anxious to impede all Canadian aid to the Republican government. On his own, King would have been less anxious to propose the act, and yet, because Britain had a similar policy, he probably would have implemented it without Lapointe's presence. Lapointe needed King's approval but did have a co-dominant voice in this decision.

Conclusion

Lapointe sought with success to include the voice of Quebec in Ottawa's reply to the invasion of Ethiopia and to the Spanish Civil War. In each case the result was to minimize Canadian intervention in foreign conflicts. When reacting to the Italian invasion, the prime minister offered greater resistance when Quebec's voice disagreed with British policy, but eventually King and Lapointe, each with a co-dominant voice, accepted compromise policies. As is seen in the next chapter, Lapointe would have more difficulty convincing King to avoid international entanglements when the interests of the empire were more directly involved.

7

Nation to Colony?

The League of Nations died a slow but certain death after the Ethiopian catastrophe. In 1938 Lapointe led the Canadian delegation to Geneva, announcing that by 'practice and consent, the system of sanctions under the Covenant had ceased to have effect. Sanctions had become non-automatic and non-obligatory.'[1] But he had not given up hope that the League would fulfil its role as an organization of conciliation. In a speech after these meetings he expressed the hope that the League would never perish: 'I may appear over-confident, but I trust that some day it will achieve its purpose.'[2] The presence of the United States, he continued to insist, was necessary for the success of the organization – not because of American military power but because discussions for peace would be more likely to succeed if all major powers participated.[3] With the impotence of the League clearly exposed to the world, Britain sought greater commitments from its friends.

The Imperial Conference of 1937

The idea of a common imperial foreign policy was again on the agenda at the Imperial Conference of 1937 in London. Britain's principal objective at the gathering was to pry out of the dominions definite commitments in case of war or at least to 'harmonize' the foreign policies of Britain and the dominions. Malcolm MacDonald, Britain's dominions secretary, stated privately that the object of the conference 'must be to get harmony on foreign policy and – in effect, therefore, – a common foreign policy, but not to attempt to get a common foreign policy in name ... It would be possible to go this far, though it must be realized that the dominions could not be expected to accept any definite commitments as regards assistance to this country in the event of war. What was necessary was to state the foreign policy of the United Kingdom, to ask the dominion delegations to indicate the foreign policies of their Governments and then hope that these policies might so harmonise that, in effect, they would be one.'⁴ King's objective of bringing Britain and the United States together as an example of economic cooperation and world peace received little attention. To what degree would the Canadian government agree to commit itself, in public or in private, to go to Britain's side if war broke out?

During the conference Ottawa maintained in public that 'Parliament will decide' policy. King told the conclave that in order to maintain Canadian unity it was necessary to avoid if possible 'participation in overseas wars or commitments so to participate.' King specified that although Canadians had preferred conciliation rather than commitments to participate in sanctions at Geneva, 'it is when we pass from the question of League to Empire war relations that we touch a really vital issue and face the possibility of definite cleavage.' On the one hand, he noted, 'there are many forces which would make for Canadian participation in a conflict in which Britain's interests were seriously at stake ... On the other hand, opposition to participation in war, any war, is growing ... No policy in Canada is more generally accepted than that commitments of any kind, involving possible participation in war, must have prior and specific approval by Parliament.'⁵

The delegations from Australia and New Zealand very much favoured greater imperial cooperation, but King remained adamant that any attempt to bind Ottawa to British foreign or defence policy would alienate Canadian public opinion and, if war broke out, be counter-productive. King argued: 'It is certain that any attempt to reach a decision, or take steps involving a decision in advance, would precipitate a controversy that might destroy national unity without serving any imperial interest, and that the decision given on an abstract issue in advance might be quite different from the decision taken in a concrete situation if war arose.'⁶ British policy-makers, who undoubtedly would have preferred a more binding commitment, understood and seemed satisfied with the probability of Canadian help.⁷

Historians who have studied the Canadian role at the Imperial Conference of 1937 focus on King and his refusal to make any commitments. Some argue that he was sensitive to the views of French Canadians⁸ or overly sensitive to these views.⁹ Others claim that he was following his own autonomist or isolationist desire to avoid commitments.¹⁰ The idea that King's ambiguous policy was a calculated strategy to alienate as few Canadians as possible as he prepared them for participation in a British war is shared by most writers – francophone and anglophone.[11] They make no distinction between the views of King and those of Lapointe. According to Hillmer, King 'had decided that ambiguity would offend the fewest. As long as there was hope for all sides, none would definitively turn against the government and begin to marshal its forces. Meanwhile King and his lieutenant, Ernest Lapointe, prepared the way for eventual Canadian participation in a British war with a cautious rearmament program and a careful balancing of support for the defence of Britain and appeals for the declaration of Canada's right to neutrality.'[12] Historians have thus implied that both men were equally willing to go to Britain's aid if war broke out. They were not.

King was indeed 'Ready, aye ready,' in 1937 to go to Britain's side in the event of a major European war. He assured the British of this support – in private – as he had at the Imperial Conferences of 1923 and 1926. He recorded in his diary after the 1937 meeting that he had 'made clear to the British Ministers that in Canada we could not and would not consider anything in the nature of an Expeditionary Force or make appropriations beyond our own security ... I stated, however, that if it became evident that Germany or any other country was guilty of aggression, I thought the voluntary feeling in Canada would assert itself in a strong way, and that it would be difficult to hold back those who would be prepared to see that aggression was stayed.'[13] After the conference King also visited Germany to warn Hitler that Canada would be with Britain.

The British leaders were pleased with King's visit to Germany, because he had promised to tell Hitler that the dominions would support Britain if it were attacked. Although, as Neatby notes, there is no evidence that Hitler understood the same thing as King when the Canadian warned him that if the freedom of any part of the Commonwealth were threatened all the dominions would rally to its defence, King did make an effort to announce Canadian support of Britain. King was not completely unaware of the danger posed by Nazi Germany. He had commented in his diary in 1936 that 'it is amazing that with this frank statement of purpose, Hitler has been permitted to go to the lengths he has,' but he hoped that Britain could stay out of European problems.[14] That King does not deserve the reputation of a naive appeaser is further suggested by the fact that his visit with Hitler was supported by such hard-line supposed opponents of appeasement as British Secretary of State for

Foreign Affairs Anthony Eden and U.S. Secretary of State Cordell Hull.[15] After the meeting, King told Hull that Hitler sought peace, and Hull said that he believed this but that if economic problems arose even Hitler would not be able to ensure peace.[16] For King, the ambiguous public policy was a strategy to alienate the smallest possible number of Canadians while he remained convinced that once the guns started firing, English-Canadian autonomists and isolationists would support Britain – as long as it appeared that their Parliament had freely decided the matter.

Lapointe, however, did not see in the government's 'Parliament will decide' statements anything other than a no-commitment policy. King recorded that, during one meeting, when he repeated that Canada did not believe in 'collective security through reliance on force,' or in a common imperial foreign policy, 'Lapointe said to me when I had finished, that he thought I had covered every point.'[17] There was no need to add that, in case of war, Canada would be at Britain's side. King also recorded that Lapointe 'strongly approved' of his trip to see Hitler – and of other Canadian initiatives to improve relations with Germany, such as plans for an exchange of six students and the signing of a provisional trade agreement in November 1936 – not so that King could warn Hitler of Canada's intention to help Britain, but as a policy, independent of Britain's, focusing on dialogue.[18]

Increased defence spending by the Liberals had concerned French Canadians, but after the conference of 1937 many expressed satisfaction with Canadian policy, which they believed signified neutrality in any British war.[19] Henri Bourassa was particularly encouraged to see R.B. Bennett step down as Conservative leader: 'Comme ça, le roi Bennett a abdiqué? Le grrrand [sic] parti conservateur s'en va à la débandade ... çela devrait vous rendre plus facile la tâche de museler les chiens impérialistes,' he suggested to Lapointe.[20] Le Soleil also considered Lapointe's presence in Ottawa crucial, not only to continue ensuring Canada's right to decide its own policy, but also to express opposition to any military participation in Europe. One editorialist, perhaps going further than Lapointe would have, suggested that Lapointe would rather sacrifice his own life than allow his country to be dragged into a foreign war.[21]

Lapointe and the Liberals passed a major test of their foreign and defence policies in the 1937 by-election in Lotbinière, when the Liberal candidate defeated a nationalist. During the campaign the Quebec lieutenant continued to insist that the increased military spending at Ottawa was for the defence of Canada only. He made it very clear that he preferred avoiding not only advance commitments but all British wars: 'S'il faut des actes pour défendre le pays, nous en sommes. Mais Ernest Lapointe ne serait plus ministre s'il y avait quelque chose de plus dans ces crédits.' In another speech he denied accusations that Ottawa was 'spending huge sums of money to send Canadians to foreign wars. It is a malicious untruth ... Those credits are for the defence of Canada ... I would not be a party to any other measure ... I am and will be opposed to Conscription. I am opposed to Canada being involved in wars, but I do not want Canada to be powerless and unable to defend itself on its own territory if ever attacked.'[22] Lapointe was pleased, he told Parliament, that this by-election had shown the other provinces that questioned the sentiments of Quebecers that the noise made by nationalist groups did not represent the voice of the province.[23] French Canadians seemed to support the government's policy, clearly understood as meaning no involvement in any British war.[24]

King's strategy reflected a sure knowledge of public opinion in English Canada. He knew that after the fall of the League, Canadians had the choice between a 'British front policy' or isolation. The isolationists seemed more numerous: in the words of J.W. Dafoe, 'the spirit of isolation is spreading in Canada like a prairie fire.'[25] But the influence of the imperialists, who enjoyed disproportionate weight in the determination of Canadian policy because of their money and social position, remained strong.[26] In addition, King knew that despite the Statute of Westminster many anglophones – even many isolationists – would not think of staying out of a major European war if Britain were in serious danger.[27] King was less aware of how opposed French Canadians were to Canadian involvement in any overseas war.

Just how different the views of King and Lapointe were on commitments to Britain became evident during the much-publicized debates related to defence policy that had made headlines just before the 1937 conference. Defence expenditures, which had been $13 million in 1935–6, grew to $33 million in 1937–8 after a decision by the Liberal cabinet in December 1936.[28] Britain had privately asked Canada to increase its defence spending in order to help Britain in case of war.[29] King favoured a 'united front' policy, as long as the appearance was maintained that Canadian defence decisions were made in Ottawa. After publicly denying the affirmations of some British politicians that the empire had given assurances to help Britain, King wrote in his diary that he did not object to coöperation: 'What is most regrettable is the fact that these statements have to be made at the most critical moment and at the very time when, if other people would not make false representations, a united front could be observed without anything being said.'[30] This policy corresponded with what the British seemed to be seeking at the Imperial Conference: no definite public commitments, but an understanding in private of harmonized foreign policies.

Lapointe, representing French-Canadian opinion, strongly opposed any spending for Canadian forces outside Canada.[31] King wrote in his diary that most ministers opposed increased spending, particularly Charles Dunning, at Finance, while Lapointe supported King as long as no money was spent for Canadian forces to be sent abroad.[32] When a French-Canadian MP challenged expenditures for involvement in overseas war, Lapointe replied that the expenditures had nothing to do with foreign wars.[33] Canada would not defend Britain, he argued, but neutrality was not possible; all countries had to defend their territories, and he therefore opposed the motion of CCF leader J.S. Woodsworth proposing Canadian neutrality. Lapointe argued that neutrality would signify 'que le Canada se sépare du commonwealth britannique ... Il y a toute la différence du monde entre la neutralité et la participation ou la non-participation à une guerre, chose que nous avons toujours la liberté de déclarer. Le Parlement canadien sera toujours libre de décider si nous prendrons part ou non à une guerre. Mais la neutralité est une tout autre chose.'[34] In private letters to King, Lapointe was even clearer: 'Every European nation looks after her own individual interest and her policies are guided by it. Why should Canada act otherwise?'[35] Lapointe believed that the increased defence spending was exclusively for the defence of Canada, while King remained convinced that it could be used to help Britain.

In 1936, when considering defence estimates, King told cabinet that Canada would have to help Britain more: 'It was amazing the extent to which many of those present spoke over and over again of keeping out of European wars and out of Asiatic wars not realizing in the least that Canada can never hope to escape a world war ... Lapointe seemed greatly concerned about Quebec, fearing the nationalistic party will soon become a solid block [sic] in Parliament against any expenditures for defence purposes. I have no fears of that if the matter is presented in its true light.'[36] King believed that Lapointe should mould the opinion of Quebecers while he reported to the Imperial Conference of 1937 with pride how he had stifled debate in Canada: 'I told them how I had endeavoured to prevent discussion on foreign affairs in Parliament by persuading members in caucus to leave the matter alone in the House of Commons.'[37]

At the conference King and Lapointe did not have the same objectives. King was clearly more inclined to make unpublicized commitments to help Britain than Lapointe, who preferred a policy of no external wars. Whether Lapointe influenced King's public policy at the conference is less obvious. Probably King, in order to reassure the English-Canadian autonomists and isolationists, would have applied the same 'Parliament will decide' policy in 1937 even without Lapointe, who realized the pressure in English Canada and was very comfortable with a policy of no commitments. Both men agreed with this ambiguous policy. A year later, when the theoretical question was a step closer to reality, when the difference between anglophone and francophone autonomists became more apparent, the different views of the two men would collide.

Munich

The absence of effective collective security measures at the League encouraged aggressive leaders such as Hitler to act. In March 1936 Germany had remilitarized the Rhineland. There seemed some justification for this violation of the Treaty of Versailles, and few people were ready to go to war over the incident. Lapointe told King after the event, which he described as an 'act of almost criminal stupidity,' that he expected that Canada would not become involved in any war as a result of constitutional ties with Britain.[38] Two years later there also seemed to be some justification for Anschluss – Hitler's annexation of German-speaking Austria – and there was not much more support for any sanctions against Germany.[39] However, as one newspaper remarked, it would be a different story when Czechoslovakia was involved.[40]

Six months later, on 12 September 1938, Hitler demanded 'self-determination' for the Sudeten Germans in Czechoslovakia, and the international reaction was indeed different. The world was on the brink of war for two weeks as Prime Minister Neville Chamberlain of Britain made trips to Germany on 15 September, on 22 September, and finally on 28 September, for a conference at Munich, where a solution was reached. The leaders of Britain, France, Germany, and Italy agreed on 30 September that Germany would occupy the Sudeten area of Czechoslovakia ... but not the areas with non German-speaking Czechs.

Chamberlain could have led the world against Hitler in a war to stop the Führer's aggressive advance. If Chamberlain had led such a mission, who would have followed? Some American historians claim that Roosevelt was seeking to stiffen Chamberlain's spine and encourage collective security,[41] but Chamberlain was not naïve enough to count on U.S. support to help push Germany out of Czechoslovakia. Nor could he depend on France, the dominions, or British public opinion, and, in addition, the British military was unprepared.[42] Winston Churchill had explained to a Czechoslovaki official in June 1938 that even though he himself 'was criticizing Chamberlain, he might well have followed the same policy if he had held the responsibilities of power.'[43] Declaring war on Hitler in September 1938 was not an option.

What Chamberlain could do was to trap Hitler, make him sign a paper affirming that Germany had no further legitimate territorial demands. This fragile piece of paper established definite limits on Hitler's aggression. The German leader's strategy had depended on propaganda that gave his aggression the appearance of justifiable action; he realized that international public opinion would hesitate to insist on sanctions against Germany. King admitted in 1941 that Canada would 'never have been able to go to war as a united' country had it not been for Chamberlain's trip, exposing Hitler's intentions.[44] Munich forced Hitler to change strategy, and rather than seeing this agreement as a great triumph the German leader considered it 'the greatest setback of his career.'[45]

The Canadian government did consider openly supporting Chamberlain's policy even if it led to war. On 23 September, a week before the agreement at Munich, cabinet – without Lapointe – favoured making a statement announcing that 'the world might as well know at once that Canada will not stand idly by and see modern civilisation ruthlessly destroyed if we can by co-operation with others help save mankind from such a fate.'[46] King asked for Lapointe's views and received the following telegram:

Cannot see that any statement should be made prior to an outbreak of war. Situation in important parts of Canada extremely delicate and requires most careful handling. Public opinion will have to be prepared not aroused by irrevocable steps. Australia and New Zealand stand in most different situation. Immediate cause of war namely minority problems in Central Europe not of a nature to enthuse our people. Submit that Parliament should be summoned, if war declared, and no definite commitment made meanwhile. Only yesterday in League of Nations I made statement based on our previous stand and constantly expressed policy that any decision on the part of Canada to participate in war would have to be taken by the Parliament of Canada in the light of existing circumstances.

I do not see how I could advise any course of action that would not only be opposed to personal convictions and sacred pledges to my own people but would destroy all their confidence and prevent me from carrying weight and influence with them for what might be essential future actions. Please consider these views and submit them to colleagues before reaching final decision. God help you. I still strongly feel that conflagration shall be avoided.[47]

King had underestimated the role that Lapointe attached to the 'Parliament will decide' policy and, surprised at Lapointe's reply, wired his lieutenant to return to Ottawa as soon as possible.[48]

A few days later, the government issued a much less binding statement, reaffirming the principle that Parliament would decide Canadian policy: 'The government is making preparations for any contingency and for the immediate summoning of Parliament if the efforts which are still being made to preserve the peace of Europe should fail. For our country to keep united is all-important. To this end, in whatever we say or do, we must seek to avoid creating controversies and divisions that might seriously impair effective and concerted action when Parliament meets. The government is in complete accord with the statement Mr. Chamberlain has made to the world today.'[49] After receiving news of an agreement on 29 September, the government congratulated Chamberlain as a 'great conciliator,' and King later felt like a cad for not having supported Britain more.[50]

Historians have not sufficiently appreciated the weight of Lapointe's telegram in the formulation of Canadian policy. Some imply, by underestimating the difference between King's preferred message and the actual statement of 27 September, that King did offer a firm commitment to go to Britain's side in the event of war with Germany.[51] Other authors argue more convincingly that Ottawa withheld a commitment but credit King, not Lapointe, with having realized that Canadian public opinion would not accept the proposed policy.[52] Neatby affirms that Lapointe, unable or unwilling to exercise a veto, 'knew that Canadian participation would be inevitable if war broke out ... He knew that the English-Canadian reaction could not be ignored and he had confidence in the political judgment of his colleagues.' Neatby concludes that Lapointe left the final decision to King, who expected 'and even anticipated this reply.'[53] Stacey agrees that Lapointe's message merely 'showed that Lapointe was deeply troubled' and postulates that King's impression, a year after the crisis, that it contained a threat of resignation was an exaggeration: 'It is hard to believe that Lapointe would have deserted King, and there is really no suggestion of it in the telegram he sent him.'[54] Hillmer and Granatstein write that King made the decisions during the crisis and that cabinet ministers agreed that they 'would have to take the country into war if Britain became involved in an armed clash over Czechoslovakia.'[55] Most historians therefore conclude that Lapointe's telegram simply confirmed King's views, supported his policy, and had little impact.

King's personal preference was clearly to commit Canada to Britain's side. Early in the crisis, on 31 August, King told Chubby Power and Ian Mackenzie 'that I would stand for Canada doing all she possibly could to destroy those Powers which are basing their action on might and not on right, and that I would not consider being neutral in this situation for a moment.' Throughout September he continued to express his intention to announce Canadian support for Britain. He recorded in his diary a conversation with the minister of labour, Norman Rogers: 'We both agreed that it was a self-evident national duty, if Britain entered the war, that Canada should regard herself as part of the British Empire, one of the nations of the sisterhood of nations, which should cooperate lending every assistance possible, in no way asserting neutrality, but carefully defining in what ways and how far she would participate.' By 23 September he informed Skelton that he was now convinced that the time had come to publicize his intentions. Skelton pointed out that this meant that Parliament would not decide, and King replied that he 'thought we would have to indicate long before Parliament met what our policy would be, though Parliament itself would decide whether that policy should be carried out.'[56]

After agreeing not to announce Canadian support for Britain, he maintained his views in private: 'Personally, I feel very strongly that the issue is one of the great moral issues of the world, and that one cannot afford to be neutral on an issue of this kind. I feel Canada would be shamed ... if, while Britain and other parts of the Empire fought on an issue of this kind, we stayed out.' He repeated to Skelton 'that if Britain was at war, we would have to accept the view that Canada was also at war, both because of the legal position – the King representing the British Empire, as a whole, and also the view that the enemy might take of the situation. The nature and extent of our participation would be for Canada's Parliament to decide.'[57] King was thus prepared to announce that Canada would be at Britain's side, and he expected Lapointe to be equally ready.

Lapointe's telegram revealed that his personal views had not changed as King had hoped. Lapointe maintained the stance that he had expressed to Parliament in May 1938: 'En quoi consiste la politique étrangère du Canada? Elle vise à nous éviter la guerre.' During this speech Lapointe had disagreed with Bennett's vision of the empire, particularly the affirmation that when Britain is at war Canada is too: 'Il a dit que nous étions tenus de remplir les obligations découlant de cette libre association. Il me semble que les mots "obligations" et "liberté" ne vont pas très bien ensemble.' Liberty, Lapointe continued, was the link that guaranteed the survival of the association.[58] In private Lapointe had told King at the same time that if war broke out cabinet would split.[59]

King assumed that by 31 August Lapointe would surely be ready to support British policy. He refused to consider the possibility suggested by Power that some Quebec ministers might resign: 'I told him [Power] that the Cabinet Ministers should realize that it would be the end of Quebec if any attitude of that kind were adopted by the French Canadians in a world conflict such as this one would be. They, as members of the Government, ought to lead the Province in seeing its obligation to participate, and making clear the real issue and what it involves. Power thought Lapointe would become so nervous and upset that he would be good for nothing, which I fear is only too true, though what he learns at the League and in France may cause him to feel differently ere his return.'[60] King thus counted on Lapointe to be more active in 'educating' Quebecers, while he continued to stifle debate.[61] But Lapointe's telegram made it clear that he did not feel differently and had no intention of leading Quebec opinion in the way suggested by King.

French Canadians, like most of the world, supported Chamberlain's peace initiatives. If war broke out, Hitler would clearly be seen as the aggressor, but it remained a European war.[62] Le Soleil thus opposed a statement of Canadian intention to help Britain: 'Dire d'avance: nous interviendrons ou nous n'interviendrons pas, ce serait provoquer, inutilement si la guerre n'a pas lieu, des controverses et des divisions au sein de notre population à un moment où l'unité est plus que jamais nécessaire.'[63] King, receiving no help from the other Quebec ministers and unable to read opinion in French Canada, was ready to proceed with the statement of 23 September until Lapointe's telegram warned of stronger opposition in Quebec than King had believed possible.

King had his eye on English-Canadian public opinion. After the statement of 27 September was issued, King wrote a revealing passage in his diary: 'I am really amazed that Dandurand and Cardin should have felt there was danger in even going that far in expressing ourselves ... The attitude of each of them was that going as far as Council had decided

would probably cost us many seats in Quebec. If it would cost the party
its whole existence, I would much rather pay that price for what I know
to be right.' Later in the day, after Hitler had agreed to meet Chamberlain at Munich, the chances of peace improved, and King began to see
the situation more clearly: 'I am mighty glad I got in the word I did
yesterday, not only that we were in complete accord with Chamberlain's
statement, but that we would want our Parliament to be prepared for
"effective and concerted action." I see now how I went as far as I did. I
was thinking of the jingos, the "Globe" and others, in asking that we
should avoid divisions and discussions that might prejudice unified action on the part of Parliament. Having concentrated my thoughts so
much in that direction, it did not occur to me that the province of
Quebec might regard the communication as indicating a determination
to participate, and for them to avoid discussions meanwhile.'[64]

The prime minister knew English Canada and expected that if Britain
decided to fight and Ottawa announced its support, 'we would have
Canada very solidly at our back, just as I am sure Chamberlain would
have pretty much the whole of Britain at his back.'[65] The events at Munich
had in fact considerably shaken public opinion throughout the world,
and English Canadians did seem increasingly ready to support Britain.[66]
Some isolationist anglophones were not, however, and Skelton, who remarked in his diary that he found King in a 'very belligerent' mood,
strongly opposed his statement.[67] But the prime minister was less impressed with this group because he had a good idea of how small a
proportion of the anglophone population its views represented.[68]

King and Lapointe clearly had different ideas about what Ottawa should
announce, and Lapointe's telegram went further than simply expressing
personal opposition to King's suggestion. Those who knew Lapointe realized that he was threatening to resign. King, better than anyone, realized the strength of the telegram, and although he wrote little about it in
his diary at the time he later acknowledged that he had understood that
Lapointe was threatening to quit.[69] Skelton also recognized the power of
the words employed by Lapointe and their influence on King: 'Good old
Ernest came across,' Skelton recorded in his diary, 'with an emphatic
rejection of any pre-war statement – must adhere to pledges to parliament – premature action would destroy his influence for what might be
essential to future action. Mr. King was surprised at his emphatic attitude, in view of Power's reports.'[70] Power had told cabinet on 23 September that he found opinion in Quebec 'much less antagonistic' to supporting Britain than he had expected.[71] Skelton added two days later that

King was 'a bit less belligerent – I think Lapointe's telegram sobered him a bit.'[72]

The difference in the views of Lapointe and King during the Munich crisis was confirmed by a minor incident at Geneva. On 20 September Lapointe sought King's permission to reduce even more the chance of Geneva'a applying coercive sanctions, but King refused: 'I agree it would be desirable as Mr Lapointe proposes to put on record our view as stated ... I do not think it desirable, particularly under present circumstances, to emphasize any remaining differences between our position and that of the United Kingdom.'[73] Neither Lapointe nor King had any interest in sanctions at Geneva, but because Lapointe also opposed Canadian involvement in Britain's problems he was much less concerned with the message that would be implied by an anti-sanctions statement delivered while Chamberlain was negotiating with Hitler. The incident was minor because the policies adopted at Geneva had become irrelevant: according to Lapointe, 'declarations of far reaching importance for the immediate future of the League are being made – but it is evident that all this work is being done in the sort of atmosphere we associate with the school room at the end of a term, the business being got through as a mechanical task whilst the minds of those engaged in it are far away, distracted by the urge of a more compelling interest.'[74]

During the crisis of September 1938 King and Lapointe differed in their views. Because the decision was taken not to issue a statement changing the 'Parliament will decide' policy to one committing Canada to go to Britain's side in the event of war, the voice of Lapointe was dominant over King's. However, Lapointe did require King's approval.

Conclusion

During the period of his career from 1930 to 1938 Lapointe was particularly concerned with representing the views of francophone Quebec. In order to slow the growing nationalist momentum he leaned more towards anti-communist policies and commitments to avoid involving Canada in European conflicts. King was not inclining in the same direction. With the two men favouring different policies, the way in which decisions were taken was crucial. The leader of the Liberals in Quebec decided questions involving his province, such as not permitting the four Spanish speakers into Quebec. But on the Foreign Enlistment Act he needed King's approval, as it also involved the other provinces. Similarly, with matters relating to Canadian policy during the 1937 Imperial Conference and the Ethiopian and Munich crises, Lapointe's voice was one of many, and he had to be more creative to make sure that it was heard. However, as the Munich crisis revealed, King seems to have concluded that 'Parliament will decide' was a commitment crucial to Lapointe's authority in his province, not to be changed without his approval. Lapointe thus had a dominant voice in this decision and a co-dominant voice on the other three.

Lapointe's task of moulding policy was facilitated by the strength of King, who was solidly in control of his party and the anglophone ministers. Parliament continued to have little opportunity to affect policy, and Skelton had influence only when his views corresponded with King's.[75] Consequently, to have a say in Canadian foreign policy Lapointe had to influence King, counting on his usual resources (ability to read the Quebec population, loyalty, speaking skills, and his control of the Quebec caucus) and increasingly on threats to resign. Lapointe did have success, and the Quebec voice was heard, not because King was sensitive to the needs of francophones but because Lapointe insisted. In contrast to the first period, when Lapointe pushed King to action, during the second, Lapointe used his influence to restrain King.

King, as prime minister, is often automatically considered the sole individual to have been determining Canadian policies while he was in office. Even at the time, King remarked that he and his colleague had both had a good laugh when they read the tribute to Lapointe during a ceremony when he was given an honorary degree at Cambridge: the statement focused on King![76] However, in each of the major questions studied in this chapter, King's final decisions were influenced by Lapointe, and the prime minister realized this. As actual war approached, King would become more eager to support the British, and the Quebec lieutenant's role would not become easier.

PART III:
FIGHTING CONSCRIPTION,
1939-1941

8

Fighting King and Cabinet

Lapointe's influence in Ottawa had risen constantly during the 1930s, but the early months of 1939 were turbulent. Increasing awareness of the dangers posed by Nazi aggression shook the established order in many countries, and Ottawa's decision-making structure was significantly altered. In Quebec Lapointe consolidated and in many ways reinforced his position within the parliamentary caucus, the provincial Liberal organization, and the province's francophones. Increased status in Quebec had meant greater influence at Ottawa during the first two periods of his career; however, from January 1939 up to his death in November 1941, Lapointe's position in Quebec meant much less to King and to a substantially anglophone cabinet preoccupied with Britain's war in Europe. Lapointe would have to rely on a variety of new resources in order to ensure that Quebec's voice was heard at Ottawa.

King the Crusader

Twenty years after his election as party leader, King's leadership was unchallenged, and he hoped to adapt the political system on which he had relied. Faced with an increasingly obvious danger to Britain, he moved away from the role of impartial umpire, reconciling regions with each other, and towards the role of crusader, fighting for what he – and English Canada – believed to be right. King felt guilty for not having supported Britain more during the Sudetenland crisis and began to assert himself. In November 1938 he insisted on increasing annual defence expenditures from $35 million to $70 million – cabinet agreed to $60 million.[1]

Concerning admission of Jewish refugees to Canada, he announced that 'the time has come when, as a Government, we would have to perform acts that were expressive of what we believed to be the conscience of the nation, and not what might be, at the moment, politically most expedient.'[2] Lapointe estimated that French Canadians might be willing to accept increased military spending and a certain flexibility in admitting Jewish refugees from Germany; however, he warned King that these policies would not be popular in Quebec.

King noted in his diary: 'I felt, as Lapointe talked, that all that he was saying simply emphasized the need for leadership, rather than breaking away from the task ... It was clear I would have to help in Quebec politics ... I told him that I thought his part and mine would be mainly that of the two most experienced in public life working together for harmonizing differences of view and that the public would have to expect our role to be somewhat different than it had been in the past.'[3] With King having decided that he should follow his instincts, his English-Canadian instincts, and 'help in Quebec politics,' problems were not far away.

In January the prime minister made his first attempt to lead Canadians: 'If England is at war we are at war,' he told Parliament.[4] The Czechoslovakian crisis of March 1939, followed by the outbreak of war in September, only made King even more likely to follow his own (anglophone) instincts, risking leaving Lapointe and Quebec with no voice. However, King remained hesitant to overrule the political advice of his Quebec lieutenant ... if Lapointe insisted. Lapointe was particularly insistent that conscription for service overseas never be applied.

During the war, King and Lapointe continued to work together, and Quebec's voice was heard, but King at certain moments risked relapsing into his crusader mode. The fall of France in June 1940 accentuated international fears of the dangers posed by Nazi Germany, leading King to remark privately: 'The one lesson I have learned in the last year or two is never to surrender my own judgment to that of any other man; to listen to all the advice and opinion possible, but hold strictly to my own view, where I feel I am at all sure of it.' Thus King, when preparing a statement in which he intended to express North American views, refused 'without a moment's hesitation' Skelton's advice – to make no reference to the United States. I told Skelton I had decided what I would say. I have so frequently been thrown off following my own judgment and wisdom in these matters by pressure from Skelton and the staff that I made up my mind I would not henceforth yield to anything of the kind.' A year later, after the death of Skelton in January 1941, King wrote in his diary that one 'of the effects of Skelton's passing will be to make me express my own views much more strongly.'[5]

Skelton was not the only actor at Ottawa with less influence during the first years of war. King on occasion expressed clear lack of confidence in the tolerance and good judgment of ministers in his cabinet. He wrote in his diary, after Skelton's death, that 'the younger and newer men in the cabinet, with the exception of Macdonald, are of very little help. Indeed it would be much easier to conduct proceedings without the presence of most of them.'[6] King's favourable impression of Macdonald would also soon become negative.[7] Consequently, King tended to seek to impose his views on cabinet much more during the period, but he could not ignore the advice of Lapointe.

King listened to Lapointe much more than to other ministers in part because he looked to his experienced Quebec lieutenant to support his own views in cabinet. For example, in August 1939 King delayed announcement of the dominion election, and 'practically all the Cabinet, I am glad to say, viewed the matter as I did, though had Lapointe not spoken as strongly as he did, some of them would very much have wavered.'[8] King believed that Lapointe felt the same way about the newer colleagues, and each man sought the support of the other in cabinet.[9] As Lapointe was not in a position to impose his views on cabinet, so too King needed Lapointe's support before imposing his policies on the Quebec caucus. 'Where differences of view have arisen,' King told an audience, 'as they inevitably must in all cabinets and all parties, Lapointe and I have worked hand in hand with a common aim, the unity of our country.'[10]

The value of Lapointe to King was again confirmed during the election of March 1940. Lapointe was unquestionably the central figure of the campaign in Quebec. He was happy to delegate to others the control of fund-raising activities: 'As far as finances are concerned,' he reminded the prime minister, 'I need not tell you that this is not my line of activities.' But he was responsible for much of the strategy and told King in June 1939 that he expected 'a difficult campaign and probably a dirty one in which I will be the main target.'[11] He was right, and after a lively public meeting King was disturbed by exaggerated stories that Lapointe had been 'attacked by hoodlums in Quebec,' but Lapointe triumphed unscathed and the Liberals won sixty-one of sixty-five seats in the province.[12] The prime minister was less dependent on Quebec, which, after accounting for 76 per cent of the Liberal caucus in 1917, 56 per cent in 1921, 60 per cent in 1925, 47 per cent in 1926, and 44 per cent in

1930, fell to 31 per cent in 1935 and 34 per cent in 1940,[13] and desired to impose his views on cabinet, but Lapointe remained too strong to be ignored.

The selection of a new cabinet affected Lapointe's ability to influence King less than it had after other elections. Lapointe relied much less on the cabinet when seeking to influence policy; he went straight to King. Against the anglophone pressure in cabinet, Lapointe seems to have received little help from his Quebec colleagues, judging by the prime minister's diary. After Rinfret's death in 1939 King noted that, despite great potential, Rinfret's place in cabinet 'had come to mean very little.' King also complained on several occasions that his other ministers from Quebec were not effective: Power was likely to go on a drinking spree at any minute and had poor judgment, Cardin was not reliable, Dandurand was over eighty years old, Casgrain was 'useless,' and Lapointe remained the only one to whom King listened. Lapointe did 'not try to debate matters in the cabinet,' according to King, and he confided to journalist Grant Dexter that he often felt isolated in cabinet, but this did not mean that he had less influence.[14]

Lapointe 'au zénith'

Lapointe's influence on the provincial Liberal organization in Quebec, substantial between 1921 and 1929, seemed to have greatly increased in 1936, when Godbout replaced Taschereau as Liberal leader in Quebec. *Le Devoir* commented in 1938 that it appeared that Ottawa now controlled the provincial wing of the party.[15] Both Lapointe and Godbout came from St Eloi, Lapointe's sister had married Godbout's brother, and both leaders shared a certain distrust of Taschereau and the conservative wing of the Liberal party. Lapointe's importance in the Quebec provincial wing of the party was confirmed during the provincial election campaign of October 1939, and after becoming premier Godbout sought Lapointe's help much more than Taschereau had.[16]

Warmer relations with the provincial Liberals gave Lapointe even more control over the distribution of patronage in the province. King consistently referred Quebec patronage requests to Lapointe,[17] meaning new responsibilities that he would often have preferred not to have. Lapointe had told King that he did not like all the patronage demands: 'Said that he personally could not stand meeting with constituents; they got his nerves on edge. He had simply to keep away from Quebec altogether.'[18] When Godbout sought war contracts for Chicoutimi, Lapointe hoped to avoid such issues and replied that this was the jurisdiction of the minister of defence, who did not consider political requests.[19] An editorial in *Le Soleil* noted that Lapointe and King were often criticized for being too public-minded and not distributing enough patronage.[20]

One of the most remarkable aspects of the election campaigns of October 1939 and March 1940 was Lapointe's readiness to defend controversial policies in francophone Quebec. During the period between 1930 and 1938, the Quebec lieutenant had been very careful to follow the voice of his province. In 1939 and 1940 he fought, and won, these campaigns on an issue that was far from receiving unanimous support in his province: Canadian participation – without conscription – in the war. This no-conscription 'pact' became the main issue in Quebec during both elections. Although Lapointe continued to emphasize the need for the government to listen to the people,[21] he was attempting to lead opinion much more than he had in the past.

In 1939 he had promised that he would resign if Quebecers had more confidence in Duplessis's Union Nationale than in his Liberal party. In 1940 he asked Quebecers whom they would like to prosecute the war effort – a government represented by men who 'in the hours of crisis, were ready to risk their political existence and their political future for the defence of unity,' or others.[22] Francophone Quebecers indicated that they did remain confident that their voice was heard through Lapointe at Ottawa. He was more solidly the voice of his province than ever. In the words of the historian Robert Rumilly: 'Les scrutins du 25 octobre 1939 et du 26 mars 1940 l'ont porté au zénith.'[23]

Not only did Lapointe have as much the confidence of his people as ever that he was looking after their interests at Ottawa, but he now had proven that, within limits, he could and would act as a leader of his people. According to Chubby Power, 'Canada was fortunate in having Ernest Lapointe in a position of power and influence in Ottawa. I doubt if any other person, certainly no one then active in Quebec politics, could ever have held the position of authority from which he was able to speak.'[24] His ability to influence Quebec public opinion made his value inestimable to King and the Canadian war effort. He had established himself as a leader whom French Canadians knew would defend their interests: he had never tried to convince them to accept any significant policy that he knew they opposed. Consequently, when he supported Ottawa's war policy and helped convince francophone Quebecers of the need to oppose Nazi Germany, he had considerable influence on their decision to accept the policy when war broke out in September 1939.[25]

There were obviously limits to this influence. The novelist E.M. Forster suggested that 'the only books that influence us are those for which we are ready, and which have gone a little farther down our particular path than we have yet gone ourselves.'[26] Similarly, Lapointe could not lead French Canadians absolutely anywhere at any speed. However, his recommendations carried great weight. This unparalleled ability, and willingness, to influence francophone Quebec provided him with an additional resource to be used in cabinet to make sure that Quebec's voice was heard.

Lapointe continued to influence King with his usual resources: control of the Quebec caucus, loyalty to the party, and ability to deliver a much more convincing speech than the prime minister.[27] More crucial during this period was Lapointe's unique ability to read and to influence the Quebec population. He had earned the confidence of French Canada, his status in his province was higher than ever, and he could present Ottawa's policies more convincingly than anyone else. As he had become irreplaceable, his threat of resignation gained weight and became a particularly persuasive means to influence King when cabinet was making the important decisions from January 1939 to November 1941.

King's tendency to act as crusader was not the only obstacle to Lapointe's influence at Ottawa, for Lapointe was bothered by poor health. Haunted by his fear that the policies he had favoured had contributed to Nazi success, he suffered an apparent nervous breakdown after the fall of France. According to T.A. Crerar, Lapointe felt 'a frightful responsibility and is stricken by the thought that he was wrong.'[28] W.A. Riddell believed that 'Lapointe realized that he had been a party to the decline of the League,' which weighed very heavily on him.[29] After a conversation with Lapointe, the journalist Grant Dexter also concluded that Lapointe was deeply affected: 'There were passages in the stream of his words which followed that were close to poetry. He spoke of the sunshine having gone out of his life, of the blood that is being shed, of the peoples who are being crushed, of the terrible things that have happened and must happen in the future.' Dexter noted that the League was a 'tender spot' for Lapointe, who again insisted that with the United States not participating, and others unwilling to enforce the covenant, the League could not function. However, Lapointe now believed that he had contributed to the failure: 'We had all been wrong in our conception of world peace, we must be prepared to fight for peace. We must keep our arms and our ability to make war and use them in the cause of peace.' Lapointe added that 'out of this war must come a new order, ending war, but it could not work unless the nations of the world meant business.'[30]

According to Dexter, Lapointe's health had suffered: 'The lines in his face are deeper and he has lost much weight, not only about the waist but in his face. His shoulders sag more than I have ever noticed them and there is a hurt look in his big brown eyes. Indeed, there is an aura of sadness about Lapointe which is quite out of character.'[31] On 11 July 1940 King greeted a Lapointe who looked tired and worn and apparently was 'worrying terribly about the war and the future.' King recorded in his diary that Lapointe 'said he did not want to add to my worries but he had come to tell me that he was afraid that he was suffering a complete nervous breakdown. Thereupon he began to cry like a child. I went over and sat beside him. Said I was not at all surprised that he felt as he did. That I knew what that kind of strain was. He then said he could not sleep and moaned in a way: Is this not too bad this had to be. He said to me in his characteristically generous way: "I hope I am not leaving too much to you and that you will be able to get along without me."'[32] King told him to take a rest.

J.L. Granatstein has written that, after this point, 'Lapointe was now more of a symbol of the Liberal Party's commitments to French Canada than a policy-making power within the government.'[33] A rumour circulated among Conservatives that he would never return.[34] The Quebec lieutenant's participation in cabinet was different; however, his health problems had never meant decreased influence on King. Many felt the stress: Skelton told King 'that last night, he had felt much the same way as though he could not stand the strain any longer,' and T.A. Crerar was 'losing his grip,' King feared.[35] Paul Bychok's interpretation appears more accurate: 'Certainly, the minutes of the War Committee of Cabinet for 1941 reveal that Lapointe did not participate actively in its sessions. But to conclude, therefore, that Lapointe was but a symbol is to misjudge Lapointe's role.'[36]

Lapointe had suffered health problems long before 1940, and his health continued to fluctuate, greatly affected by news of the war. Before its outbreak Lapointe had seriously considered resigning rather than supporting Canadian participation, and this decision caused him great stress. On 18 February 1939, King wrote in his diary that he 'felt, as [Norman] Rogers remarked later in the evening, that there was a sort of rebirth in his [Lapointe's] interest in politics.' Two days later Lapointe confirmed to King that he was 'wholly pleased about continuing on,' that he had been bothered by his 'indecision and the fears concerning his own health ... Having made the decision to continue, he has picked up ever since.' In early 1940, as the situation in Europe deteriorated, King noted that Lapointe was not looking well, but three weeks after his breakdown following the fall of France Lapointe called King to say that he was in the best of shape and ready to return.[37] Lapointe told Dexter to inform J.W. Dafoe that he was on the job and would remain so for 'some time to come.'[38]

He continued to have ups and downs the following year. In February 1941 he spent three weeks in hospital.[39] In June 1941, when Hitler launched his attack on the Soviet Union, which King believed would ensure Hitler's doom, King remarked that 'Lapointe looks remarkably well and said to me he felt exceedingly well. Gotten over all his nervousness, is really in much better shape.'[40] Four months later, when it looked as though the Soviet Union might not hold out much longer, Lapointe's health again declined.[41] Whether Lapointe's health was affected by news of the war is difficult to prove; however, it is clear that his health fluctuated greatly – as it had throughout his career when he was under great stress.

At times the prime minister indicated that he made a definite connection between how much responsibility each minister assumed and how much influence that minister would be allowed in the decision-making process. For example, King opposed allowing Luxembourg's government to establish itself in Canada during the war. Lapointe was in favour, according to King, and 'as others seemed to share his view, except Crerar, I agreed ... I wanted to make it clear that others could have their say too but would also have to take their responsibility.' A few months earlier Power had suggested that all ministers should submit their resignation, to give King a free hand, and only Lapointe opposed the suggestion, on the grounds that this would just increase the prime minister's responsibility, and King agreed.[42]

King knew that Lapointe had been hoping to retire to the Senate since 1935, and just by remaining in cabinet the minister of justice demonstrated a loyalty to King that the prime minister appreciated. In 1940, during the election campaign, Lapointe feared for his health and again sought a Senate seat. After the election he was less anxious to go to the upper house, but Ralston hoped to be named chief justice of the Supreme Court. King remarked that 'Lapointe himself might have pressed for that post had he been other than the unselfish man that he is.' Three months later, King wrote: 'Lapointe, as always, was very considerate though he, himself, would like to be relieved of Justice. Would welcome being simply President of the Council which would mean a position without any duties whatever.' In September 1940 Lapointe asked again about the Senate, and King, counting on his loyalty, replied that a seat was there for him anytime he wanted, though his staying in the Commons for the debate on peace after the war would be appreciated: 'He said he could not go through another election, and this with a look of positive pain in his face ... As always, he acquiesced but I noticed did so in this without any words ... Lapointe has never liked too much in the way of final responsibility.'[43]

'Loyalty' was a word that King repeated often when praising Lapointe's career. In a 1940 letter to Lapointe, King commented on their twenty-one years of success: 'How much all of this is owing to your loyal co-operation in the leadership of the party ... you and I alone know, but, I imagine, I know even better than you.'[44] And King was glad to have Lapointe in cabinet: 'Within the limits of our system,' King announced during a 1939 tribute to Lapointe, 'his collaboration has been practically [that of a] co-Premier.' Two years later King wondered what it would mean if 'Lapointe and I' ceased to control government policy.[45]

During this period of upheaval, Lapointe's liberalism, and his style of leadership, changed significantly. He increasingly saw the need for effective Canadian participation against Germany and that such effort required certain limits on civil liberties. Because so much was at stake, he was more willing to lead the French-Canadian population than he had been; however, he was not willing to lead his people in the direction chosen by King. The support of the Quebec lieutenant, for certain policies, remained conditional on the inclusion of a Quebec voice in these policies.

French-Canadian Concerns

Although Lapointe's approach had changed and he spent less time seeking to influence cabinet and more time seeking to influence King, his interests remained virtually unchanged. For example, in January 1941 Lapointe ordered War Services to print $5,000 worth of prayer books to be used during the 'day of prayer for victory' event endorsed by Cardinal Villeneuve, archbishop of Quebec. When King heard of the project, and got the bill for it, he immediately ordered a stop to it: $5,000 'for prayer books to be used in Roman Catholic mass, and only in the province of Quebec, would set the heather on fire – Orange lodges, Ku Klux Klans, etc.' King felt that he should have been consulted and suggested that Lapointe, who 'seemed very disappointed' at the cancellation of the printing, reopen the matter in council. The Quebec lieutenant in earlier years might have sought the support of cabinet against King but, knowing what he could expect, replied that it would be wiser not to discuss the question in cabinet.[46] This was a minor incident, but Lapointe's lack of confidence in cabinet concerning francophone-anglophone matters is also apparent in more important questions.

French-Canadian representation in the civil service continued to fall further and further behind English-Canadian as the government grew – largely because of the war effort – and anglophones hired other anglophones.[47] Ensuring equal opportunity for francophones in Ottawa became more important and more difficult. When a new chairman of the Radio Commission was being chosen, Lapointe preferred René Morin to General Odlum, who, Lapointe noted, 'has expressed views about the French-Canadians that would impair his efficiency in such a delicate position where he will have to deal impartially with both races.'[48] Lapointe warned King and the whole cabinet during the first months of the war that the lack of francophones – 'the percentage is infinitesimal' – named to the various war commissions would hurt the war effort and be disastrous politically.[49] The presidents and directors responsible for hiring bring in people they know, Lapointe complained: 'The great trouble is that they do not know French-Canadians.' King agreed that the problem was caused by 'leaving everything to appointees whose circle of acquaintances are, for the most part, among English-speaking circles.'[50] The problem extended into the armed forces, where French-speaking officers were very rare,[51] largely because of the lack of training schools for francophones, Lapointe argued.[52]

King, on his own, was not greatly concerned with the problem. Francophone rights remained a low priority for King, who considered Dandurand 'a bit fanatical on these matters' of bilingual texts and the use of French in the government.[53] When pushed by Lapointe, the prime minister asked all ministers to make 'adjustments ... in order that a fair share of the positions in the agencies related to our war effort will be held by French-speaking Canadians.'[54] Francophone Quebecers appreciated the efforts of Lapointe, who, one editorialist noted, 'favorise dans toute la mesure de son influence et de son autorité le bilinguisme au Canada. Et par là il fait l'oeuvre d'un champion de l'unité nationale.'[55] But successes were rare, and resentment in the province grew.[56]

Lapointe often battled with anglophone ministers, particularly C.D. Howe, whose Department of Munitions and Supply was not known for its bilingualism. Oscar Drouin, an MPP at Quebec City, told Lapointe that with only three francophones among 100 employees in the department, Howe was making a name for himself in Quebec like Sam Hughes (francophobe minister of militia during the First World War), and Lapointe wrote to Howe seeking greater bilingualism in the department.[57] In cabinet Lapointe insisted with success that recommendations for appointments of legal advisers to all departments be approved by him, because Justice was his responsibility and because Howe was hiring few French Canadians.[58] In June 1940, Howe's department awarded major construction contracts in Quebec City to Montreal anglophones rather than to the local firms that were available. Lapointe again complained: 'I earnestly believe that this kind of action will lead to great troubles.'[59]

A year later Lapointe was again criticizing Howe for the dismissal of two francophone purchasing officers in Quebec City; Howe claimed that they lacked competence, but Lapointe believed that they were fired to make room for the unilingual anglophone choices of the chiefs of branch. Howe acknowledged that understanding French might be an asset in Quebec City but affirmed that no francophones were competent; Lapointe suggested that 'out of over three million French Canadians it is possible to find one who is competent in the business of purchasing. The first essential requirement to meet the difficulty is goodwill.'[60] King tended to support Howe, who, he believed 'has done his best,' and felt that Lapointe 'takes these matters in a very personal way', however, he understood Lapointe's frustration with the rest of the cabinet. 'The truth is,' King added in his diary, 'that several members of the Cabinet are really of little help, and being unfamiliar with past controversies are apt to review old things that have been often settled.'[61]

Lapointe, realizing more than King the dangers of such problems in Quebec, was probably more exasperated by cabinet colleagues than King realized. Lapointe's impatience with the anglophone ministers peaked in October 1941, when Minister of Finance J.L. Ilsley appointed a Montreal Conservative to a key commercial position. Lapointe emphasized that appointing a Conservative was not the problem – the Liberals had appointed many – but Montreal Liberals were up in arms because the person named was a partisan organizer with close connections to Duplessis's Union Nationale. 'Surely,' Lapointe complained to Ilsley, 'in a matter of this importance I might have been consulted.'[62] The same day Lapointe wrote King complaining about the 'amazing appointment' by Ilsley: 'Do you not think that this came as a result of the absence of French-Canadians from Quebec on the various boards which advise the Ministers? I have been protesting so often in the past and with such indifferent success that for the last few months I have not said a word about it, seeing that it is a useless waste of energy.' Lapointe added that 'the appointment of a French Canadian to the Unemployment Insurance Commission is long overdue. Mr. McLarty has always said that he was waiting that the organization is complete before doing that, but the result is all the appointments are made everywhere by the present [anglophone] commission ... I am receiving resolutions and letters from all the public bodies and from citizens all over the Province asking that the appointment be made immediately.'[63]

After 1938 Lapointe remained as eager as ever to fight for francophone services, and as uninterested in economic questions – unless they concerned Quebec. At least once, in November 1940, when he insisted that the 25 per cent tariff on boots be modified, he even threatened to resign.[64] Earlier, at the request of Cardinal Villeneuve, Lapointe had warned Ilsley that the idea of exempting theatres, hotels, and dances from an electricity tax imposed on retirement homes, orphanages, convents, and monasteries 'would be impossible to defend' and had to be changed.[65] Two weeks later Lapointe again wrote Ilsley and seemed to threaten resigning: 'I assure you that it would be impossible for me to explain to my province the exclusion of these classes from the list of privileged institutions.'[66] Lapointe again showed interest in an economic issue in 1941, when Ottawa considered modifying its Unemployment Relief programs. The Quebec lieutenant warned King that with many employable people still unemployed in Quebec, it would be 'unthinkable that agreements which have been entered into with Provinces and Municipalities ... should be abandoned.'[67] His interest in economic questions was thus limited to those that risked dividing anglophones and francophones.

Similarly, his interest – and influence – in matters in his Department of Justice were greater when they involved provincial autonomy or francophone rights. A strike in July 1941 at an aluminum plant in Arvida, Quebec, revealed how Lapointe and King had to work against cabinet colleagues to protect provincial rights. Lapointe, like King, was more hesitant to rely on force and compulsion against a Catholic union in Quebec than others in cabinet. King recorded in his diary that, 'without Lapointe beside me, I would be in the most difficult of all positions.'[68] Howe, Ilsley, MacDonald, and Ralston all favoured greater intervention without waiting for provincial consent. Lapointe warned that Ottawa had to be careful at Arvida – and at Hamilton and in Nova Scotia, where other labour disputes were occurring – not to provoke labour problems throughout the country.[69]

The strike had serious repercussions on the war effort when the aluminum hardened in the pots, causing several million dollars of damage and three weeks' delay in production of aluminum needed for airplane construction. The president of the Confédération des Travailleurs catholiques du Québec (CTCQ) told Lapointe that he sought a solution and hoped to cooperate in the interests of the war effort,[70] but Howe was convinced that the factory at Arvida had been seized by saboteurs, probably 'foreigners,' and insisted that Ottawa immediately send troops.[71] Lapointe told King that 'Howe has allowed himself to be deceived by the Aluminum Co. and his statements have precipitated a storm in Quebec.' He strongly opposed the heavy-handed intervention into a Catholic union labour dispute.[72] Some observers considered Howe's accusations of sabotage inconsistent with the facts and accused him of having sought to profit from the situation to obtain the right to call out the troops in every case that might come up. Premier Godbout also told King that Howe's statement did injustice to Quebec and to the Catholic union, but Godbout was even more upset about the dominion intrusion into provincial jurisdiction.[73] Order was re-established within a few days at Arvida, but Howe, despite much evidence to the contrary (such as an RCMP memo concluding that conditions of pay, not sabotage, had provoked the strike),[74] continued to refer to 'enemy alien sabotage' and to seek more powers to intervene rapidly in disturbances. Most ministers sided with Howe, but King wrote: 'Lapointe and I, fortunately, are keeping our minds on situations as they may develop, and watching questions of jurisdiction and procedure, which others seem to think should be ignored just because there is a war.'[75]

The strike at Arvida also revealed how isolated Lapointe was from his colleagues concerning francophone rights during the war. The chief conciliation officer sent to the Chicoutimi region by Minister of Labour Norman McLarty was a unilingual anglophone.[76] Lapointe informed McLarty that this was 'a great mistake ... The matter is not even susceptible of argument.' McLarty replied that more francophone officers would be sought, but when the job openings were advertised bilingualism was not listed as an essential qualification. Lapointe again wrote the minister of labour warning that 'this situation cannot be tolerated much longer ... Really, I cannot conceive that the question has even to be considered.'[77]

Lapointe and King also opposed their cabinet colleagues during the discussion of strategy for the calling of a Dominion–Provincial Conference to discuss the Rowell-Sirois Report. As Ontario Premier Mitchell Hepburn opposed many elements of the document, King and Lapointe preferred to postpone the meeting and let the situation settle until acceptance of the proposals seemed more likely.[78] But, according to Lapointe, the 'hot heads' in cabinet insisted on confronting the Ontario premier and risking disunity. Lapointe had told Grant Dexter that he feared that an open confrontation with Hepburn would destroy the formation of a national consensus on the issue.[79] As King and Lapointe expected, the conference, in January 1941, failed.[80] King recorded in his diary his speech to cabinet after the failure: 'I said I thought I had been unfair to myself and to them in not resisting more strongly ... Both Lapointe and myself had, as a result of our experience, counselled against trying to hold a conference on the Sirois report. They had seen we were right in the position we had taken, but wrong in yielding to them.'[81] Clearly, King appreciated Lapointe's presence in cabinet.

International affairs, of course, dominated this period. After the fall of France many anglophones became less interested in ensuring a minority voice in Canadian policy. Their priority was to help Britain win the war: pressure for Union government[82] and for overseas conscription grew, as did English-Canadian resentment of Quebec's influence in preventing these measures. Lapointe's agenda was also dominated by international affairs; however, he remained most concerned about questions that might push apart francophones and anglophones. He was particularly interested in attempting to remove the appearance (and the reality) of British influence over Canadian policy. Lapointe suggested appointment of a Canadian-born governor general, but King refused, arguing that no Canadian was acceptable. Both eventually agreed to the appointment of Lord Athlone.[83] Lapointe also favoured a Canadian flag, the right to modify the constitution in Canada, and the end of appeals to the Judicial Committee of the Privy Council in London.[84] Lapointe 'instantly approved' King's proposal to appeal for peace to Hitler in late August 1939 because it was constructive and 'meant Canada taking its own position as a nation, not following in the trail simply of what the British government might wish.'[85]

Lapointe made almost no contribution to other major foreign policy debates, most notably those concerning relations with the United States. When King and Roosevelt signed the Ogdensburg agreement on 18 August 1940, establishing a permanent Joint Board of Defence, neither cabinet nor the Canadian Chiefs of Staff were consulted. Lapointe also appears to have had little input into the Hyde Park Declaration of 20 April 1941 – the economic corollary of Ogdensburg. Both greatly affected Canada's future, but Lapointe left King on his own during these negotiations.[86]

Conclusion

After Munich, King was firmly leader of his party and sought to support British policy as much as possible. Lapointe remained the only actor at Ottawa strong enough to influence the prime minister considerably. He ensured a Quebec voice in policy, but he had to insist. The resources that he relied on to influence King remained similar, but his demonstrated ability to influence francophone Quebec added considerable weight to his threats of resignation. King needed Lapointe.

9

Sacred Pledges:
The No-Conscription Pact

During the weeks following the Munich settlement, Ernest Lapointe saw no reason to modify Canadian foreign policy. At a meeting of the League of Nations Society in Canada in November 1938 he joined the majority of Canadians in expressing his approval of the settlement and his 'admiration of the great Statesman whose courage, tenacity, patriotism and gallantry brought it about ... Through his efforts, and I wish to give credit to the powerful help he received from others, a world war was averted.' Lapointe was more convinced than ever that Canadian policy was appropriate: if war should come, Parliament would consider Canadian participation, but there would be no automatic commitments to Britain or to the League in advance. He continued to insist that the element of coercion in the League should be 'done away with' so that all countries could join the organization to negotiate.[1]

The prime minister also admired Chamberlain's efforts. A year into the war, King and Lapointe both agreed that Chamberlain had been unfairly treated because both realized fully how important the Munich agreement had been in preparing public opinion for war against Hitler: King 'was glad to hear Lapointe say that he felt as I did about the injustice done Chamberlain in so many quarters. He said in most ways he preferred Chamberlain to Churchill.' In 1941 King told Churchill that he thought Chamberlain had been unjustly treated, that he had tried to rearm Britain, and that 'if he had not gone to Munich, the situation would have been much worse.'[2] But the Sudetenland crisis had an entirely different effect on King, who became convinced that war was coming and that Canada should commit itself openly to be at Britain's side. King's declaration in Parliament in January 1939 – 'If England is at war we are at war'[3] – demonstrated how far he had drifted from the previous

Canadian policy, to which Lapointe and many others still clung. Skelton noted in his diary that King's statement 'has provoked profound alarm and anger not only in Quebec but among all nationalists.'[4] The test of whether or not it would be possible to reconcile the views of King and Lapointe within a common policy arrived in March 1939.

Ottawa's Reaction to the Invasion of Czechoslovakia: The Pact

On 15 March 1939 Nazi Germany invaded the rest of Czechoslovakia, revealing to the world Hitler's aggression. Munich had set definite limits on what the world would consider to be 'justified' German expansion, and Hitler now passed these limits. In Britain the government introduced conscription for the first time during peace and, with France, guaranteed Poland's borders. Public support in Britain and France for this guarantee was greater than would have been possible in September 1938. The United States also took some limited action against Germany: Secretary of State Cordell Hull remembered that 'in line with our policy of "methods short of war" to manifest our condemnation of acts of aggression, the Administration now took a series of steps following the swallowing up of Czechoslovakia. We refused to recognize the conquest and continued to receive the Czech Minister ... We suspended the trade agreement with Czechoslovakia ... [and] increased duties on imports from Germany.'[5] These methods indeed fell far short of war.

In Canada, the government's reaction would reveal whether King and Lapointe had reconciled their views. Ottawa decided to announce publicly the policy that became known as 'the pact.' On 20 March 1939 King declared Canadian support for Britain: 'If there were a prospect of an aggressor launching an attack on Britain, with bombers raining death on London, I have no doubt what the decision of the Canadian people and parliament would be. We would regard it as an act of aggression, menacing freedom in all parts of the British Commonwealth.' When Lapointe spoke on 31 March he announced the same policy but put much more emphasis on Canadian interests and much less on helping Britain.[6]

During his speech of 31 March the minister of justice emphasized, more than King, Canadian interests: 'Whatever decision is reached on a question of this kind must be on the basis of putting Canada first in our national policies, as Canada should be also first in the hearts of her people.' Canada had the right to be neutral, but the exercise of that right would mean that it would have to forbid enlistment on Canadian soil and the raising of money for war relief, intern British sailors and war vessels in Canadian ports, and remove the British trade preference. This would be possible, if Canadians decided on it, but, Lapointe asked, 'would it be in the interests of Canada to do it?' Of course most Canadians would not desire neutrality, Lapointe continued, and the minority should try to comprehend how the majority felt; but the majority should also 'understand the feelings ... of the French Canadians of Quebec.' Lapointe asked English Canadians to understand that French Canadians 'have only one country, one home. None of them would say that he is "going home" when he leaves Canada.'[7] More important, Lapointe and King – who spoke again on 30 March – promised that conscription would never be applied. A commitment to participate if Britain went to war against Germany united with the commitment never to apply conscription was the pact that both Lapointe and King could accept.

Many historians credit King with preparing public opinion by planning a strategy that relied on Lapointe's insistence that Canada could not be neutral in a British war and on King's determination that there be no conscription. According to Hillmer and Granatstein, 'King and Lapointe were pursuing a deliberate, co-ordinated strategy with their speeches of 30 and 31 March.'[8] Granatstein describes Lapointe, playing 'good cop, bad cop' with King, not only as the more insistent of the two that Canada could not be neutral but even as the more imperialist.[9] Most often, whether they acknowledge any minor role for Lapointe, historians (most notably H.B. Neatby) see the presentation and formulation of both parts of the pact as a plan of King's.[10] According to Granatstein and Bothwell: 'King's backing and filling, his evasions and hesitations, do not make inspiring reading. But his actions, particularly between 1937 and 1939, indicate his sure grasp of the public mood.'[11]

The interpretation that the prime minister formulated both parts of the pact is improbable; his principal concern was to commit Canada to be at Britain's side in the event of a major war. After King's 'when Britain is at war' speech, Skelton feared that it would be difficult to reconcile this stance with previous policy. 'Skelton then said,' according to King, 'that Sir Wilfrid was always driven with the Imperialists on one side, and the Nationalists on the other, and sought to take a middle position. He did not see why I should not do the same. I replied to him that was exactly what I was doing – by my silence last session on one side, and emphasis on the other, I had been shoved into an extreme nationalist position which was not my position nor that of my party.' He knew that his autonomist staff opposed his 'when Britain is at war' speech, but he expected that the country and cabinet would support him. King told cabinet: 'I knew what the intelligentsia view would be, and that I knew what a handful they were compared with the country as a whole, and that my business was to tell Canada of her dangers. Not of theories that could not save the lives of the people.' King later regretted having listened so much to Skelton and not having gone even further in his pre-war speeches.[12]

Nor is the interpretation that King devised a strategy to maintain unity – whereby he presented the no conscription part of the pact while Lapointe presented the no-neutrality part – supported by an examination of his views and actions. King admitted in his diary that the general impression held by the press gallery – that Lapointe, on 31 March, had spoken much more effectively than he (King) had on 30 March – was 'perfectly true.' King told Lapointe that he 'thought the speech was really the crowning one of his career. It will give him [Lapointe] a real place as a world statesman.' King continued to criticize himself for not offering a sufficiently strong promise of support to Britain. 'Lapointe made an excellent speech this afternoon. He went much further than I did in making clear that Canada could not be neutral in a war in which Britain might be engaged, more particularly at a time like the present. That is obviously true, and I have all along felt that I should have made that part of my speech more emphatic than it was ... I think he was right politically and every other way. I think I have lost to a certain extent in being so vague in places. I feel that my own position, this year, will suffer as it did last year from an impression of aloofness so far as relations between Canada and Britain are concerned, though not anything like the same extent.'

In an effort to console himself, he reasoned that he and Lapointe together had 'built a substantial support for the structure of Canadian unity ... If I had made the speech Lapointe made, the party might have held its own with the Jingos in Ontario, but would have lost Quebec more or less entirely. If he had made the speech I did, he might have held Quebec, but the party would have lost heavily in Ontario and perhaps some other parts on the score that Quebec was neutral in its loyalty. Together, our speeches constituted a sort of trestle sustaining the structure which would serve to unite divergent parts of Canada, thereby making for a united country.'[13] Because King announced this supposed strategy in his diary after the speeches had been delivered, it seems that he was merely attempting to reassure himself that the consequences of his poor performance would not be too serious. Lapointe's speech had been stronger than King's in promising both no conscription and no neutrality.

Hitler's invasion of the rest of Czechoslovakia seems to have convinced Lapointe that war was coming. After King congratulated him on his speech, the Quebec lieutenant replied 'that it would help to prepare the way for Canada playing her part, should war come as he more or less believes it will.'[14] Lapointe seems to have estimated that enough French Canadians believed that war was coming – and that Hitler was the aggressor – that the time was now appropriate for a clear statement of Ottawa's new policy. He supported King's statement of 20 March – he 'supposed there would be hell to pay for it [in Quebec] but it could not be helped'[15] – and, more important, Lapointe himself presented very strongly the argument that Canada could not remain neutral in a British war.

The Quebec lieutenant also spoke out strongly against conscription. He announced: 'I think I am true to my concept of Canadian unity when I say that I shall always fight against this policy; I would not be a member of a government that would enact it; and not only that, but I say with all my responsibility to the people of Canada that I would oppose any government that would enforce it.'[16] Lapointe devoted a full page of his seven-page speech to the subject, and his firm promise was much clearer and more convincing than the prime minister's two-sentence no-conscription pledge, lost in over twenty pages of promises to many groups. King announced that 'the present government believes that conscription of free men for overseas service would not be a necessary or effective step. Let me say that so long as this government may be in power, no such measure will be enacted.'[17] That was it. Because he was prime minister, King's two sentences carried great weight; but he was not nearly as emphatic as Lapointe with his no-conscription vow.

Canadian public opinion appeared to accept the pact described by King and Lapointe in March, but for varying reasons. French Canadians were particularly pleased with the firm no-conscription guarantees in half of Lapointe's speech, although some would have preferred a more independent policy: 'Que ça plaise ou non à l'Angleterre ... nous préférons mourir au Canada que de mourir en Europe pour servir les intérêts de l'Empire. Nous ne répéterons pas Vimy.'[18] Letters to Lapointe from French Canadians, and editorials in Le Soleil, confirmed that when French Canadians read about the pact they supported the no-conscription policy and remained hopeful that Canada could be 'independent' from Britain.[19]

English Canadians were glad that Lapointe came out so strongly affirming that Canada could not be neutral in a British war. In fact, many seemed to have heard only this half of the speech: Globe and Mail emphasized that Lapointe had rejected neutrality, 'in a speech far more British than anything Prime Minister King has said on Canadian foreign policy.'[20]

The British high commissioner to Canada also referred to 'Lapointe's speech on neutrality.'[21] R.B. Hanson, leader of the Conservative party in the House of Commons in January 1942, presented a tribute to Lapointe, referring to his 'great' speech of 31 March 1939, on 'the question of Canadian neutrality' during war.[22] Some English Canadians would have preferred a policy more aligned with Britain: 'Many of us in Ontario feel that with the proper leadership our French-Canadian compatriots of Quebec would stand with us and behind Britain in any trouble but do not feel they are getting either from the Church or State the leadership that should be theirs.'[23] There undoubtedly remained a fundamental difference of opinion between the two solitudes, but the no-neutrality with no-conscription pact defined in late March 1939 seemed to be accepted by a large portion of both groups.

To appreciate the degree to which Lapointe's voice was present in the pact of March 1939, it is necessary to study his reaction to King's speech of January 1939. After his speech, the prime minister was surprised to find that 'Lapointe did not like the words: "When England is at war, Canada is at war."' King seems to have agreed with Power, who 'did not think there would be the opposition in Quebec that Lapointe feared. Cardin also agreed to this.' The prime minister protested that all had agreed to the statement at an earlier meeting: 'Lapointe asked if he was there at the time, and I said yes. He added that he must have been asleep.'[24] Lapointe threatened to resign, but King's account of the confrontation indicates that he remained unaware of the views of Lapointe and Quebec.

The prime minister believed that Lapointe accepted the idea that Canada would enter Britain's war. King wrote in his diary that Lapointe realized that Canada would be swept into war by emotions, 'that it might be necessary for some of [the ministers] to consider whether they could do better in the way of steadying the people in their own parts, by being out of Cabinet, rather than in it – helping to explain the situation, etc ... There was no disagreement on Lapointe's part as to what would have to be done by Canada. All he seemed concerned about was whether he could remain in the Government, knowing what the feeling would be in his province.' According to King's version of the cabinet meeting, Lapointe 'seemed very fearful that we were going to make the statement at once, and said he saw no necessity for rushing into a statement of where we stood until we had to.'[25]

But Lapointe did disagree as to what would have to be done by Canada. He announced during a speech to delegates at a meeting of the Confédération des travailleurs catholiques du Canada (CTCC) on 21 January

1939: 'Je remarque cette phrase dans votre mémoire: La CTCC est opposée à la participation du Canada à toute guerre extérieure. Je partage votre opinion.'[26] Lapointe particularly opposed King's announcing in public, before war broke out, the anglophone view of what Canada should do.

After his Quebec lieutenant threatened to resign, King promised that he was willing to work with him 'to get our views so accommodated that there could be no need for anyone to go out.' Lapointe began to consider the possibility of accepting Canadian participation but, despite what King believed, had not yet decided to remain in a cabinet led by a prime minister so unwilling to accommodate the minority voice. King told cabinet that if French Canadians left, it 'would mean an inevitable demand for National Government [and conscription]. That if they wished to avoid a situation of that kind it would be [best] for us all to stay together and not let the control of Government in a crisis of the kind pass into the hands of jingos and Tories. This seemed to make an impression,' King believed.[27]

But Lapointe was less impressed than the prime minister thought. In early February, Lapointe went to see Skelton, who described the meeting in his diary: 'Lapointe came in ... asking me to try to prevent the Prime Minister making any more breaks [from the 'Parliament will decide' policy]. I said that was hard for me to do if fifteen colleagues in Cabinet couldn't – Lapointe said unfortunately some of the fifteen were worse than King, but that the Prime Minister was fooling himself if he thought Cardin and he agreed. He made it clear that whatever the government as a whole agreed, individual members would have to decide what stand they would take and he had made no commitment on that point.'[28] Lapointe, more than Skelton, was willing to accept the engagement that Canada would not be neutral in a British war, if he had something that he could present to Quebec. What Lapointe suggested to Skelton was the promise that there would be no expeditionary force sent overseas. King had also written in his diary that 'we were all agreed that we would not countenance any expeditionary force nor would we countenance conscription. This was not mentioned but will have to be understood later.'[29]

King was aware of the need to re-establish Lapointe's confidence. In mid-February cabinet favoured Canadian withdrawal from the League's General Act and optional clause because Britain had decided to withdraw from these agreements and urged others to follow. King realized the risk to Canadian autonomy of following so closely the British policy, but he and cabinet were quite willing to do so. Only Lapointe, more aware of the need to prove to Canadian autonomists that Ottawa was not following Britain's foreign policy, was firmly opposed. 'As Lapointe felt strongly on the matter,' King wrote in his diary, 'I said I was quite agreeable to have his views govern, and the rest of the Cabinet did like-wise, though, I think, practically all were equally of my point of view.' King added that refusing Britain's request 'might occasion adverse comment in the event of a serious situation developing later on,' but after cabinet refused to follow Britain King reasoned that the fact that Australia also refused 'will save us from invidious criticism. Moreover, I do think,' King added, 'that the British have changed their own attitude too often and have rather unreasonably expected us to follow them in every twist and turn.'[30] Although the issue was relatively unimportant, Lapointe was probably reassured that Quebec's voice could still be heard and shortly after decided to remain in cabinet.[31]

After the invasion of 15 March 1939 the pact – particularly when presented by Lapointe – received a much warmer welcome in English and French Canada than had King's January declaration. King could not understand why. He complained in his diary that 'all that Lapointe said [on 31 March] was exactly what I was saying at the time that others were critical of my quoting Sir Wilfrid's statement: "When Britain is at war; Canada is at war."'[32] Both speeches had suggested Canadian support for Britain in a European war, and King did not appreciate the French-Canadians emphasis on the no-conscription promise and other aspects of the speeches: Lapointe's defence of the policy, the emphasis on Canadian interests, and the fact that it was announced after Hitler invaded Czechoslovakia. Lapointe thus adapted King's 'when England is at war' impulse and made it more acceptable to French Canadians. Of course, the main difference between the declarations in January and in March was the no-conscription promise, and, given King's mood, it seems that Lapointe was responsible for convincing King of its necessity. If King made any no-conscription promise at all he did so grudgingly, without emphasis, and clearly in response to Lapointe's threat to resign.

Lapointe's influence on the Canadian government's decision to announce the pact after Germany's invasion of Czechoslovakia was substantial. King's voice was also vital, but others had little influence on King. The pact represents a compromise. Lapointe, who preferred maintaining the 'Parliament will decide' policy, accepted the reality that Canada would not be neutral in a British war but insisted that a no-conscription promise be included in the policy. King, whose main interest was to announce support for Britain, accepted the no-conscription policy. Both voices were co-dominant.

Application of the Pact

The no-neutrality, no-conscription pact had helped minimize disunity in Canada in March 1939, when the question was academic. English Canadians had emphasized the no-neutrality aspect and during the late spring of 1939, while a tour by King George VI and Queen Elizabeth encouraged imperial emotions,[33] continued to call for a clearer statement of support for Britain. During a meeting with the prime minister in April, High Commissioner Sir Gerald Campbell, speaking for Britain, 'asked point blank,' according to King, 'if I would make a statement in the House tomorrow to the effect that Canada was behind Britain's efforts and would support her in whatever course she took.' King refused.[34] French Canadians, less emotionally affected by the royal tour,[35] emphasized the no-conscription aspect of the pact. Would Ottawa's pact be respected in September, when the question was no longer academic?

In August, Germany was threatening Poland, the country that Britain and France were committed to defending. At a cabinet meeting in Ottawa on 24 August 1939 many anglophones still preferred to make an immediate declaration of support for Britain. Finally, all ministers agreed that the government would make no public announcement before war broke out; but all also agreed that Canada would participate if war were declared.[36] On 1 September Germany invaded Poland and ignited the Second World War. Britain declared war on 3 September, and the Canadian government now had to act. King and Lapointe announced that Parliament would be summoned and would decide Canadian policy. A week later, on 10 September, Canada declared war on Germany, after its Parliament – not Britain's – had so decided. King, on 8 September, and Lapointe, the following day, both announced that there would be no conscription. Parliament had accepted the pact.

Most English-Canadian historians credit the prime minister with the application of the pact, which ensured Canadian unity. Some praise King for the unity: according to Stacey, 'the parliamentary and national decision arrived at in September 1939 was the greatest achievement of Mackenzie King's career.'[37] Granatstein specifies that King had decided in September 1938 that Canada would participate, but pressure from two other anglophones, Skelton and Christie, 'often forced him to hedge and trim.'[38] Others blame King for being too preoccupied with pleasing Quebec and neglecting the war effort. Donald Creighton argues that in 1939 King, rather than asking Canadians for 'the all-out effort needed to defeat Germany,' sought merely 'a modest effort which would keep Canada politically quiet and the Liberal party in power.'[39] P.B. Waite writes that 'King preferred Lapointe's passive belligerency to the real war preferred by most English Canadians.'[40]

French-Canadian historians also credit King with the decision – although most suggest that Lapointe also had a certain influence – but they do not believe that unity existed. The decision to participate was forced on Quebec against its will and, in the words of Michel Brunet, 'rappela aux électeurs canadiens-français que leurs représentants au parlement fédéral constituaient une minorité soumise aux pressions du Canada anglais.'[41] Denis Bertrand writes that French Canadians were 'presque unanimement opposés à la participation, mais sans chef, incapables de s'exprimer dans une forte réaction collective.'[42] Journalist André Laurendeau writes that the pact was useless because Lapointe had entered the compromise having already fulfilled his part.[43] In short, English Canadians argue that King gave Quebec what it sought (a limited war effort, including a no-conscription promise), while French Canadians claim that the prime minister gave English Canada what it sought (participation and an insincere, temporary no-conscription promise). Almost all focus on the role of King.

If French Canadians accepted the pact, they did so not because of the efforts of King, whose concern was to support Britain. During his crucial speech to Parliament on 8 September he repeated the policy that Canada could not be neutral, and, even though this time he did stress that the government's interest was to defend Canada, his one-sentence promise never to apply conscription was again lost in the twenty-two pages that he delivered.[44] At the end of 1939 he wrote in his diary that with his stance on conscription and because he had gained the confidence of the people of Quebec, 'I think I may claim to be responsible in no small measure for the unity of Canada at this time and certainly for the united manner in which the country has entered the war at the side of Britain.'[45]

Lapointe realized, much more than King, how crucial appropriate presentation of the pact would be. When Lapointe spoke to the House on 9 September, although he presented the same policy as King, his speech was much more effective. Lapointe argued, as in March, that it was 'impossible, practically, for Canada to be neutral.'[46] Lapointe's argument that the world would assume that Canada was a belligerent was confirmed when Roosevelt called King to ask whether Canada was at war.[47] Lapointe was also much more forthright than the prime minister in suggesting the possibility of an expeditionary force. Many Canadians, including Quebecers, were volunteering for service, he said, and he asked: 'If the need comes, does any member of the house think any Canadian government, whether this or any other, could stop the thousands of volunteers who would like to fight for Britain and France?'

Lapointe also provided an infinitely more convincing no-conscription pledge than King: 'The whole province of Quebec – and I speak with all the responsibility, all the solemnity, I can give to my words – will never agree to accept compulsory service or conscription outside Canada. I will go farther than that: When I say the whole province of Quebec I mean that I personally agree with them. I am authorized by my colleagues in the cabinet from the province of Quebec [Cardin and Power] to say that we will never agree to conscription and will never be members or supporters of a government that will try to enforce it. Is that clear enough?' He added that if they were forced to resign, 'I question whether anyone would be able to take our place.'

Lapointe's speech was seen at the time and later by historians as an appeal to French Canadians to support participation. Many anglophones, as in March, heard only the appeals to Quebec that Canada could not be neutral;[48] the *Globe and Mail* remarked that the 'expected French-Canadian rebellion vanished' with Lapointe's speech.[49] J.A. Hume, secretary to the national war services minister, remembered Lapointe's 'when Britain is at war, Canada is at war' speech.[50] More recent interpretations have continued along the same line: Granatstein, for example, describes how King's 'too long, too boring' speech was 'greatly exceeded in impact by Lapointe's masterly oration and plea for Quebec to support the war.'[51] Pickersgill writes that 'the most influential speech of the special session was made by Lapointe. It was addressed to French-Canadians and was an appeal for Canadian unity.'[52]

However, Lapointe realized that a major obstacle to French-Canadian acceptance of the no-neutrality part of the pact was the *mentalité* in English Canada. He thus appealed mostly to anglophones to accept the no-conscription part of the pact. He prefaced his speech with the warning that he would be speaking in English, 'because most of my remarks are addressed rather to the English-speaking majority in the house.'[53] Lapointe's address made it clear to anglophones that francophones would not accept conscription, and French-speaking Quebecers, knowing that Lapointe would defend their views, were more willing to accept the pact.

The immediate reaction to Lapointe's speech revealed that Parliament was not unanimously behind the pact. J.C. Landeryou, Conservative MP for Calgary East, followed Lapointe saying that Hitler 'has challenged the British empire, and that is why we [the Conservative party] have urged upon the government the necessity of universal conscription of finance, industry and man power.' Liguori Lacombe, Liberal MP for Laval-Deux-Montagnes, then followed Landeryou with a different plea: 'Si la neutralité du Canada doit s'effacer à l'avantage de l'unité nationale, j'affirme que ce serait payer trop cher une communauté de sentiments dont le maintien aurait pour prix l'irréparable désastre et la ruine de notre pays.'[54] However, despite the opposition, most members did accept Ottawa's policy, or their interpretation of it. Public reaction was similar.

English Canadians would not accept neutrality in the war against Hitler. Some sought to defend 'civilization,' others to defend Britain, and most saw no difference between the two; they would not have entered a war to defend Danzig – when King heard that Winston Churchill and Anthony Eden were coming into the British cabinet in the summer of 1939, he feared that this meant war and that Danzig was not worth it – but in September 1939, when Britain was at war, English Canada was at war.[55] Skelton had said in March that 'if we go into any European war it will be simply and solely on the grounds of racial sympathy with the United Kingdom,' and in August he complained that 'the first casualty in this war has been Canada's claim to independent control of her own destinies.'[56] King tried to convince himself that more noble – and independent – motivations fuelled English Canada's support of the mother country. During the Munich crisis he had written, 'I do not agree with Skelton's view that it would be sympathy for Britain that would be the determining factor for Canada going into war. I believe the determining factor would be the determination not to permit the fear of Force to dominate in the affairs of men and nations.'[57] But even King must have realized the strength of imperialist emotions and how this separated anglophones from francophones, who were less emotionally attached to the British Empire and less eager to accept participation in war. In 1939, few North Americans recognized the dangers to the Western Hemisphere: in the United States, for example, a poll estimated that only 5 per cent of Americans believed that their country should enter the war.[58] There was thus, in francophone Quebec, limited enthusiasm for what was seen as a 'British war.'[59]

Certain considerations encouraged French Canadians to accept Canadian participation. Hitler's aggression led a *Le Soleil* editorialist and many others to conclude that if he were not stopped he would continue to invade other countries.[60] The Nazi–Soviet non-aggression pact, signed 23 August 1939, also helped by turning many anti-communists in Canada against Hitler.[61] King had been warning Britain of Canadian opposition to British attempts to seek an alliance with the USSR, and he told Campbell: 'Certainly our people would not want to fight to help Russia.' There was 'considerable opposition in Canada,' King added, 'to the manner in which the United Kingdom appears to be becoming entangled with Balkan and Eastern European countries and above all with Russia.' When he heard that the Germans and Soviets would sign a pact, King 'felt instantly a sense of relief.'[62] Lapointe must have been even more relieved. In addition, the influential Cardinal Villeneuve supported the war against Germany and increasingly publicized his position.[63] However, the promise of no conscription, made forcefully by Lapointe, and the delay in announcement of support for Britain helped many French Canadians accept the pact.[64] 'I believe the majority in my province trust me,' Lapointe announced during his speech of 9 September, 'I have never deceived them, and I will not deceive them now.' He added that if his stand meant 'his political death,' as some told him, 'at least it would not be a dishonourable end, and I am ready to make sacrifices for the sake of being right.'[65]

During the crucial period between 24 August and 10 September Lapointe's guidance of King had ensured maximum support in Quebec for the pact in two ways. First, it was Lapointe who remained most insistent that the anglophones in cabinet respect the pact. During the meeting of 24 August, when King asked for comments on Ottawa's policy in the event of war breaking out, Lapointe led the opposition against Ilsley, Mackenzie, and Rogers, who preferred to issue immediately a statement declaring Canadian support for any British policy.[66] That the prime minister listened attentively to the judgment of Lapointe on such questions is suggested by the Canadian decision to send an expeditionary force overseas: as late as 30 August King repeated his earlier intentions that there would be none, but when the idea received greater support in cabinet than expected on 7 September (Lapointe did not object), an expeditionary force was mobilized for service overseas.[67] Regarding the vital no-conscription promise, anglophones in cabinet preferred to say nothing about conscription, despite earlier promises. King recorded that 'Lapointe said he would have to be outspoken on this point,' and King agreed – after Lapointe had spoken.

Second, Lapointe had ensured maximum support in Quebec for the pact with his help during presentation of the policy. The prime minister's first speech of the war, on 3 September, would be crucial. Four days earlier King had outlined to cabinet what he intended to say and found general agreement that Canada would participate in the war, but Lapointe had some advice. He suggested beginning with the dangers to Canada before mentioning the intention to side with Britain, and then coming into the larger issue – the cause of freedom. King agreed, as did the cabinet.[68] But Lapointe wanted to make sure that he had been understood, and he wrote to King the next day, repeating that any declaration would have to be prepared 'with extreme care' and must emphasize the dangers to Canada before talking about siding with Britain, while not forgetting to announce that Parliament was free to decide.[69] Even as Lapointe read on air the French translation of King's statement on 3 September, an eight-second pause during his address indicates that he still suspected that the prime minister might sneak in a 'when Britain is at war, Canada is at war' comment. The Quebec lieutenant, who had not been able to read the statement in advance,[70] was racing through the text when he froze: 'Vendredi dernier le gouvernement, au nom du peuple canadien, a annoncé que dans le cas où le Royaume uni serait engagé dans une guerre dans ses efforts pour resister à l'aggression ... [silence for eight seconds as Lapointe reads ahead to verify the text before continuing] ... il demanderait au parlement, dès que ce dernier sera reuni, son authorisation pour la coopération efficace du Canada au côté de la Grande Bretagne.'[71] King had indeed followed (closely enough) Lapointe's advice in this case, but the Quebec lieutenant was watching him carefully.

Two months later, when preparing another statement of war objectives, King told Skelton that 'I should like to have Lapointe present in the cabinet when this statement is being finally discussed. He will himself desire that, and, without him, I might encounter difficulties which I should like to avoid.'[72] Lapointe would continue advising King to avoid too great an emphasis on the need to help Britain.[73]

Even more important than his guidance of King was Lapointe's own presentation of the pact. As in March, Lapointe again 'stole the show' from King during the debate in Parliament. J.W. Dafoe of the *Winnipeg Free Press* referred to Lapointe's address of 9 September, which had stirred him to the depth of his 'emotions,' as 'about the most effective I ever heard. I've searched my memory for a parallel,' he wrote Lapointe, 'without finding one though I have heard not a few of the famous addresses of the past half century ... a landmark in Canada's history.'[74] According to André Laurendeau, if adverse reaction to the pact was minimal in Quebec it was because of Lapointe's intervention, on 9 September and afterward.[75] The Quebec lieutenant's speech helped convince many Quebec MPs to accept the pact, and an opinion poll conducted in the comté d'Argenteuil on 9 September 1939 indicated that Quebecers also accepted the policy: 20 per cent opposed all participation, while 65 per cent favoured collaboration 'within our means.'[76] Chubby Power remarked that during the election campaign of 1940 the 'unofficial "no-conscription" pact, made by Lapointe on our behalf, was generally considered to be in force.'[77]

Thus when Ottawa applied the pact in September 1939, Lapointe's voice was important. He continued to oppose conscription and, with his speech of 9 September and his guidance of King between 24 August and 10 September, ensured the effective presentation of the policy in a manner that emphasized Canadian interests. King, on his own, would not have been able to present the policy nearly so effectively; however, he did accept the advice of Lapointe, whose voice was thus co-dominant with King's. The Quebec lieutenant could not impose his will concerning such a question, and he clearly needed King's approval. The minority had confidence that its voice was being heard and would continue to be heard by the majority. How much confidence Quebecers had in Lapointe and in Ottawa's pact would soon be tested more precisely.

'La vraie voix du Québec': Lapointe or Duplessis?

Lapointe's position as voice of Quebec had been consolidated with the application of the pact, but it was seriously challenged when Quebec Premier Maurice Duplessis called an early election three weeks after Canada entered the war. Duplessis hoped to capitalize on Quebec's opposition to conscription, to participation in the war, and to the pact. Lapointe's voice at Ottawa depended on the anglophone ministers' recognizing that he spoke for his province, and a win by Duplessis would seriously undermine his credibility. A new Union Nationale government at Quebec City would also hamper dominion–provincial cooperation in the war effort. How would Ottawa react?

Lapointe, with his colleagues Cardin and Power, announced that the Quebec ministers would have to leave cabinet if Duplessis were elected. Lapointe declared his intentions in public at the end of September, arguing that Duplessis had decided to campaign against the federal government 'et particulièrement des mesures prises pour assurer l'efficacité et le succès de l'effort du Canada dans le présent conflit, [ainsi] un verdict en sa faveur serait un verdict contre nous.'[78] In private, Lapointe told King that a Duplessis win would indicate that Quebecers no longer had sufficient confidence in him; 'that if Duplessis carried the province, it would be equivalent to a want of confidence both in themselves and as federal ministers, and that they would feel it necessary to withdraw from the Cabinet as having lost all the influence in Quebec.'[79]

When Lapointe announced, with Power and Cardin, that they would resign their seats, the campaign changed immediately.[80] On 30 September Le Soleil agreed with the Globe and Mail that Lapointe, during his speech of 9 September, had spoken for Quebec more than had Duplessis, who was attempting to create dissension on a life-and-death question.[81] The campaign became in large part a contest between Lapointe and Duplessis over who spoke for Quebec, with those accepting the pact backing Lapointe and those opposing it supporting Duplessis, who seemed to oppose participation as well as conscription. At a speech at Trois-Rivières he announced: 'Je dis qu'un vote pour M. Lapointe c'est un vote pour la participation et pour la conscription.'[82] The dominion ministers did not resign. The provincial Liberals won 54 per cent of the votes and sixty-nine of the eighty-six seats.[83] Lapointe, in reply to a letter of congratulations, told Skelton that 'you are right in thinking that the most urgent work to do is to kill the nationalistic separatist movement that has been allowed to grow for some time. I believe it has now received a deadly blow.'[84] The blow had not been fatal, but Duplessis would be less of a problem for the Canadian war effort during the next five years. Godbout was pleased to share credit for the win with Lapointe: the result, Godbout announced, showed the good sense of the Liberal program, and 'il constitue de plus une approbation de l'attitude tenue dans le domaine fédéral par ceux qui ont toujours été les défenseurs de nos droits et les champions de l'unité nationale.'[85]

Many historians, both anglophone and francophone, agree that Lapointe played an important role in the decision to confront Duplessis and in convincing Quebecers that the federal government represented the best guarantee against conscription.[86] There is, however, a tendency among anglophone historians to imply that the Quebec lieutenant was simply acting under King's orders. In the words of Granatstein, King 'had managed the Quebec election well.'[87] Bliss writes that without 'King's' no-conscription strategy Lapointe would have been powerless.[88] At the same time, francophone authors imply that Lapointe and the francophone ministers in Ottawa were centralist traitors, deliberately misleading Quebecers in the interest of the anglophone majority. Durocher accuses Lapointe of blackmailing Quebecers and suffocating provincial autonomy.[89] Brunet argues that French Canadians realized that they had no choice and had to submit to the blackmail, but that the French-Canadian nation, 'humiliated,' realized as never before its state of political subordination.[90] In short, Lapointe is not always given the credit he deserves for being both influential and a defender of French-Canadian interests.

The prime minister had almost no say in the matter of how Ottawa would reply to Duplessis's challenge. He opposed the idea of Lapointe, Cardin, and Power putting their seats on the line and did all that he could to prevent them from doing so: 'I do not agree that our Ministers should leave the Federal Cabinet if Duplessis wins,' he wrote in his diary, and a few days later he added that he again 'impressed very strongly' on them that they should not commit themselves.[91] King and other Liberals, such as Brooke Claxton,[92] feared that they would lose, as Duplessis was heavily favoured to win.[93] But Lapointe, Cardin, and Power did not listen to King, who did not fully appreciate the threat to the authority of the federal ministers.

It was Lapointe who decided Ottawa's policy. Chubby Power claimed that he had decided that the Quebec ministers should put their seats on the line, that 'Cardin was very hesitant in accepting this, and Lapointe, though less hesitant, was not enthusiastic.'[94] This interpretation is conceivable; however, Power was not shy about giving himself credit and afterward had repeatedly insisted to cabinet that he had been responsible for winning the Quebec election. According to King, Power 'said something to Lapointe about his having made the speeches, but that he, Power, had really won the election.'[95] Regardless of who first had the idea of putting the seats on the line, Lapointe believed strongly that Duplessis's act was 'straight sabotage,' which could possibly have led to riots and bloodshed in Quebec.[96] If Duplessis were elected, Lapointe told cabinet, he would continue to hurt Ottawa's war effort.

During his campaign speeches, Lapointe defended the pact in the same way he had in March and September. On 9 October he told a crowd: 'Nous avons au Canada une différence de mentalité qui rend des compromis nécessaires ... Si nous apprécions et comprenons leur mentalité, ne sommes-nous pas en meilleure posture pour leur demander de respecter aussi le sentiment unanime de notre province sur une question comme celle du service obligatoire?' Lapointe repeated that he had devoted his entire life to national unity, had always defended provincial autonomy, and had never let the people of his province down: 'Je ne vous ai jamais trompés. Je ne vous ai jamais menti.' He insisted that he would not let them down on conscription: 'Nous sommes le rempart entre vous et la conscription. Nous sommes la muraille qui vous protège,' he told his audience.[97]

Attacks against Duplessis were not uncommon during Lapointe's campaign speeches. The minister of justice accused Duplessis of calling the election to distract the attention of the population from the financial problems of the province. Lapointe ridiculed Duplessis's accusation that the federal ministers could not prevent conscription: 'Il essaie de vous effrayer mais que propose-t-il? Son acte ne ressemble-t-il pas à celui du malfaiteur qui crie "Au feu" dans le seul but de créer une panique?'[98] Lapointe repeated that Duplessis had supported Meighen in 1921 (and had even been paid by the Union government, in 1918, to prosecute persons refusing conscription),[99] could do nothing at all to prevent conscription, and was just making trouble; but, Lapointe added, if Quebecers thought that Duplessis could better defend their interests he himself would understand and resign. His threat to quit was not new to King, but it was the first time that he used this resource in an attempt to influence the people of Quebec.

Quebec's 'humiliation' was not at all evident when it voted for Godbout, and Lapointe, in 1939. According to *Le Soleil*: 'Nous convenons volontiers que le service public présentement rendu par l'honorable Ernest Lapointe est le plus important de notre histoire.'[100] The French-Canadian press, much more than the English-Canadian, considered that provincial issues also played a role in Duplessis's defeat,[101] and *L'Action catholique* warned that Quebec was not writing a blank cheque for participation. Nevertheless, the intervention of King's ministers did influence voters, and this effort was clearly decided on and orchestrated by Lapointe. According to André Laurendeau: 'L'élection provinciale d'octobre 1939 fut dominée par un homme d'Ottawa: Ernest Lapointe ... Je me souviens de l'avoir suivi, maudit, mais secrètement admiré.' Laurendeau specifies that although three dominion ministers entered the campaign only one dominated: 'Ils étaient – il était la barrière, la muraille, le rempart,' against conscription.[102] Daniel Johnson, Union Nationale premier in the 1960s, agreed that Lapointe's intervention turned the tide for Godbout.[103]

The English-Canadian press saw little more than the issue of participation.[104] The *Ottawa Journal* and the *Globe and Mail* wrongly suggested that conscription would now be accepted with no difficulty.[105] Because most anglophone newspapers concentrated on questions involving the war effort, they credited Lapointe with the decision to confront Duplessis and with the victory. According to the *Saskatoon Star*, 'his oratory, his influence and his clear enunciations of the alternatives facing the electors of the Province were the most important factors in swinging the tide.'[106] King received many letters from anglophones asking him to congratulate Lapointe for winning the election; one judge even offered to create a private fund of $100,000 for the Quebec lieutenant, but King replied that this would not be necessary.[107]

King and Lapointe had not shared the same views as to how to reply to Duplessis. Lapointe had determined Ottawa's strategy, but King hoped to share the credit. Forgetting his opposition to Lapointe's strategy and his fears of a win by Duplessis, King congratulated himself in his diary: 'My own feeling has been right [all] along, as I said to Lapointe at the outset, that I thought we would score a great victory.' The results, King believed, showed the 'confidence of the Quebec people in Lapointe and myself and our Federal administration, in the matter of not permitting conscription.' At the end of the year King believed that Lapointe, Cardin, and Power deserved credit for the victory, but 'they will be the first to say that that result would never have been what it was had I not taken, at the last Session and at the Special Session, the stand I did on conscription, and had I not, over the years ... gained the confidence of the people of Quebec.'[108] Lapointe confided to Grant Dexter that he did not appreciate King's taking credit for the reaction to Duplessis: 'Of course,' Lapointe complained, 'after these events which have taken my strength, those who opposed me have quite happily shared in any credit that was going.' It was the only time Dexter could remember Lapointe's 'taking a dig' at King, and because he repeated it two or three times it obviously 'rankles in his mind,' Dexter concluded.[109]

At times King also realized how important was his Quebec lieutenant's reacting to Duplessis's challenge. He wrote in his diary before the vote that if the Liberals won, Lapointe would hold a position higher even than that held by Laurier in the esteem of Canada.[110] King repeated his comments in a letter to Lapointe during the campaign: 'No man in the history of Canada will hold a higher place than yourself – not even our beloved chief, Sir Wilfrid, for none has ever had quite so significant a part to play as is yours at the moment.' King continued in this letter, wishing Lapointe a happy sixty-third birthday, that 'It seems to me that Providence has reserved for you this particular year as the highest peak in your great career.'[111] On 25 October he congratulated Lapointe: 'The success has been due in no small measure to your courageous and truly statesmanlike endeavours in the interests of Canadian unity.'[112] He repeated this statement in his diary.[113] The next time Lapointe threatened to resign, King would be even more interested in adapting policy to accommodate his lieutenant. Lapointe's voice was clearly dominant over King's in the decision to confront Duplessis in 1939. His will became Ottawa's policy. In addition, the question concerned exclusively Quebec matters, and Lapointe did not need King's approval to carry out his decision.

Conclusion

The pact was thus applied and successfully defended in Quebec in 1939. There was opposition throughout the country: many French Canadians clearly preferred neutrality, and many English Canadians, conscription. As Duplessis had done in 1939, Ontario Premier Mitchell Hepburn challenged Ottawa's pact in January 1940. 'I trust you will pardon my apparent impatience at the lack of a whole-hearted and full out war effort,' Hepburn told Lapointe, adding that the situation was more serious than most realized.[114] King and Lapointe met Hepburn's challenge, calling and winning an election in March 1940 largely on the war policy. Lapointe's role in the strategy to confront Hepburn was less predominant than in that vis-à-vis Duplessis, but King realized the value of having Lapointe on his side. After Lapointe and King agreed that some action was necessary, such as an election, the decision was clearly left to King. When King told Lapointe that he would dissolve Parliament, Lapointe was doubtful about the wisdom of the move, but acquiesced; King said that he would prefer that he agreed, and Lapointe did.[115] Despite opposition in all parts of the country, the majority of both the major linguistic groups supported the pact. During the 1940 campaign Lapointe reiterated how important it was to have his province behind him, so that he could speak with authority in cabinet.[116] He added that the voice of Quebec had never been so well understood in the other provinces: 'Le verdict que vous avez rendu en octobre dernier a consolidé la Confédération.'[117]

During the formulation and implementation of the no-neutrality, no-conscription pact in 1939, Lapointe and King did not share the same views. They came to agree on the policy, but, like most members of the two cultural groups, they accepted the agreement as a compromise between their divergent views. King was so alienated from the French-

Canadian *mentalité* that he did not appreciate the difference between Lapointe's March speech and his own January 'when Britain is at war, Canada is at war' speech. By threatening to leave King, Lapointe was able to persuade him to apply the pact, and by threatening to leave Quebecers, he was able to persuade them to accept it. Lapointe had ensured that Quebec's voice was included in King's policy in 1939, but would he be able to continue to do so when the 'phoney war' in Europe turned real?

French Canada and the Fall of France

In the spring of 1940 the danger facing the world became suddenly and dramatically apparent. The speed and success of the German blitzkrieg on Holland and Belgium shocked many people, but it was undoubtedly the collapse of France in June 1940 that convinced Canadians that the situation had become critical. Lapointe and King were shaken and quickly ordered more soldiers overseas. The Second Canadian Division was sent to England; a third division was mobilized, and almost immediately the greater part of a fourth. M.J. Coldwell, the new leader of the Co-operative Commonwealth Federation (CCF), remembered the time in April 1940 when King and Lapointe had briefed him: 'They told me they were giving orders to send over all the old Ross rifles in the Lindsay [Ontario] arsenal, and from Valcartier [Quebec] to Britain because the British were short of defensive weapons ... It was then that they realised, as all of us were bound to realise, that we were in the midst of a great struggle.'[1]

King was shocked, primarily because of the new dangers facing Britain. In late May he began to fear that Britain and France would lose the war, and after France fell his concern for the motherland increased: 'My heart is very sad at the loss of France, and above all at the appalling situation with which the British Isles are faced from now on ... My heart aches for the people in the British Isles.' He added that the priority for Canadians had 'changed now to the stage where defence of this land becomes our most important duty.' Throughout the summer and crucial autumn of 1940 the prime minister recorded his concerns that Canada would be attacked and 'that Britain may be beaten down in this struggle. With all the forces arrayed against her, as they are, I really cannot see how she can hope to win, short of some miracle of Providence.'[2]

The reaction of O.D. Skelton indicates how upsetting the news was even to English-Canadian autonomists. Abandoning any hesitation he had felt about Canadian participation, Skelton – according to King – adapted his views: 'It amuses me a little to see how completely some men swing to opposite extremes. No one could have been more strongly for everything being done for Canada, as against Britain, than Skelton was up to a very short time ago ... He now sees that the real place to defend our land is from across the seas.'[3] The Canadian war effort would change in many ways, and it would not be easy for Lapointe to ensure that a French-Canadian voice would continue to be heard in the evolving Canadian policy over relations with Vichy France, dealing with subversive groups in Canada, conscription for the defence of Canada, and the move towards a 'total war effort.'

Relations with Vichy France

The First World War hero Maréchal Philippe Pétain, who had assumed the direction of the French government, sought armistice terms on 17 June 1940. The terms imposed by Germany and accepted on 22 June were severe: Paris and northern France became a zone of German occupation, while Italy occupied south and eastern France; Pétain would remain leader of a 'sovereign' French government, soon established at Vichy, with control over the French Empire (mostly in North and West Africa and Indo-China) and the French navy, which was to be demilitarized. In addition, the French army would be reduced to 100,000 men, and 'occupation costs' paid to Germany. General Charles de Gaulle remained determined to fight and established a Free French resistance movement in London. There were other French resistance movements, but this group became the best known, and the Canadian government would thus have to decide whether to support Pétain or de Gaulle.

The British government had no doubts about whom it would support. In July Prime Minister Churchill, fearing that the French navy would fall into the hands of Germany, ordered the French to turn over their fleet to the Allies. When French Admiral Darlan refused to sail the fleet to the British, because he feared that this would lead to the total occupation of France and North Africa, Churchill approved a British attack on French ships at Oran, in North Africa. France ordered a retaliation by air on the British at Gibraltar and on 5 July broke off relations with Britain. According to Churchill, 'the genius of France enabled her people to comprehend the whole significance of Oran, and in her agony to draw new hope and strength from this additional bitter pang.'⁴ Anglo–French tensions placed the Canadian government in a particularly uncomfortable situation. While being careful to emphasize that the action was directed against Germany and not France, Ottawa approved of the British attack. King defended the action in a public declaration, in which he also praised the French sailors for resisting. In no country, he added, had 'the calamity of France received more understanding sympathy than in Canada.'⁵

Another British–French conflict was narrowly averted in September, much to the relief of Canadian leaders. An expedition, with the goal of establishing de Gaulle in the West African city Dakar, was planned by the British Admiralty and the Free French movement. When Britain informed Canada that after an upcoming operation Vichy might declare war against the Allies, King warned of how serious this would be for Canada and appealed to Britain to act cautiously. King and Lapointe agreed that 'a declaration of war against France would have serious repercussions in Canada. The Vichy government was still the government of France.' Cabinet decided to send a telegram stating Canadian concern with any action that might harm relations with France.⁶ The attempt to install de Gaulle in Dakar was unsuccessful, and King was glad that 'we placed ourselves on record in advance against a move of the kind.'⁷

Ottawa preferred to avoid any actions against Pétain's forces throughout 1940, and cabinet agreed that all efforts should be made to maintain friendly relations with the French government, 'so long as there were no open break between the Vichy government and the government of the United Kingdom.'⁸ In June the *Emile Bertin*, a French ship that had been sent by the previous French administration to deposit gold in the Bank of Canada, was ordered by Pétain to sail the cargo, said to be worth 100 million British pounds, to Martinique. As the ship was in Canadian water, Britain wanted it to be held, with force if necessary, but Ottawa let the ship sail. 'I opposed the use of force,' King told Ralston and Power after they briefed him on the situation, 'pointing out the folly and injury it would be for any ships of Canada starting firing on a French ship.' King would tell René Ristelhueber, the French minister in Canada, only that he preferred that the vessel stay and deposit its cargo in the Bank of Canada as planned.⁹

The Canadian government also refused other British requests in July and August for French gold held in the Bank of Canada. King wrote in his diary that Sir Frederick Phillips of the British Treasury was in Ottawa 'to see if Canada might not be willing to turn over to the British government the gold deposits made by the French government,'¹⁰ but Ilsley and

Ralston shared King's view 'that we were trustees in the matter and could not consider giving any undertaking of the kind.'[11] Britain also asked Canada to stop French trawlers near St Pierre and Miquelon. The British, according to King, hoped to prohibit the French marketing their catch, 'prevent food getting to France and elsewhere and also to hold the vessels for British use and the Island of St. Pierre and Miquelon for de Gaulle.'[12] Canada again refused the British request.

Ottawa was no less opposed to British demands to support various programs of de Gaulle in Canada throughout 1940. Requests for a program to train Free French pilots in Canada were refused. Power opposed the idea because of technical considerations – it would take too long – as well as political considerations: opposition in Quebec. In October the Cabinet War Committee decided to study further the possibility of training de Gaulle's pilots but refused the request to press St Pierre and Miquelon to declare support for de Gaulle. It was also decided that Ottawa would provide no assistance for any of de Gaulle's fund-raising in Canada.[13]

In 1941 the situation changed. After Pétain began collaborating with Germany beyond the terms of the armistice treaty, Ottawa became less hesitant to cut relations and to encourage de Gaulle. Le Devoir was warned in February 1941 that its support for Vichy would no longer be tolerated by the censor.[14] Britain sought and received Canada's permission in February to send one of de Gaulle's envoys, Commander Georges Thierry d'Argenlieu, to make contacts in Canada.[15] In 1941 Ottawa was clearly supportive of de Gaulle's resistance movement and willing to end relations with Vichy France, but did not. Churchill's voice became decisive on this question.

Britain had no contact with Vichy and had encouraged Canada in late 1940 to send Pierre Dupuy, the former first secretary in Paris and now acting chargé d'affaires to France in London, to meet Pétain and report on the situation. The British prime minister was pleased with Dupuy's mission and throughout 1941 was 'quite emphatic' that Canada keep the contact.[16] In May King told Ristelhueber that Pétain's stated intention to collaborate further with Germany meant that Canada would have to act, but Churchill still wanted to keep the contact and King agreed that Canadian policy 'should be determined by the reply received from the United Kingdom.'[17] In August the Cabinet War Committee again proposed to end relations with Vichy; 'however, the previous decision to continue to receive a French Minister had been greatly influenced by Mr. Churchill's view of the value of Mr. Dupuy's contacts with Vichy,' and Churchill, asked again, repeated his preference 'to have a window on that courtyard.'[18] This window proved to be embarrassing at times: the Free French in London were annoyed, as recognition of their organization was doubted;[19] some other parts of the British Empire, in July 1941, were 'amazed' that Canada still had relations with Vichy,[20] and Ralston, increasingly uncomfortable with the contact, asked Churchill's permission to announce that Canada maintained relations on orders of the British.[21] But King was proud that a Canadian played such an important role: 'As Churchill himself cabled me, Dupuy was the one effective link the British government had with the Vichy government.'[22]

King also left the Canadian reaction to de Gaulle's invasion of St Pierre and Miquelon in December 1941 in Churchill's hands. After Lapointe's death in November 1941, King, who had two years of Lapointe's warnings of the explosiveness of the situation fresh in his memory, had personally opposed de Gaulle's take-over, but many in cabinet – particularly the three Nova Scotians – had favoured the idea when it had been discussed in early December. King noted that Ralston and Macdonald approved, and 'Ilsley, of course, was all for fight regardless of anything else.' After de Gaulle's take-over of the islands, King told U.S. Secretary of State Cordell Hull that Canada would agree to his request to order de Gaulle out, if Churchill agreed, but Hull preferred not to bring up the question with Churchill. The next day King was pleased that Vichy exonerated Canada, and a difficult situation was avoided.[23]

In November 1942 Pétain's open support for Germany made any further contact impossible. After Pétain appointed Pierre Laval prime minister in April, congratulated the Germans for Dieppe, and opposed an American landing in North Africa in November, the United States ended relations, followed by Canada on 9 November 1942. King was pleased that Canada had separated itself from Vichy without severing any relations with the French people.[24] The evolution of the Canadian position raises an important question: when deciding the extent to which it would support Pétain or de Gaulle (as Churchill preferred), why did Canada follow Britain in 1941, but not in 1940?

Most anglophone historians focus on King's role. They argue that anglophones favoured de Gaulle, and francophones, Pétain; most complain that the prime minister again allowed Quebec to dominate Canadian policy.[25] Donald Creighton argues that King's stated reason for not delivering the French gold in the Bank of Canada to the British – that the money was there on trust – was a disguise. What moved King, according to Creighton, was 'his political dependence on the Province of Quebec ... He was always hypersensitively alert to the moods of his faithful Quebec, and he was well aware now that French Canada differed radically from English Canada in its attitude to the new Pétain government in France ... Everyone of any consequence knew that King's excuse was a hypocritical evasion, and that his refusal was really dictated by his sedulous concern for public opinion in Quebec.'[26]

Francophone historians comment on the different views of anglophones and francophones, without acknowledging any attempt by Ottawa to include both voices in Canadian policy.[27] Robert Rumilly considered that the British and Canadian propaganda was consistently slanted towards de Gaulle – who had established himself in London – and consistently critical of Pétain, whom he thought a loyal Frenchman: 'La propagande auprès de la province de Québec atteint au délire. Elle s'en prend plus à Vichy qu'à Berlin, à Pétain qu'à Hitler.'[28] Few historians have acknowledged that Lapointe played a major role by interpreting for King the 'Quebec voice,' which – without dominating – was definitely heard in Canadian policy.[29]

The two men had quite different views. King, right from June 1940, undoubtedly would have preferred a policy more supportive of Britain against Pétain. After the terms of the armistice were announced, the prime minister recorded in his diary: 'It practically is an entire surrender to the German government. Pétain, and I think his colleagues, are a Fascist group ... All this will be very hard for Britain.' Like most English Canadians, he had supported the British attack at Oran. A week later King again referred to Pétain as a fascist who had betrayed France, and he never changed this opinion, while he saw in de Gaulle and his stand 'the kind of purpose and stand' that his own grandfather had taken. During a visit to Ottawa in 1944, de Gaulle presented King with a photograph of himself, which King placed beside that of his grandfather.[30] Conversely, Lapointe – in 1940 – respected and thought highly of Pétain, the hero of Verdun, while he had a 'thorough distrust and dislike of de Gaulle.'[31] During public speeches Lapointe emphasized that he had confidence that Pétain, who had presented him with medals during a ceremony at Vimy in 1937, would not help Germany and that 'La France, envahie et mutilée luttera jusqu'au bout.'[32]

In 1940 King was aware of the need to move slowly. He had to consider the British policy and the potential advantages to that country of keeping a line of communications open; he had to take into account the position of American policy-makers, who kept relations with Vichy and were very suspicious of de Gaulle. Above all, King realized the potential danger to Canadian unity. Skelton gave King credit for reading the situation and preserving unity, praising King, who 'has his faults but I do not know any public or business man who could do half as well in keeping a cabinet and parliament and country together.'[33] King could read the situation with some skill, but he needed Lapointe to make clear to him exactly how hesitant Quebec was to oppose Pétain and to support de Gaulle.

Canadians were divided on the question of whether to support Pétain or de Gaulle. Anglophones were more inclined to support de Gaulle's resistance movement,[34] and some had a hard time believing that anyone could support Pétain. Minister of National Defence J.L. Ralston, for example, had travelled through Europe and became convinced 'that the French heartily hated Hitler.' He thus argued that 'in reckoning de Gaulle's usefulness Ottawa must not forget that [he] is not alone.'[35] Ralston concluded that all Canadians had the same view and that Pétain had no support in Quebec; to help Lapointe he forwarded a poll which suggested that 98 per cent of Quebecers favoured de Gaulle over Pétain.[36]

However, francophones in Quebec initially supported Pétain strongly, while de Gaulle was more or less unknown.[37] The Canadian minister to France, Georges Vanier, was not impressed by Pétain, whom he considered defeatist, but he thought that de Gaulle lacked political judgment.[38] Elisabeth de Miribel, a Frenchwoman working with de Gaulle, visited Quebec in August 1940 to assess the situation and found that most people 'esteemed and venerated' Pétain, while the Free French were described by some as 'mercenaries of England.' Vichy propaganda in Canada reinforced the impression that de Gaulle was a British puppet.[39] *Le Soleil* repeated throughout the summer of 1940 that the Catholic hero of Verdun sought to make the best of a bad situation, and his motives were not questioned – as de Gaulle's were. When the newspaper criticized Vichy, in late 1940, it portrayed Pierre Laval, not Pétain, as the traitor. In 1941, as the influence of Germany at Vichy became more apparent, support for de Gaulle grew and Pétain's motives began to be questioned. A month later, while de Gaulle's popularity increased, the paper openly opposed Pétain.[40] The tide had turned, but as late as July 1942 Pétain remained as popular as de Gaulle.[41]

To understand the Quebec population, King needed help. In 1940 Lapointe had told the Cabinet War Committee that 'a declaration of war against France would have serious repercussions in Canada. The Vichy government was still the government of France. As yet General de Gaulle had no great prestige in this country.'[42] After Britain requested in October that the Canadian government seize French trawlers near St Pierre and Miquelon, Lapointe replied: 'For the life of me I cannot see how we can do what they ask; this is an act of war and we are not at war with France.'[43] Ralston favoured the action requested by the British, but King strongly opposed it, even before he had heard from Lapointe, and was glad to learn from Skelton 'that Lapointe was strongly of my view.'[44] King also opposed the British request to seize French gold before he had heard from Lapointe. King later was pleased that Ottawa had refused the British request: 'If we had seized the French gold as I had been pressed to do by the British Government, it is doubtful if this present position [referring to the contacts between Ottawa and Vichy] would ever have been reached. The chances are the French would themselves have joined with Germany.'[45] However, both decisions seem to have been motivated more by his preference for inaction than by his limited understanding of francophone Quebec's views.

In addition to rejecting action against Pétain, Lapointe also opposed helping de Gaulle in 1940. He told the Cabinet War Committee in late September that in Quebec 'General de Gaulle had no prestige. His broadcast appeal to French-Canadians [of 1 August] had been regarded as an insult ... Marshal Pétain and General Weygand stood high. They were known and respected by French-Canadians, as men of courage and integrity.' Lapointe added that the fall of France was a tragedy and that there was no criticism of Britain at the time, 'but the violent attacks which had been made upon Pétain and Weygand since the capitulation, had been bitterly resented.'[46]

The next day Ralston sent Lapointe a proposal recommending promotion of de Gaulle in Canada, adding that he imagined that Lapointe would turn down the idea, and Lapointe did not disappoint him: 'I certainly disagree with the suggestion that there should be under governmental auspices some kind of a committee to further General de Gaulle's aims in Canada. This would be a great mistake and nothing would be more dangerous than to start a controversy in Quebec as between Pétain and de Gaulle.' Lapointe repeated that the appeal made by de Gaulle to French Canadians in August 'was a blunder and it is fortunate that more publicity was not given to it.' The minister of justice had not yet finished. If Ralston really wanted to help the war effort, then he should do more to support Lapointe's attempts to establish a propaganda agency for presenting war aims to French Canadians ... without provoking controversies: 'Everything has been done with regard to publicity and information as far as English speaking Canadians are concerned, but very little was done where it was most needed, namely in French speaking Canada. May I add that the best agency for propaganda would be to recognize the French-Canadian minority in all war activities, in army position, in war contracts, etc. Nothing could be more disastrous than to bring outside English speaking firms to execute contracts in French speaking localities as this has been done too frequently. In other words, French-Canadians must be made to feel that they are of Canada as well as in Canada.'[47] Lapointe had complained earlier about the lack of public information on war aims in Quebec.[48] King was pleased with Lapointe's letter and said that he 'agreed with its every word';[49] however, on his own King would have been less likely to oppose support for de Gaulle.

When Lapointe delivered a radio speech to France in October 1940 he made no attempt to promote de Gaulle's group. His objective was to reassure the French that Canada understood the difficult situation and knew that the French would not help Germany: 'Nous connaissons trop bien le coeur de la France pour douter un seul instant de sa loyauté,' Lapointe announced, adding that he had confidence that France 'ne se dresserait jamais contre les Britanniques, contre nous, Canadiens-français, dont tant de fils reposent en terre de France depuis vingt-trois ans.'[50]

Lapointe's role became particularly important in 1941 when Canada considered changing policy. How far were francophones willing to change? and how fast? The situation was extremely delicate, and King would need Lapointe's approval for any action. Norman Robertson, the new under-secretary of state at External Affairs, first asked for Lapointe's approval of the Free French mission of Georges Thierry d'Argenlieu and then informed King that Lapointe agreed as long as no public speeches were made.[51] Lapointe confided to d'Argenlieu that Ottawa was shifting from Pétain to de Gaulle but would have to move slowly because of opinion in Quebec. In May 1941 d'Argenlieu telegraphed to de Gaulle: 'Canadian mission happily completed. Perfect relations established with the highest personalities Government Ottawa and Province and Cardinal Villeneuve. According to reliable witnesses, French Canadian opinion strongly shaken and leaning towards us.'[52] The mission had been successful, but there remained much support for Pétain.

From mid-1941 another representative of de Gaulle, Colonel Martin Prevel, was also present in Ottawa, working in the Department of Munitions and Supply and making informal contacts. Robertson admitted to King that this was an anomalous situation but added: 'It was, however, expressly approved by Mr. Lapointe and the War Cabinet.'[53] Lapointe had told the Cabinet War Committee in May that he had made arrangements for informal contact between Canadian officials and adherents of the Free French movement, who were unable to use normal diplomatic channels. Finally, on 13 August 1941, when Pétain announced that he hoped for closer collaboration with Germany, Lapointe told the Cabinet War Committee that ending diplomatic relations 'would present no difficulties in so far as Quebec was concerned.'[54] Although many Quebecers still supported Pétain, opinion had become sufficiently divided that Quebec would no longer see action against Pétain as a decision of the English-Canadian majority being imposed on the voiceless minority.

Lapointe made another speech to the French people in September 1941 and again appealed to the honour of Pétain and the French: 'Dès la signature de l'armistice, nous étions convaincus que jamais le vrai peuple français ... n'accepterait volontairement de pactiser avec l'ogre aussi fourbe que féroce, qui occupe son territoire.' But he now added clear support for the French resistance: 'Il vous reste encore la présence dans la lutte de tous ces Français libres, qui se battent magnifiquement pour vous en votre nom.'[55] He repeated in this and other speeches his confidence that France would not collaborate with the 'ferocious beast.'[56]

The voice of francophone Quebec was heard in Canadian policy towards Vichy France. In 1940, for their varying reasons, King's views coincided with Quebec's concerning British requests to oppose Pétain. King would have preferred to offer more help to de Gaulle, but he was prepared to agree that Canada not help the Free French. The Quebec lieutenant knew when the moment arrived to consider a change and at what speed to effect the change without losing public support in Quebec, and King, who was also listening closely to Ralston and Churchill, considered that questions related to Vichy particularly affected Quebec, and he followed closely the advice of his lieutenant.

Reacting to the Fifth Column

The fall of France also significantly affected the official Canadian reaction to subversive groups in Canada. In November 1939 cabinet had considered amendments to the Defence of Canada Regulations severely limiting the freedom of certain groups. It accepted a watered-down amendment in January. In late May 1940, when the possibility of a French defeat began to be considered seriously, some Canadians began to panic. Many feared that enemy groups in Canada – a fifth column – were working against the Allied war effort, and pressure for government action grew. The expression 'fifth column' was used during the Spanish Civil War by Franco, who boasted of having four columns of soldiers advancing towards Madrid and a fifth column of fascist supporters already in the city, ready to fight. Large rallies across Canada, particularly in English Canada, sought more actions against subversive activities: demonstrations in Calgary, Montreal, and Vancouver attracted 7,000 people in each city at the end of May, while on 9 June 50,000 demonstrated in Toronto.[57] The Canadian government did act. The Cabinet War Committee agreed that more police were needed to fight the fifth column, and on 5 June 1940 Nazi and communist organizations were banned. The arrest of Canadian fascist leaders came shortly after the arrest of Britain's fascist leaders.[58]

Because the measures strengthened the powers of the Canadian government to act in the interest of the Allied war effort, readers of English-Canadian history might expect that King, more than Lapointe, fought to implement them. According to Stacey, from the moment the King government was re-elected in 1935 a pattern of disagreement emerged in cabinet that would persist, 'with the representatives of Quebec always on the side of holding back and an English-speaking group – invariably including Ilsley – always on the side of greater activity and effort. On the eve of war, one group would favour commitment and the other delay. During the conflict the same division constantly recurred.'[59] This generalization, repeated by other English-Canadian historians, is not true.

If the Canadian government did not ban Canadian subversive groups until June 1940, it was because King opposed the action. In November 1939 Lapointe had presented an order-in-council to cabinet to suppress subversive activities. Aimed at communist and Nazi groups, the proposed amendments to the Defence of Canada Regulations sought to increase the powers of the Royal Canadian Mounted Police (RCMP) during the war. King favoured the principle of Lapointe's recommendations but, fearing that they went too far, joined other ministers in opposing the proposal. He noted in his diary that he felt that Lapointe, 'while very nice about it, was a little disappointed at not getting the order through at once.' King suggested a committee to investigate the situation, but Lapointe, alone in cabinet, refused and insisted strongly on the necessity of the measures as proposed. Two days later Lapointe was again strongly in favour of his proposal, which Euler, Mackenzie, and Power strongly opposed. Lapointe continued to insist on action, and King to resist. 'I am surprised at how fearful Lapointe is in these matters,' King wrote in his diary, 'and how reactionary he is prepared to become during the war period. I think it is in part a nerve strain and less power of resisting demands of his officials.'[60] That the minister of justice was too weak to oppose his officials seems very unlikely, given that he was strong enough to fight the entire cabinet.

In December Lapointe suggested a new draft, which, he pointed out to King, included five significant changes: first, 'no mention is made by name of any association or group'; second, subversive activities are defined as those 'prejudicial to the efficient prosecution of the war or to the safety of the state'; third, the powers given to 'Police Heads or to persons authorized by the Minister to permit searching houses' are eliminated; fourth, the officers of an association will be guilty of any offence 'committed by, or on behalf, or in the name of their association'; and finally, 'when officers of an association shall have been convicted on indictment, the Court may in its discretion declare such association an illegal one, subject to appeal to the Court of Appeal.' Lapointe added that 'this would have the effect of placing the responsibility on the Courts of the land rather than on the Government, and I believe this should meet approval and remove certain objections to my previous recommendations.'[61]

King still thought that Lapointe's proposal was too arbitrary and went too far,[62] but in cabinet Lapointe was not completely alone. Minister of Labour Norman McLarty agreed with the recommendations: 'I have always felt that in connection with the prosecution of the war we could not effectually carry on our war effort on one hand and on the other mollycoddle our Communists and Fascists.'[63] Finally, King accepted the proposal in early January: 'Power, Crerar and I opposed it pretty strongly,' he wrote in his diary, but 'I saw it was useless to continue discussion and allowed it to pass, stating that I did so out of regard for Lapointe, but was strongly opposed to the recommendation itself as unnecessary.'[64]

It was Lapointe who was responsible for the strengthening of Ottawa's powers to deal with subversive activities at this stage. Technically, Pierre Casgrain, as secretary of state, was responsible for many of the actions against enemy aliens, but most questions in the House were directed to Lapointe.[65] Power later wrote that he had found the measures too strong and was surprised that Lapointe had been pressing for even more restrictive legislation: 'I was fully aware that King in principle felt as I did; but I was also aware that he could not vigorously oppose Lapointe, who had been his right-hand man ever since he became prime minister.'[66]

In late May 1940 it was thus the minister of justice who became the target of calls for more severe measures against subversive groups, even though, as Lapointe told the House of Commons, until recently all critics had complained that the laws were too arbitrary and severe. His call for a committee to consider further steps was immediately approved by King.[67] It was now Lapointe who was asking Canadians to 'remain calm' and to avoid 'hysteria.' Even the RCMP believed the situation under control, as 200 Nazi sympathizers had been arrested in September 1939. Lapointe called Mitchell Hepburn reckless for announcing that Nazis in the United States were preparing to attack Ontario.[68] An RCMP investigation of complaints that Germans in British Columbia were a threat proved groundless, as did many similar complaints in other parts of Canada, 'indicating the nervousness of the general public,' as S.T. Wood, the RCMP commissioner, suggested to Lapointe in July.[69] Some francophones requested censoring of *Life Magazine*, which had stated that King was being blackmailed by the 'pro-Axis French-Canadian minority' and that 'Ottawa's job is to declare independence from the Axis transmission belt in French-Canada.'[70] Other francophones wrote Lapointe asking him to censor anti–French-Canadian comments in English-Canadian newspapers. Former Quebec premier L.A. Taschereau asked him to warn the anti-British priests in Quebec; Lapointe replied that this had been done.[71]

In June 1940 Lapointe and King knew that outlawing the Fascist party would be accepted by English Canadians, while outlawing the Communist party made the measures more acceptable to French-and English-Canadian anti-communists. In fact, Lapointe's principal interest in December 1939 had been to act against the Communists, as suggested in his letter to King, when he used Tim Buck, the Communist leader, rather than Adrien Arcand, the Fascist leader, as an example. Lapointe told King that making the officers of an association responsible for acts of their association 'would cover the case of Tim Buck in the name of whom and of the Communist Party of Canada the circulars were published recently which have given cause to such disturbance.'[72] J.W. Pickersgill, King's secretary, writes in his memoirs: 'King clearly did not like the proposals [making groups illegal] but said Lapointe felt the ban on the Communist Party was politically essential in Quebec. For the prime minister, what was politically essential was to keep Lapointe in the government.'[73]

Of course, many francophones opposed Nazi groups, and many anglophones feared communism: George Drew, the Conservative leader in Ontario, was not alone in calling for more steps 'to check communism which he felt to be a far greater danger than Nazism.'[74] The attorney general of Ontario also sought greater protection against communist propaganda as soon as war broke out.[75] In cabinet, Howe, Ilsley, Macdonald, and Ralston in 1941 all sought tougher action against labour at Arvida, in Hamilton, and in Nova Scotia, where, Macdonald claimed, 'the communist element amongst the miners' caused the strike, although Lapointe, with RCMP reports as proof, disagreed.[76] By combining the two extremist groups – as Lapointe had done in September 1939, when he interpreted the Canadian war effort as a fight against Nazi Germany 'and Bolshevist Russia, who looms upon the horizon' – the justice minister ensured maximum support for Ottawa's policy. He told Parliament that only communists in Quebec opposed the war, and he did not want them on his side.[77]

There was opposition in June 1940 – and even more a year later – to the government's action. The *Globe and Mail* had criticized Ottawa for complacency in the spring of 1940, but in March 1941 it was attacking the government for overreacting, for running roughshod over civil liberties. It continued to imply that Quebec dominated the making of such policy – an accusation denied by *Le Droit*.[78] The *Canadian Tribune*, which Lapointe had acted against a month earlier, also found the measures too arbitrary.[79] Lapointe told one critic that 'it is my unhappy lot to have the final discretion in that matter and I have been criticized at the same time from those who thought I was too strict and dictatorial, and those who claimed that I was endangering the country by leaving dangerous people at large.'[80] Lapointe added that he would never intern labour leaders for their activities,[81] that he remained a liberal, and that he hoped to be trusted to some extent during the war. The minister of justice followed closely the application of the law, intervening on occasion for or against certain individuals.[82] Despite the opposition, most Canadians realized that with the fall of France the war had changed and that severe measures were understandable.

King was characteristically reluctant to admit that he had changed his mind. He was, however, eager to note that 'no one was stronger than Skelton was against the Defence of Canada regulations. Equally [secretaries] Pickersgill and [Arnold] Heeney, and others around me. Now, Skelton begins to see the need of even going further in some ways than we have thus far gone.'[83] Lapointe would have preferred stronger measures but because he needed the approval of King and cabinet, he agreed that they could water down his initial proposals to amend the Defence of Canada Regulations. Lapointe did make the policy stiffer than cabinet wanted, because King realized that the question was important in Quebec, but unlike the Padlock Law it was also prominent in the rest of

Canada, limiting Lapointe's influence. After the fall of France he had no difficulty in obtaining cabinet approval for measures against subversives.

Conscription for the Defence of Canada

With the fall of France, all aspects of the Canadian war effort were re-evaluated. Anglophone pressure for overseas conscription – identified in the minds of many as an essential element of a total war effort – suddenly intensified when the danger to Britain became more urgent. Conscriptionists in cabinet insisted, as a minimum, on mobilization for the defence of Canada. Francophones, shaken by the fall of France but still identifying the conflict as a British Empire war, still opposed being forced overseas, but would they accept conscription for the defence of Canada, if it were presented correctly? The Canadian government faced another delicate decision.

On 18 June 1940 Ottawa announced the introduction of the National Resources Mobilization Act (NRMA), which became law on 21 June 1940. This measure, according to King, would 'confer upon the government special emergency powers to mobilize all our human and material resources for the defence of Canada,' but 'no measure for the conscription of men for overseas service will be introduced by the present administration ... Let me emphasize the fact that this registration will have nothing whatsoever to do with the recruitment of men for overseas service.' Lapointe repeated his pledge to resign if conscripts went overseas, but mobilization to defend Canada was necessary. Lapointe also pointed out that in the newspapers calling for compulsory service 'c'est toujours la conscription des hommes qu'ils réclament. Les journaux qui sont plutôt les organes des intérêts financiers du pays se gardent bien de parler de la conscription de leurs propriétés et de leurs richesses.'[84]

Some anglophone historians, who seem to imply that a total war effort required that conscripts be sent overseas, argue that King's government 'held back' from a total commitment to help the Allies in June 1940 because of its 'sensitivity to the concerns of Quebec.'[85] As usual, they give King the credit, or the blame, for reading the concerns of Quebec: according to Stacey, 'King's foremost interest throughout the war was the maintenance of his pre-war pledge against conscription for overseas service. He stood his ground until late in 1944.'[86] Francophone historians, far from acknowledging the presence of a Quebec voice in the NRMA, interpret the bill as another step in the predetermined and inevitable march towards imposition of overseas conscription by the anglophone majority. According to Michel Brunet: 'De 1939 à 1944, les Canadiens français du Québec ont pris la mesure réelle de leur influence dans un pays qu'ils avaient cru être leur patrie.'[87]

King of course hoped that Quebec would accept the measure, but on his own he was not sufficiently skilled to judge the opinion of that province. In fact, he wrote in his diary that although he believed that the promise of no conscription would ensure unity, he also thought that some French-Canadian MPs would bolt from party ranks. On 17 June, King told the Conservative leaders R.B. Hanson and Grote Stirling, who came to see him demanding mobilization of 'all the manpower and all the material resources of this nation for the sake of the Mother Country and for the defence of Canada,' that any form of conscription remained out of the question. But that night Lapointe agreed 'that we should have a measure that would enable us to call out every man in Canada for military training for the defence of Canada.' King added that 'it was a relief to my mind, in that it amounts to what is right in the matter of mobilization of all resources.'[88] Power was also strongly in favour of military training in Canada to defend the country, as were Crerar, Howe, and Skelton. If Lapointe had decided on overseas conscription, it is probable that King would also have considered this to be right.

Lapointe added two essential elements to the NRMA that made it acceptable to French Canadians. First, he appreciated more than King how great was the difference for French Canadians between conscription for service overseas (which would be seen as helping Britain) and conscription for the defence of Canada. When Hanson demanded mobilization of manpower 'for the aid of the Mother Country and for the defence of Canada,' King did not seem to have made any comment that would indicate that he realized how much of a difference there was between the first and second parts of this proposal. King replied that he would not change his view on conscription.[89] He insisted in cabinet that it 'be made quite clear that mobilisation of manpower for the armed forces would not extend to service overseas, for which the voluntary method should be continued.'[90] The following week Lapointe again reminded the Cabinet War Committee that 'the government's primary responsibility was to provide for the defence of Canada and that if this country were denuded of protection, the government would be held responsible.'[91] The committee agreed that no more commitments would be made for overseas, without full consideration.

Second, Lapointe influenced the timing of the NRMA. The possibility of national registration was discussed in caucus on 5 June until Lapointe warned of 'the devilment it would make of the situation in the province of Quebec.' King added that during this caucus meeting he had stressed the 'need for co-ordinating voluntary work' to prevent calls for conscription. Lapointe, after Dunkirk, had agreed that an organized voluntary effort would be the only alternative to conscription.[92] On 17 June, after Pétain announced that he was seeking armistice terms, Lapointe estimated that Quebec would now accept the measure, and it was introduced the following day.

French Canadians were shaken by the fall of France, and most did accept the NRMA. Even Maxime Raymond – who had opposed Canadian participation in September – voted for the bill. The country was in danger, and conscription was acceptable to defend Canada. Germany had become more menacing, and the emotional attachment to France was not completely unimportant. In the confusion of June 1940, André Laurendeau remembered, French Canadians seemed willing to accept almost anything.[93] French Canadians, however, remained strongly opposed to conscription for overseas service and counted on Lapointe to resist anglophone pressure.[94] A vocal minority, unaware of the seriousness of the crisis, did oppose the NRMA. René Chaloult, MLA for Lotbinière, doubted that Canada was in danger: 'Parce que monsieur Lapointe l'a dit, dans un moment de ferveur impérialiste, cela ne suffit pas à me convaincre.'[95] Chaloult proposed a motion in Quebec's legislature against the NRMA, which was easily defeated by Godbout's majority. This vote reminded King of how significant the Quebec election had been for Canada's war effort: 'No one will ever be able to say what service Lapointe and Cardin and Power have rendered in that province.'[96]

Montreal's Mayor Camillien Houde encouraged citizens not to register as required by the NRMA, but few followed his advice. Even Ottawa's internment of Houde received more support than outrage in Quebec in 1940.[97] When cabinet had had to decide how it would react, Lapointe had been absent and King and Cardin had hesitated to act against Houde. King noted that advisers in the Department of Justice preferred that the provincial government act, but cabinet agreed to arrest Houde, and the prime minister was worried: 'I can see in the whole business possibility of riots and serious difficulties throughout the Province of Quebec.' Two days later Lapointe returned from vacation, and although Cardin and other ministers feared reaction in Quebec, Lapointe had no hesitation and immediately signed the necessary orders,[98] confident that Quebecers would support him, and they did. Lapointe anticipated Quebecers' reactions much more accurately than anyone else in cabinet.

Most anglophones had accepted in September 1939 the fact that conscription would never be applied for overseas service, but this was when all assumed that the Allies would win the war. The events of May and June 1940 led many to believe that this restriction, which was seen as a limit on a total Canadian war effort, should be removed. The Conservative MP Tommy Church complained that the NRMA did nothing to help Britain.[99] Conservative leaders R.B. Hanson and Grote Stirling pressed King to impose overseas conscription: Hanson suggested to King that Lapointe might be as good a member of cabinet as Howe, Ilsley, Power, and Ralston, 'if he would do more in urging his own people to accept compulsory service.' King disagreed, arguing that 'Lapointe was rendering greater service [by] refraining from that. That he was extraordinarily helpful in his experience in every way.'[100] At the time, most anglophones seemed satisfied that some action had been taken: Skelton and Howe noted that the need for 'large numbers of skilled industrial workers' could not be neglected.[101]

Lapointe not only influenced King by reminding him how intolerable overseas conscription would be to French Canadians in Quebec, he also guided King when Ottawa applied the NRMA for the defence of Canada. He had delayed introduction of the measure and emphasized that it was intended exclusively for the defence of Canada. Lapointe and King appreciated that the no-conscription promise had been made to Quebec and that any changes to this promise would need the approval of Lapointe, who thus had the final say in such decisions.

Total War Effort and the Pact, 1941

After the fall of France many Canadians agreed that the country should commit itself to a total war effort – a term open to many interpretations. The voices of those who considered that such an endeavour required conscription to support a 'Big Army' overseas became louder in the spring of 1941. Ottawa's decision to continue resisting this pressure was motivated by two considerations. First, the Canadian government estimated that any benefits gained by imposing conscription for military service overseas would be overshadowed by the damage that would be done to the impressive war effort in Quebec. Second, if too many men became committed to the army, other essential elements of the country's war effort would suffer: the air force, the navy, and agricultural and industrial production. Exactly how big the Canadian army should be was not decided, but cabinet did decide, in the summer of 1941, that it would not be the sole priority of the country's total war effort. When Minister of National Defence J.L. Ralston, the main force in cabinet pushing for greater emphasis on the army, presented the program for 1942 to the Cabinet War Committee, he met a brick wall – the army proposed to increase the overseas force from four to six divisions. Lapointe was absent from the meeting, but King strongly opposed the proposals, including the suggestion that no further mention be made of the no–overseas conscription promises.[102]

Few anglophone historians refer to either Quebec's impressive war effort or the country's agricultural and industrial contribution when explaining Ottawa's decision to resist pressure for conscription overseas. C.P. Stacey, author of two of the three volumes of the Department of National Defence's official history of the Second World War, has implied that Quebec barely participated at all in the war: 'A crisis which moved English-speaking Canada to great sacrifices moved French Canada only slightly.'[103] The authors for whom overseas conscription seems to be the sole criterion of a serious contribution to the Allied cause argue that King resisted committing Canada to a total war effort because of his preoccupation with public opposition in Quebec.[104]

Other anglophone historians, and most francophone historians, do consider that Canada's war effort was total in 1941 and that overseas conscription would have hampered it. Some point out the participation of Quebecers on the homefront: on the farms, in the factories, and in buying war bonds in approximately the same proportion as the other provinces.[105] Others emphasize French-Canadian participation, which should be seen as surprisingly substantial, they argue, once the obstacles that French Canadians faced are recognized: of twenty-eight training centres in Canada, in the summer of 1941, only one was French speaking and two were bilingual; francophones had to speak English to join the navy and the air force; the percentage of French-Canadian officers was low; and the recruitment strategy of the Wartime Information Board, with appeals such as 'le Canada au côté de l'Angleterre,' was not effective.[106] While there were no official numbers recorded, it appears that about 161,000 French Canadians volunteered during the war, representing about 20 per cent of the Canadian armed forces – more than during the First World War and also more than the 13 per cent that they represented in the civil service.[107] These historians conclude that, despite the inequalities, French Canadians contributed considerably to the war effort and justifiably counted on the King government to respect the no-conscription promise.

King had never been, and in the summer of 1941 was not, opposed to overseas conscription. During the war of 1914–18 King had written in a New York newspaper: 'It is perhaps not surprising that the rest of Canada sees in the Quebec attitude nothing but disloyalty, and is more determined than ever to make certain that Quebec shall not prevent the Dominion from doing its entire and splendid duty to the men at the front.'[108] During the war of 1939–45 King did not oppose conscription on ideological grounds. J.W. Pickersgill remembered that King 'had no personal conviction that conscription was wrong in itself. He admitted to me privately that he thought conscription the fairest system of recruitment.' To obtain overseas conscription with a united country, King commented in 1942, would be 'the biggest triumph of the war.'[109]

In the early years of the war, King did oppose conscription, fearing its effect on unity. He argued in the Cabinet War Committee that machines more than men were needed: 'It was essential that we concentrate upon the production of the weapons of war, ships and the obtaining of superiority in the air.'[110] How much his own reading of Quebec public opinion and how much the continual warnings of Lapointe shaped his conclusion are difficult to determine precisely; however, King was clearly more interested in helping Britain and less interested in Canadian unity than Lapointe.

King continued to believe that Canadians thought, as he did, that the country was fighting for Britain and should do everything possible to help it. The title that he selected for a book describing the country's effort – Canada at Britain's Side – was translated as Le Canada et la Guerre when it appeared in French. When cabinet considered the policy that Canada would take in the event of a Japanese attack against the United States, Power and Skelton favoured announcing that it would declare war against Japan to respect joint defence commitments with the United States, but King disagreed: 'I took strong exception to it ... I contended such a statement would be construed as a North American policy rather than a British Empire policy ... I thought our position would be that we would stand by the side of Britain.' The next day King added that the 'people of Canada will want our action based not on North American solidarity but upon Canada as a part of the British Empire in what it is fighting for in this war.' In King's view, Canada was at war because Britain was at war, but he did not believe that Canada was at war to save the British Empire. King insisted that if Britain itself was in danger Canada should do everything possible to help it; however, Canada would decide to what degree its own interests were involved before helping Britain fight to save its colonies, and thus King, like Lapointe, refused to send troops to the Suez.[111]

The Canadian government's unwillingness to consider overseas conscription in 1941 was clearly influenced by Lapointe's persistent, strong opposition to the measure. He insisted often that his support of the war without conscription represented Quebec opinion, that Quebec had done – and would continuing doing – its work, and that conscription would only destroy its impressive war effort.[112] When Lapointe accepted the extension of compulsory military training for home defence only, in January 1941, he made it clear that this was intended 'not as a prelude to conscription for service overseas.'[113] He repeated to the Cabinet War Committee in May 1941 his promise to resign if the measure were considered; he personally could never accept conscription 'under any circumstances,' not only because of the pledges that he had made but because it 'would wreck the Canadian war effort, destroy the national unity, and might even mean civil conflict.'[114]

As he encouraged Quebecers to continue to participate – and Lapointe's words greatly aided recruitment[115] – the promise that overseas conscription would never be applied became an essential element of his appeals.[116] In May 1941 he told a radio audience: 'Je suis toujours pour l'enrôlement volontaire, pour service en dehors du Canada ... Mes compatriotes de Québec, je serai fidèle aux promesses sacrées que j'ai faites. Vous pouvez compter sur moi. Je sais que je puis, moi aussi, compter sur vous, et que vous accomplirez volontairement et fièrement le devoir que la patrie vous demande.'[117] Lapointe fought to eliminate the obstacles to greater French-Canadian participation, such as the lack of francophone officers and the impression that Canada was fighting Britain's war: 'Nous ne nous battons pas pour tel ou tel peuple,' he told a radio audience, 'nous nous battons avec tous ceux qui luttent encore pour la défense d'un idéal chrétien, d'une civilisation humaine et de la liberté de l'individu.'[118]

When opposing overseas conscription, Lapointe also emphasized the non-army elements of the war effort. Britain, since the outbreak of war,[119] had favoured aid in the air rather than a huge Canadian army, and Lapointe and Dandurand were anxious to publicize this fact. Lapointe asked the Cabinet War Committee in February 1941 whether 'in view of the emphasis which the United Kingdom government continued to give publicly to the provision of ships and planes, it might not be of greater assistance were Canada to divert to these purposes resources at present being utilized in the Army expansion programme.' Ralston and General

H.D.G. Crerar opposed Lapointe's suggestion.[120] Crerar did not wish to reduce the army but did favour in September 1940 'a longer and more thorough training for a smaller number of men,' rather than the inefficient thirty-day NRMA scheme. He even argued that 'our first objective in military organization must then be to produce the arms and equipment we need for our Army ... Therefore at this stage nothing in the way of military training should be allowed to interfere with production.'[121] In June 1941 there was no shortage of volunteers to maintain the army,[122] and when Ralston presented army recommendations to increase its size,[123] Lapointe again strongly opposed this suggestion in the Cabinet War Committee: 'Large numbers of inadequately equipped men must not be sent against machines merely to satisfy public clamour.'[124]

French Canadians participated surprisingly well, but the pact remained crucial to this effort.[125] The impression that Canada was at war because Britain was at war proved difficult to change. Oscar Drouin informed Lapointe about anti-war propaganda delivered by some priests and warned that 'les progrès de cette propagande terrible qui est en train de faire perdre l'unité du Canada' should be stopped.[126] As late as 1942, 60 per cent of French Canadians believed that Canada was at war because the Commonwealth was at war;[127] however, this did not mean that they opposed the war. There were perhaps as many anglophones who held the same view and strongly supported the war effort. In August 1942 almost all Quebecers (89 per cent, according to one poll) agreed that Canada was doing everything possible to win the war, while only 44 per cent of the rest of Canadians agreed.[128]

Many English Canadians continued to see the no-conscription promise as a limit on a total war effort. A Department of National Defence memo noted that the 'quite untrue rumour [that the Quebec regiments contained mostly anglophones from Quebec and Ontario] is having an unfortunate effect on recruiting.'[129] Many English-Canadian newspapers – not all – repeated that Quebec was not doing its share.[130] Ironically, the minister of national defence does not seem to have been eager to get more conscripts from Quebec. Journalist Grant Dexter reportedly heard Ralston complain that 'there is only limited room in our army for these men [French Canadians]. They can't speak English. We have no French [-Canadian] officers to handle them. Their fighting ability is questionable etc. etc.,' and Ralston sought conscription only to get more men from the English-speaking provinces.[131] That the armed forces were not prepared to accommodate the large number of francophones that conscription would bring was also suggested when some recruits were given permission to join the Free French because their English was not good enough for the Canadian services.[132]

King referred often in his diary to the increasing pressure coming from English Canada for overseas conscription.[133] If only Lapointe would use his influence to convince French Canadians to support conscription, anglophones such as R.B. Hanson and Premier Duff Pattullo of British Columbia argued, Canada would be able to contribute without restriction to the Allied cause. Pattullo claimed to know French-Canadian opinion better than Lapointe or did not care about the minority voice: why talk of 'French Canadians,' Pattullo asked, when we are all Canadians? And if Ottawa agreed to overseas conscription, this decision would receive the 'general approbation of the people of Canada.' Lapointe replied that overseas conscription now would be 'a calamity,' ending unanimity in the war effort: 'Permit me to beseech you not to unwillingly assist the campaign of those who play politics with the issue.'[134]

Lapointe received many letters on the subject from the anglophone public. A representative of the Weston Shops Ex-Servicemen's Association sent him a resolution arguing that conscription was necessary for unity because 'the average French-Canadian is as much concerned in winning this war as are all other Canadian citizens.'[135] In reply to another letter, from a Montreal accountant who had suggested that Lapointe was the one man who could and should convince French Canadians to accept conscription, Lapointe answered: 'I claim I know the Province of Quebec as well, if not better, than any other man and I have discussed that question with all the leaders civil and religious. I may assure you that you are wrong in the conclusion which you seem to have reached, and that in the interests of our war effort it is better not to do what you suggest.' Lapointe added that Australia, Canada, and South Africa had diverse populations that were united behind the war effort, but each would be less so with conscription.[136]

Other English Canadians, notably in cabinet, were not at all sure that Canada's role in the war required overseas conscription. Most ministers disagreed with the notion that the country's most effective contribution was the sending of as many men as possible overseas, as the army requested; only Ralston did not question the advice. King, according to journalist Grant Dexter, complained that Ralston often 'stood up for the generals, fought the cabinet in their behalf ... "I have talked to him again and again. I have asked him not once but many times why he does not tell the generals what we, the cabinet, think instead of continually telling us what the generals think. Generals are almost invariably wrong."' T.A.

Crerar, Howe, and Power were impressed by Churchill's request not for more men but for greater industrial production: 'Give us the tools and we'll finish the job,' he had urged. Even Angus Macdonald agreed, arguing during the Cabinet War Committee meeting of 29 July 1941 that Canada's top war priority should be ships, then air, followed by industry, with the army last.[137]

Lapointe's influence was very present in Ottawa's decision to continue resisting pressure to apply overseas conscription, as King had no objection to sending conscripts overseas. Decisions concerning Canadian policy towards France and overseas conscription were not unrelated. Lapointe told the Cabinet War Committee on 20 May 1941 that 'in view of the deterioration of relations with France, it was all the more important that the position of Quebec should be appreciated' concerning overseas conscription.[138] In the spring and summer of 1941 King, and most anglophones in cabinet, did agree with Lapointe that conscriptionist pressure should continue to be resisted; however, Lapointe did not need King's approval. The question involved a promise made to Quebec, and King would not have changed policy without the approval of Lapointe, who remained opposed till the day he died.[139]

Conclusion

Lapointe's views, like those of francophone Quebecers and many other North Americans, evolved in the period between January 1939 and December 1941. From the hopes that war could be avoided to the realization of the need to resist Hitler's Germany with force, Lapointe increasingly saw collective security, and even conscription for the defence of Canada, in a different light. He did not, however, change his mind about conscription for overseas service. Francophone Quebecers lived the same events, and Lapointe continued to represent their evolving views at Ottawa.

King remained more concerned with English-Canadian views. In June 1941 Churchill wanted King to visit England, but Lapointe opposed the idea, invoking to High Commissioner Vincent Massey the dangers to unity if King were absent: 'As far as Quebec is concerned King is the leader whom they will trust exclusive of all others.' King described the threat to unity that his absence would create in different terms to Massey. Going to England would oblige him to invite Lapointe to become acting prime minister, and if relations between Britain and France or conscription became an issue, 'the whole province of Quebec would immediately be centred out for attack by extreme elements in the other provinces and Lapointe himself would be made the target of abuse. This would certainly mean a complete change in the present whole hearted cooperative attitude of the entire province of Quebec in Canada's war effort ... Indeed it is only by the two of us working so closely together that Canada's national unity has remained up to the present time what it is.' Lapointe's concern was Quebec, King's was English Canada. When Germany attacked the Soviet Union a week later, raising the embarrassing issue in Quebec of aid to the USSR, King was glad that he had not left: 'Were Mr. Lapointe acting in my absence, the situation would become doubly difficult for him to cope with.'[140] King's fear of the impression of Quebec domination in the party remained a constant limit on Lapointe's influence in cabinet.[141]

Ottawa's method of deciding policy was less complicated during this period than it had been in the previous two periods. King was much stronger and more willing to impose his anglophone views on cabinet ... if he could. Only Lapointe was strong enough to resist King when push came to shove, and he relied much less on others (francophone ministers and caucus) to sway King. In addition to his loyalty, speaking ability, and threats of resignation, Lapointe had earned a new resource in this period: much more than earlier, francophone Quebecers looked to him to represent their interests. Being irreplaceable, in poor health, and thus anxious to retire, Lapointe was able to influence the prime minister.

During this final stage of his career, Lapointe had established a role in cabinet that gave him the final say on certain important questions. Concerning Ottawa's reaction to subversive groups – a compromise between the views of King and those of Lapointe – they shared co-dominant voices, as they did in March and September 1939, when they agreed on the no-neutrality, no-conscription pact. Once the pact had been applied, Lapointe became guardian of the francophone voice in the pact, and any modification would require his approval. He thus possessed a dominant voice in the decisions to apply the NRMA in 1940 and to resist calls for overseas conscription in 1941. He also determined the degree to which Canada would support the Free French movement and whether or not to confront Duplessis in the provincial election of 1939. King was able to maintain unity, as he followed Lapointe's advice on these questions of particular importance in francophone Quebec, but could he do so without Lapointe?

Epilogue: King without Lapointe

How important the influence of Ernest Lapointe had been in Ottawa was suggested after his death on 26 November 1941, when William Lyon Mackenzie King began making decisions without his lieutenant. During Lapointe's last month the prime minister had begun to fear that 'should he not recover strength enough to help me, at least in Council, I shall be in a desperate plight,' and he had offered to lessen Lapointe's burdens in cabinet.[1] King recorded in his diary what he had told Lapointe on his deathbed: 'But for him, I would never have been Prime Minister nor would I have been able to hold the office as I had held it through the years. That there was never a deeper love between brothers than existed between us.' He used the metaphor of 'a large pine tree ... with its strength and its sheltering limbs' to describe what Lapointe had meant to his career: 'I naturally felt deeply what it was going to mean to me by way of loss that this great, strong, towering, sheltering gift of God should be struck down and no longer present at my side.' King added that 'only the belief that a higher spiritual presence could remain, could possibly sustain me in such a loss coming on top of that of Skelton, Rogers and Tweedsmuir.'[2]

Throughout late November and the early days of December, King was constantly aware of how handicapped he was without Lapointe to guide him. When the lieutenant-governor of British Columbia sought King's advice on a critical matter, King commented: 'In considering this particular question, I realized how much Lapointe's absence was going to mean to me in dealing with difficult matters of this character.' When discussing the possible seizure of St Pierre and Miquelon by de Gaulle's group, King noted that 'in these situations, I am terribly handicapped having no French colleague at my side. This is a matter that peculiarly affects the province of Quebec.' When dealing with a strike at Kirkland

Lake, when anglophone pressure in cabinet grew for overseas conscription, and during the plebiscite campaign in February 1942, King repeatedly commented on how much he missed Lapointe.[3]

King remained heavily influenced by what Lapointe had counselled during his life and still sought his guidance. On 1 December 1941 he awoke and immediately wrote down the following words from a dream: 'Which makes possible meanwhile return my colleague to public life.' King was not sure but thought that maybe 'this signified Lapointe's continued help from beyond coming to me in the way of a much needed colleague at Ottawa.' He had told Lapointe 'that I was as sure as could be that whichever of us went first, that we would keep in touch with each other. He said: I believe that.' As King spoke about the life hereafter, Lapointe asked: 'Do you remember the time that our government was sworn in, and you and I went down to the cemetery to Sir Wilfrid's grave, each of us with a flower, and I turned to you and said: would it not be nice if Sir Wilfrid could see us together here. He [Lapointe] said: you turned to me and spoke in a very earnest way, saying: but he does see us. He is right here with us. I am sure of that. He said: You were very emphatic.'[4]

The day Lapointe died King read from his Bible and underlined the following: 'Behold, I am with thee, and will keep thee in all places whither though goest. Also when God takes away that which He has given you, he knows well how to replace it either through other means or by himself.' Four days later King dreamt of 'seeing a group of men all dressed in black in the forefront of which, standing out by himself as the leader and spokesman, was Lapointe ... They seemed to be just in front of Laurier House near the stone step like a delegation. The thought came to my mind that the group signified Lapointe and others in the Beyond coming with some message. When I opened the little book, the vision came back to my mind as my eyes fell on the passage for yesterday: "My sons be not now negligent for the Lord hath chosen you to stand before Him, to serve Him" ... The passage for today has the words: "We are troubled on every side, yet not distressed." I seemed to get further confirmation of the vision throughout the day.'[5] In a parliamentary eulogy King praised Lapointe's loyalty, repeating that he owed Lapointe his nomination and much of his own success.[6]

A New Voice for Quebec in Ottawa

A replacement would be hard to find because Lapointe had come to mean so much to the Quebec population, which depended on him to represent it at Ottawa. The tributes to Lapointe after his death reveal how francophone Quebecers had seen his role. One author emphasized that Lapointe never went too far ahead of French-Canadian public opinion; another remarked that Lapointe, characterized by his honesty, speaking ability, and 'simple bon sens,' had learned English 'tout en restant typiquement Canadien-français.'[7] L.-Philippe Picard, Lapointe's former secretary, elected MP for Bellechasse in 1940, agreed that understanding and interpreting the thoughts of his people were central to Lapointe's role at Ottawa.[8] In the words of Adélard Godbout, 'Il a été la voix de son peuple.'[9]

King knew that Lapointe's loss was felt by the people of Quebec. Referring to the funeral, King noted in his diary: 'I do not think at any stage of the visit of the King or Queen to Canada, or at any funeral in Canada heretofore, not excepting Sir Wilfrid's or Sir John Macdonald's, there was a larger number of people gathered in the buildings and on the streets, or more in the way of genuine expression of affection and reverent remembrance. I felt as we walked along how much one owes it to be true to the people.'[10] King, however, did not have the same idea as the people of Quebec as to what was needed to replace the loss eventually.

King attempted to lure Godbout to Ottawa, as Lapointe had suggested, but the premier of Quebec was reluctant. Lapointe, while he was still alive, had told King, according to King's diary, 'I can see no one to take my place except Godbout at some time in the future.' King indicated that he agreed. Cardin, not well known or appreciated in English Canada, not liked by King, and in poor health, was not considered. King argued that someone was needed 'who could speak with authority of the whole Quebec position.' On 29 November 1941, King seemed to prefer the Quebec lawyer Louis St Laurent, despite being warned by Dandurand that 'St. Laurent lacked a certain political sense.' King felt that St Laurent 'is perhaps the very man most needed as I must get someone outstanding for the position of Minister of Justice. It is owing to the French, the Bar, the Government and the country that the Minister of Justice should be a man of exceptional legal attainments.' The next day King was convinced that Godbout was needed: 'I am perfectly sure that if Godbout does not come, the whole situation in Quebec will deteriorate, and that will mean a deterioration of Quebec's position in the Dominion, and a deterioration of our war effort.'[11] He told Godbout: 'You are the only one to succeed Lapointe,' and if he did not accept, 'there is a great danger of the Quebec point of view being insufficiently emphasized, if not altogether overlooked.'[12]

King continued for another week to seek Godbout, who considered that his English was not adequate and that he was needed in Quebec City. King recorded in his diary that Cardin, Dandurand, and Godbout all agreed that St Laurent 'would make an exceptionally able minister of Justice and would be a national figure.' Godbout considered his 'character a fine one ... though he might not be a political leader in the province.' Godbout also mentioned that his connections with large corporations might hurt the government. All agreed that he 'would be the most fitting next to Godbout of any successor.' Finally, King asked St Laurent, who accepted the task on 5 December 1941. When King offered him the position, St Laurent mentioned that 'he did not think that he would be particularly popular among the people there [in Quebec East, because he came from the Eastern Townships] ... Also he had been associated with the big interests and there would be prejudice on that score.' King insisted that what was needed was 'someone who could speak to the provinces of the Quebec point of view; interpret the Quebec point of view to the provinces. That he would be exceptionally good for that purpose.'[13]

Most anglophone historians consider that King made an excellent choice. According to King's biographer, H.B. Neatby, 'Lapointe had seemed irreplaceable but almost overnight he had been replaced.' Neatby argues that St Laurent's prestige, like Lapointe's, rested on the fact that King had chosen him. However, Lapointe's prestige had been founded on much more than King's appointment. For example, King had tried to increase Cardin's prestige in the province, without success, showing that more than his support was needed to make a lieutenant. Neatby notes that King did approach Godbout but made little effort to convince the premier, preferring St Laurent.[14] Granatstein implies that the cabinet was even stronger when St Laurent replaced Lapointe, right from 1941.[15] Brian Nolan agrees and lists St Laurent's qualifications in terms that would have pleased most English Canadians in 1941: he spoke eloquent English, was a corporation lawyer, 'and best of all, did not oppose conscription.'[16]

Most francophone historians disagree. Robert Rumilly, for example, describes St Laurent's qualifications in terms different from those used by Nolan: 'Il est plus à son aise en anglais qu'en français. Il est devenu l'avocat des grosses compagnies anglaises de la région québécoise. Intellectuellement honnête, il n'a pas la mentalité d'un Canadien français et ne verra pas d'inconvénient à la centralisation fédérale.'[17] Genest notes that Godbout was a much better speaker than St Laurent and adds that if

Quebecers had known that Godbout was the first choice, they would have thought that the first choice was the best.[18] André Laurendeau concludes that after Lapointe's death 'il est sûr que sa disparition affaiblit le parti de "l'unité nationale."'[19]

The French-Canadian population in December 1941 knew little of Louis St Laurent. According to Chubby Power, St Laurent disappointed crowds accustomed to the inspiring oratory of Cardin, Lapointe, Rinfret, and others. He adds that 'St. Laurent enjoyed a great reputation as one of the foremost lawyers in Canada ... but he had never taken any part in politics, and thus lacked Lapointe's experience and knowledge.'[20] In the words of one newspaperman: 'He just isn't a politician, that's all.'[21] Quebecers did not come to consider that he presented the Quebec voice in cabinet, because most did not even know that he was a minister. As late as 1945, in reply to the question, 'Do you happen to know the names of any of the members of Mackenzie King's Ottawa Cabinet?' 52 per cent of Canadians named Ilsley, 43 per cent A.G.L. McNaughton, 24 per cent Howe, and 21 per cent Macdonald. St Laurent was not named.[22] He was not recognized by French Canadians as a defender of their interests at Ottawa, he rarely sought to remedy the many obstacles encountered by French Canadians in the civil service and armed forces,[23] and his refusal to commit himself against conscription overseas did not help him become more popular.[24]

After Godbout had refused him, King had not insisted.[25] Had the prime minister convinced him that speaking perfect English was not necessary, and that he was needed in Ottawa more than in Quebec City, he might have accepted the invitation. But King did not push; he even stated later that he and Lapointe had agreed that St Laurent was 'the one person in Quebec' to fill the post.[26] Even though he clearly desired unity, King was left on his own – with his pro-British instincts. His judgment of what Quebec would accept was in no way comparable to Lapointe's. St Laurent would later be a great asset in cabinet, in his own role: according to J.W. Pickersgill, 'Mackenzie King regarded St. Laurent as the ablest man who had ever sat in a Canadian cabinet and so did I.'[27] But in December 1941 he did not replace Lapointe as the voice of Quebec in Ottawa.

The Plebiscite of 1942

King would now have to decide, alone, whether or not to continue resisting pressure for overseas conscription. In early November 1941 the pressure from the Conservative party grew when Arthur Meighen returned as Conservative leader.[28] In cabinet, immediately after Lapointe's death, Macdonald wanted to know why French Canadians objected to the measure, and King explained. Ralston continued adamant, but King resisted, still influenced by Lapointe's warnings: 'Mentioned that I had Lapointe's last letter in my pocket,' he told cabinet, 'saying he was ready to fight very strongly if conscription became an issue.'[29] Rather than revealing how much King was committed to preserving unity, these incidents suggest the danger to unity: King's role in cabinet was to reconcile the regions, not to present their views, and he was particularly unqualified to present Quebec's views. A few days later, when Japanese planes bombed Pearl Harbor, anglophone pressure for conscription in Canada increased. Maybe the situation had changed for French Canadians, thought King. On 9 December King told cabinet that R.B. Hanson had suggested that 'it was Lapointe's influence which had held Quebec against conscription, but [Hanson] did not think they would feel that way if I asked it.' Some anglophone ministers agreed, but Cardin and Dandurand warned that no leader could get Quebec to support conscription.[30]

King had been considering the possibility of a plebiscite ever since he had learned in mid-November that Lapointe would not live, and he appears to have decided on a vote in mid-December 1941. He told cabinet that 'if there was a referendum as there might be, I, for one, would speak very strongly against supporting conscription on the ground that it would divide the country.' However, the Quebec ministers offered little resistance to the proposal, although Cardin saw 'difficulties,'[31] and King's views became Canadian policy. Cabinet decided, in January 1942, to ask Canadians to release it 'from any obligations arising out of past commitments restricting methods of raising men for military service.' Almost overnight King's no-conscription policy became 'conscription if English Canada wants it.'

King called the plebiscite, and in February he felt, according to journalist Grant Dexter, 'absolutely sure that the plebiscite would carry.'[32] But the French-language campaign, asking francophone Quebecers to have confidence in King, was a disaster. King argued on one occasion that the issue was not conscription at all and in another speech that removing the restriction on conscription would 'help overcome a source of irritation and disunity in our country.'[33] As should have been expected, the vote divided the country. With anglophones voting four to one in favour and francophones four to one against, the global result in Canada was 63.7 per cent 'yes' and 36.3 per cent 'no.' Cardin, the leading French-Canadian minister since Lapointe's death, believed his prestige in the province weakened by the results, and when King told cabinet on 8 May that he would notify Parliament of his intention to amend the NRMA to allow conscripts to be sent overseas, Cardin decided to resign. Bill 80, introduced on 11 May, passed in early July by a vote of 158 to 54; forty-eight French-Canadian Liberals, along with six CCFers, opposed it. Cardin said that his colleagues did not appreciate Lapointe's fight, and King agreed. King's promises that conscripts would not be sent, unless necessary, convinced Ralston that the country was run by Quebec but did nothing to reassure French Canadians.[34]

English-Canadian historians, except Desmond Morton, rarely argue that the French-Canadian voice became weaker in Ottawa after the death of Lapointe.[35] They describe the decision to call the plebiscite, like previous Canadian foreign-policy decisions during the war, as another of King's masterful political manoeuvres. Because King had found someone to replace Lapointe, and the French-Canadian voice continued to be heard, these authors explain King's sudden reversal of policy without referring at all to Lapointe's death. Most often they invoke Meighen's return as Conservative leader and the Japanese bombing of Pearl Harbor to explain King's sudden impression that conscriptionist pressure was too strong and had to be dealt with by calling a plebiscite.[36] Creighton adds that the casualties to the Canadian army in Hong Kong (1,975 men) 'had strengthened the demand, if not the need for more combat manpower.'[37] The death of Lapointe, for most anglophone historians, did not mean the end of Quebec's voice, which for them remained strong.

French-Canadian historians do not consider that Quebec's voice was heard in the decision to call the plebiscite of 1942. Most consider this decision as the incident that not only shook French-Canadian confidence in the dominion ministers, but destroyed any confidence that existed. According to Laurendeau, Quebecers saw them as spokesmen of King and English Canada.[38] René Lévesque argued in 1963 that 'Lapointe's' broken promise was still rankling in the minds of many French-Canadians who had great doubt and distrust in the role of their ministers at Ottawa.[39] However, opposition at that moment was not strong enough to fuel any significant resistance to liberal war policies. Consequently, some see Lapointe's death as important, but most agree that it changed little in Ottawa's policy, which had been moving inevitably towards conscription for service overseas since 1939. In the words of one author: 'Les promesses non conscriptionnistes d'Ernest Lapointe et d'Adélard Godbout ne seront qu'un rempart de paille devant la raison du loyalisme et la logique du jeu politique fédéral où la loi du nombre s'impose toujours.'[40]

French Canadians' confidence in the no-neutrality, no-conscription pact evaporated as their voice disappeared from policy. They saw the war differently after Pearl Harbor; instead of a British war, the conflict became much more international, and closer to home.[41] But they continued to insist that the dominion government respect the pact, which had become a major symbol of their voice in Ottawa's decisions, and in this respect Pearl Harbor had changed nothing. From the moment the plebiscite was announced, French Canadians felt betrayed.[42] In a letter to the American minister in Canada, Quebec's lieutenant-governor, Sir Eugène Fiset, remarked that French Canadians felt it 'strange that within a very few weeks of the death of Mr. Lapointe, Mr. King should be asking a release from his solemn pledges.' Rumours even circulated that Lapointe had been shot by conscriptionists.[43]

King received little guidance from his francophone ministers for two reasons. First, when they were consulted, francophones in cabinet, far from exerting the strong, clear pressure that Lapointe had, were uncertain of Quebec public opinion and indecisive. Cardin, the Quebec minister most opposed to the idea of a plebiscite, said that he 'was not going to betray all that he and Lapointe had done to try and have the province of Quebec come into the fight.' A week later Cardin seemed less firmly opposed, as all other Quebec ministers had accepted the idea. Shortly afterward, King 'found that Cardin and Dandurand were looking with disfavour on even a referendum as certain to create the feeling that the Government·was countenancing conscription for overseas.' St Laurent, instead of speaking for French Canadians, advised the prime minister that he 'did feel that we should hold firmly to our policy of not resorting to conscription, but should not tie our hands absolutely in case of a situation that might arise of which we had no knowledge at the moment.' St Laurent added that the measure might be necessary if the United States entered the war enforcing conscription.[44]

Second, and even more revealing of the contrast between the influence of St Laurent and that of Lapointe, St Laurent was barred from the meetings of Cabinet War Committee, which discussed policy and made Ottawa's decisions. From December 1941 until after the plebiscite, in April 1942, St Laurent, on King's instructions, was not invited to these crucial meetings.[45] Until mid-May 1942, French Canadians were represented in this group by the minor minister J.E. Michaud from New Brunswick ... against six to eight anglophones. Between Lapointe's death and St Laurent's acceptance into the committee on 14 May 1942, three weeks after the plebiscite, it met forty-one times. Michaud alone represented French Canada thirty-one times, five times old Senator Dandurand accompanied him, and five times there was no French Canadian present. The anglophones usually included King, Crerar, Howe, Ilsley, Macdonald, and Ralston. Power was also present at times.

What would Lapointe have done? This is a question that many asked at the time. In cabinet, opponents of conscription for service overseas repeated Lapointe's warnings, while those ministers in favour argued that, given the new circumstances, Lapointe would have adapted his views. During the campaign St Laurent, in one speech, hoped to identify Lapointe with the 'Oui' side, quoting the parts of Lapointe's speeches that emphasized Canada's war effort.[46] The 'Non' side quoted the parts of Lapointe's speeches where he talked about conscription, and it seems certain that his voice would have continued stiffening King to resist pressure for conscription.[47] Meighen's return provided a focus for the pressure, but many English Canadians still opposed the idea. Pearl Harbor was a shock but, unlike the fall of France, was a turning point that would aid the Allied cause; Churchill's reaction to the attack was: 'So we had won after all!'[48] If action was necessary, Lapointe, who in 1939 had spoken out strongly against any plebiscite that risked balkanizing the country, would have been able to see something that King could not.[49] Even if King had insisted on a plebiscite, Lapointe in exchange would have obtained something – perhaps a question asking a compromise from both groups – to show that French Canada's voice was heard.

The Reinforcement Crisis of 1944

The conscription question came to a head with the reinforcement crisis in November 1944, three years after Lapointe's death. However, the most important decision in the shift from the no-conscription policy to the sending of Canadians overseas was made by King on 3 December 1941, a week after Lapointe's death. The 'Big Army' proposed by the military and always resisted by Lapointe was suddenly accepted by King.[50] Cabinet approved the plan a month later, but with King's support and no French-Canadian voice – St Laurent remained outside during Cabinet War Committee meetings – there was little opposition. The Canadian war effort changed fundamentally: in addition to its vital industrial and agricultural effort, the country was now committed to maintaining a Big Army in constant need of reinforcements. T.A. Crerar felt that if the number of men suggested were drawn into the army, 'production of essential war materials and foodstuffs would suffer.'[51] Many in cabinet suspected that conscripts would be needed eventually.

The crisis arrived in stages. In September 1942 King began to fear that maybe the Big Army was too big and risked hurting other areas of the war effort. 'I feel very strongly we have gone much too far particularly in relating to the army. It makes a desperate effort for everything else,' he confided to his diary.[52] In late October 1944, as expected, the army sought reinforcements, and English-Canadian pressure for conscription became increasingly insistent. The more than 600,000 Canadian volunteers overseas were insufficient, according to many English Canadians, who were equally if not more interested in political considerations.[53] In cabinet, battles continued as Howe insisted on men for industry, while Ralston continued to see conscription as the only answer. On 1 November 1944 King accepted Ralston's 'resignation,' but the new minister at National Defence, A.G.L. McNaughton, soon made the same suggestion, and when the military and anglophone pressure became insistent, with the Quebec voice at Ottawa still silent, cabinet began to bend to the political pressure.[54]

On 22 November 1944 King abandoned his no-conscription policy. Judging the attitudes of Quebecers on his own, King believed that because he had delayed the measure, and because the anti-conscriptionist McNaughton had replaced Ralston, French Canadians would be more willing to accept the sending of conscripts overseas. He recorded in his diary that he now considered 'a situation of civil war in Canada would be more likely to arise' if Ottawa did not enforce conscription.[55] On 23 November, 16,000 conscripts were sent overseas. Chubby Power, the last remaining minister of the triumvirate that had defended the no-conscription policy during the Quebec election of 1939, had been unable to influence King's decision, and he resigned. It was limited, it was late in the war, but it was conscription for military service overseas. The pact was broken.

Although King's decision to send conscripts overseas occurred three years after Lapointe's death, it is perhaps the single event that has determined the interpretation of Lapointe's influence in Canadian history. Anglophone historians agree that the Quebec voice was heard in Canadian conscription policy from 1939 to 1944, ensuring Canadian unity, and thus Lapointe's death changed nothing. Francophone historians agree that French Canadians had no voice in the dominion decisions of 1942 and 1944, but they minimize Lapointe's position in Canadian history by retroactively dating this absence of voice in conscription policy to 1939.

Anglophone historians are almost unanimous in considering that Quebec's voice was heard in this decision of November 1944, and that Quebecers accepted it. Some, who emphasize that there was a military need for overseas conscription, criticize King for paying too much attention to the minority voice and for having dangerously delayed application of the measure. According to Stacey, the no-conscription promises were unrealistic and were never made with the intention of being respected. Quebec had dominated Ottawa's policy, and the province therefore could not, and did not, disagree with the measure in November 1944: 'Mr. King's essential hold on the Province of Quebec remained unshaken.'[56] Other anglophone historians praise King for listening to the Quebec voice, which was thus present in the decisions to hold the plebiscite and to send conscripts overseas.[57] According to J.M.S. Careless, French Canadians supported King, who 'had held out against compulsory service to the last and had yielded finally to the necessity of majority rule ... The Liberal leader had saved both national unity and his party.'[58]

The assumption that French Canadians accepted the 1944 sending of conscripts overseas is not shared by francophone historians, who talk of near-unanimous opposition. In the words of Pariseau and Bernier: 'Les Canadiens français, minoritaires au sein de la fédération, se virent à nouveau forcés d'admettre que dans les démocraties la minorité cède toujours à la majorité.'[59] Canadian policy was decided by anglophones, most francophone historians argue, and the Quebec voice was not heard. Michel Brunet and others include Lapointe in the generic term 'les ministres fédéraux,' who were no more – and never had been any more – to Quebecers than impotent spokesmen of the anglophone majority. When Lapointe announced the pact and campaigned in the provincial election in 1939, he was simply making empty promises that he was powerless to honour, as the majority brought in conscription in stages.[60] One author even blames Lapointe directly for the measure of 1944.[61] Quebec voted for King's Liberals in 1945, but not because it remained confident that its voice was heard in Ottawa. Interest in federal politics declined after the war, and many turned to Duplessis to defend their interests. The breaking of the conscription promise was neither accepted nor forgotten.[62]

French Canadians in November 1944 did not believe that they had a voice in the decision to send conscripts overseas. Polls indicate that they remained as opposed to the measure as they had been in April 1942 and

September 1939.[63] In the House of Commons thirteen French-Canadian MPs from Quebec voted for their party's measure, eight abstained and thirty-four voted against it. Liberal MP for Lotbinière since 1940, Hugues Lapointe, Ernest's son, was one opponent. He spoke as his father would have: 'I believe I truly express the sentiments of the people whom I have the honour to represent,' he said, adding that King remained the best of the dominion leaders but that Quebecers could not 'forget the breaking of a pledge which to them was sacred.'[64] King noted in his diary that after the speech he decided that St Laurent should reply, 'otherwise we were letting Lapointe become the voice of Quebec in voting against the administration.'[65] But the voice of Quebec was not to be expressed by a speech from Louis St Laurent, with words put into his mouth by King.

No minister was able to represent the voice of Quebec during the crisis of 1944. St Laurent, who was asked not to help the provincial Liberals during the provincial election campaign of 1944, was still a long way away from enjoying the confidence of Quebecers that Lapointe had earned. St Laurent had suggested to a journalist in 1942 that, 'provided that the need for conscription could be reasonably proved, Quebec would accept it under King.' In 1944 Quebec clearly would not accept the measure, but St Laurent said that he would support it, even though he feared his party's losing every seat in Quebec.[66] This was a stance that Lapointe would never have considered: as voice of Quebec, he saw his role as representative of the people, leader at times, but never too far ahead of opinion.

It is difficult to imagine what Ernest Lapointe could have done at this stage. Some believed that this stage never would have arrived had he lived. L.-Philippe Picard, Lapointe's former secretary and MP for Belle-chasse from 1940, suggested to Parliament on 29 November 1944 that 'his weight in the councils of the nation would have strengthened the will of the Prime Minister to prevent some of the measures which have divided us and at times taken our minds away from Canada's wonderful accomplishments in the war. Never has a man's passing away been so sadly felt, especially when we realize that his presence might have been such an agent of cohesion and of unity.'[67] In January 1942 King paid tribute to Lapointe, predicting that his contribution to national unity would become more and more obvious.[68] King had often thought that Lapointe exaggerated Quebec's opposition to certain proposals, but he would agree to follow Lapointe's advice when pushed. With Lapointe no longer there, King, following his English-Canadian instincts, made questionable decisions, which left Quebec with no voice at Ottawa, illustrating just how important Lapointe had been.

Conclusion

During the fifteen years or so that he was a minister, from 1921 to 1941 except during the summer of 1926 and from 1930 to 1935, Lapointe sought Canadian unity. Two very different visions of Canada collided on many major questions of foreign policy, and Lapointe attempted to demonstrate that the voice of the francophone Quebec minority could be heard in the decision-making process in Ottawa. He was not responsible for the important changes in Canadian foreign policy between 1921 and 1941; international events, economic influences, domestic pressure, and the combined influence of many actors – particularly King – shaped these changes. However, in the individual decisions that led to the loosening of ties within the British Empire/Commonwealth and to French-Canadian participation in the Second World War, Lapointe played a crucial role.

How influential was the voice of Lapointe? A brief statistical demonstration will not answer this question. However, the seventeen decisions analysed in this study indicate that he succeeded in every case in his attempts to include a francophone Quebec voice. Usually King agreed and both voices were co-dominant, but in six decisions Lapointe's voice was even stronger than that of the prime minister.

The seventeen decisions and the strength of Lapointe's voice vis-à-vis King's were:

1　refusing to commit Canadian troops for Chanak (co-dominant)
2　insisting on signing the Halibut Treaty alone (co-dominant)
3　clearly defining the status of dominions at the 1926 Imperial Conference (co-dominant)
4　opposing Article X of the League Covenant (co-dominant)
5　favouring acceptance of the optional clause in the Geneva Protocol (co-dominant)
6　seeking a seat on the League's Council in 1927 (dominant)
7　repudiating Riddell's proposal for sanctions against Italy (co-dominant)
8　adopting the Foreign Enlistment Act vis-à-vis the Spanish Civil War (co-dominant)

9 refusing to make commitments to Britain at the 1937 Imperial
   Conference (co-dominant)
10 refusing to make commitments to Britain during the Munich crisis
   (dominant)
11 making the no-neutrality, no-conscription pact (co-dominant)
12 applying the pact (co-dominant)
13 defending the pact, confronting Duplessis in 1939 (dominant)
14 supporting the Free French movement (dominant)
15 banning subversive groups (co-dominant)
16 accepting conscription for the defence of Canada (dominant)
17 resisting pressure for overseas conscription (dominant)

One question in which it may appear that King imposed his voice over
Lapointe's was the decision in early 1939 to commit Canada to be at
Britain's side if war broke out. However, when the policy was officially
announced, it also included the promise that conscription would never
be applied – an addition that Lapointe had imposed – and his voice was
thus co-dominant with King's. Subsequent decisions involving the pact
are not easy to classify.

The first two cases in which Lapointe's voice was dominant over King's
are relatively straightforward: about seeking a seat on the League Council and refusing to make commitments during the Munich crisis, the
Quebec lieutenant disagreed with the prime minister, threatened to resign, and convinced King to change his mind. King had the final say yet
decided to yield to Lapointe. When Ottawa replied to Duplessis during
the provincial election campaign of 1939, the decision involved Quebec,
and Lapointe had the final say. But regarding the pact, the situation was
more complex. In 1939 Lapointe needed King's approval before he
announced the no-conscription pact (he had promised for years that
there would be no conscription, but it did not become official policy
until 1939); however, any decision to amend this part of the pact, the
part clearly directed to Quebec, seems to have fallen within Lapointe's
sphere of influence. Thus King needed Lapointe's support when intro-
ducing the NRMA and when considering any change to the no-conscription policy in 1941. The prime minister also seems to have considered
recognition of the Free French a question involving Quebec's interests,
and Lapointe seems to have had the final word.

Because King and Lapointe eventually both agreed on most policies, it
may appear that Lapointe did nothing to change the policy that King
would have adopted had he been alone. This would be a mistaken as-

sumption. When two voices are co-dominant on a decision, they are not necessarily in favour of the same policy. King and Lapointe did agree easily on certain decisions – such as the no-commitment policy during the Chanak incident and during the Imperial Conference of 1937, the signing of the Halibut Treaty, and opposition to Article X – but they did not seek the same policy in any of the seventeen decisions. King, though a Canadian autonomist, favoured a much closer connection to Britain than Lapointe, who hoped to cut the ties as quickly and as completely as possible. This difference was most apparent when defining dominion status and debating the optional clause in the late 1920s. King would bend to pressure by Lapointe – and later take credit for the compromise as his policy, most notably during the Ethiopian crisis – but on his own King, who saw Canada as 'one of the English-speaking Dominions,'[69] would have acted much differently.

Lapointe did not dominate the decision-making structure in Ottawa. He could not convince his anglophone colleagues to accept equality for francophones in the civil service or the army. He rarely attempted to influence economic policy – unless it directly and obviously affected the interests of Quebec. But he was certainly not an anglophone stooge, manipulating or betraying his people to promote the imperialist policy of the anglophone majority. Using a variety of resources, adapting to the evolving decision-making structure during three distinct phases of his career, despite almost constant resistance from King and most anglophones in cabinet, he fought not for a dominant but for a representative voice for francophone Quebec in Ottawa.

King looked at the world as an anglophone, while Lapointe saw it as a francophone. That King, given his views of Canada and the empire, is known as the 'national unity' prime minister suggests how great was the influence of Lapointe. Realizing how important it was for francophone Quebecers to know that their views were not ignored by the majority, Lapointe devoted much of his career to guiding the 'national unity' prime minister through many political mine-fields. It was not an easy task, but for most of the period from 1921 to 1941 Lapointe ensured that Quebec's voice was heard in Canadian foreign policy.

Notes

Introduction

1 Charles Taylor, *Reconciling the Solitudes: Essays on Canadian Federalism and Nationalism* (Montreal: McGill-Queen's University Press, 1993), 187–90.

2 Allan Gregg, 'The New Canada,' *Maclean's* 4 Jan. 1993, 28. Glen Allen, 'Articles of Faith,' *Maclean's* 22 March 1993, 18–19.

3 Michel Brunet, in *Québec*, 286, writes that whenever national unity has triumphed 'c'est parce que les Canadiens français se sont inclinés devant le Canada anglais.' Donald Creighton, in *Forked Road*, 69, argues that the conscription debate in 1941 confirmed 'the basic doctrinal truth that French Canada possessed rights superior to those of English Canada.'

4 Frank Underhill, 'Concerning Mr. King,' *Canadian Forum* (Sept. 1950), 121–2, 125–6.

5 Bliss, *Right Honourable Men*. J.L. Granatstein, 'The 100 Canadians,' *Maclean's* 1 July 1998, 24.

6 'Rizzuto promet, Chrétien fulmine,' *Le Nouvelliste*, 23 Oct. 1993, 1; Anthony Wilson-Smith, 'Ottawa's Fresh Faces,' *Maclean's* 5 July 1993, 7. English, 'French Lieutenant,' 194.

7 National Archives (NA), Ottawa, Lapointe Papers, vol. 61, file A4, Canon H.J. Cody, president of the University of Toronto, in official program, *Banquet offert au Très Honorable Ernest Lapointe*, 18 Feb. 1939, 1, said: 'In every important issue, domestic, imperial and international, during the past twenty years, Mr. Lapointe has played a distinguished and often a decisive part.'

8 Neatby, 'Historians,' 4.

9 The books referring to King (360), Skelton (110), and Lapointe (52): Wigley, *Transition* (42-11-1); Eayrs, *Defence*, vol. 1 (64-10-2); Stacey, *Conflict*, vol. 2 (146-36-23); Veatch, *League* (66-39-26); Glazebrook, *External Relations*, vol. 2 (17-4-0); and Granatstein, *Britain's Weakness* (25-10-0).

10 Brunet, *Québec*, 270. Bertrand, 'Politique extérieure,' ii. Monière, *Idéologies*, 286. Gravel, 'Québec militaire,' 108.

11 Groulx, *Histoire*, 2: 329.

12 NA, Chisholm Papers, vol. 19. Chisholm interview with Lévesque, c. 1962.

13 Pierre Elliott Trudeau, *Federalism and the French-Canadians* (Toronto: Macmillan 1968), 166.

14 Bernard Saint-Aubin, *King et son époque* (Montreal: La Presse 1982), 261. Linteau et al., *Québec*, 2: 132–42. Rumilly, *Histoire*, 39: 157. Laurendeau, *Crise*, 18–21. Brunet, *Québec*, 269.

15 Eayrs, 'Low, Dishonest Decade,' 76–7. See also Stacey, *Conflict*, vol. 2. Hooker, 'In Defence of Unity,' 33.

16 Slobodin, 'Tangled Web,' xv, 496–7.

17 Neatby, 'Historians,' 12. Neatby, 'Unity,' 54–70. Granatstein, *Canada's War*, vii.

18 See Granatstein and Bothwell, 'Self-Evident National Duty,' 213–14. Neatby, 'Unity,' 54–70. Thompson and Seager, *Canada*, 314. Granatstein, *Canada's War*, vi. Waite, 'French-Canadian Isolationism,' 135.

19 Slobodin, 'Tangled Web,' viii. See also Eayrs, *Defence*, 1: 25. Stacey, *Conflict*, 2: 3–14.

20 Stacey, *Conflict*, 2: i. Thompson and Seager, *Canada*, 41.

21 Granatstein, *Canada's War*, 420. See also English, 'French Lieutenant,' 185.

22 Bliss agrees with H.S. Ferns: 'In terms of understanding the political problems of Canada and in knowing what the Canadian people as a whole were willing to accept from a government, Mackenzie King was miles ahead of any of the active participants in politics.' Bliss, *Right Honourable Men*, 128.

23 Veatch, *League*, 18. See also Gibson, 'Cabinet of 1935,' 114. Granatstein, *Canada's War*, 207.

24 Neatby, 'French Canada,' 5. See also Neatby, 'Historians,' 12. Neatby, *King*, 3: 128.

25 W.A. Matheson, *The Prime Minister and the Cabinet* (Toronto: Methuen 1976), 151–2.

26 Hillmer and Granatstein, *Empire to Umpire*, 151. Hilliker, *Affaires extérieures*, 1: 204. Whitaker, *Government Party*, 36.

27 Esberey, *King*, 189.

28 Granatstein, 'King and His Cabinet,' 179.

29 Nolan, *King's War*, 27.

30 Hamelin, in Hamelin, ed., *Dandurand*, 6. Lloyd, 'Dandurand,' 581–606.

31 Cook, *French Canadian Question*, 147–8.

32 Bychok, 'Lapointe,' 11–14, 34, 294–6.

33 Neatby, 'French Canada,' 8.

34 Lemieux, *Éléments*, 7, 54.

35 Ibid., 6, 14–16, 38. Dahl, *Analysis*, 29–31.

36 King diary, 28 March, 23 Nov. 1919.

37 *Time*, 7 Jan. 1946, copy in NA, Picard Papers, vol. 1.

38 Pickersgill, 'King's Political Attitudes,' 19.

39 Martin, *Very Public Life*, 1: 362.

40 Neatby, 'French Canada,' 5–7. Gibson, 'Cabinet of 1935,' 114. Neatby, *King*, 3: 128. Bruce Hutchison in Bychok, 'Lapointe,' 19. Chisholm, 'Never,' 3. Bothwell, *Canada and Quebec*, 63.

41 Dahl, *Analysis*, 33.

42 Ibid., 37. Lemieux, *Éléments*, 30.

43 Stacey, *Conflict*, 2: 4, 73. Dickinson and Young, *History of Quebec*, 245.

44 Dahl, *Analysis*, 26–7.

45 On the importance of the size and weight of a minister's domain, see Bakvis, *Regional Ministers*, 14.

46 NA, Chisholm Papers, vol. 19, Chisholm interview with Power, 1962. Power, in Ward, ed., *Power*, 133, 377.

47 Journalist Léopold Richer, in *Nos chefs*, 45–51, wrote that Lapointe, the most important defender of his people's interests at Ottawa, 'domine dans la vie politique fédérale. Dans l'esprit de ses compatriotes, il a succédé à sir Wilfrid Laurier.'

48 *Maclean's*, 1 Aug. 1929, in NA, Lapointe Papers, vol. 75.

49 King diary, 6 March, 26 Nov. 1919. C.P. Stacey, *Mackenzie King and the Atlantic Triangle* (Toronto: Macmillan 1976), 53. Neatby, *King*, 2: 197.

50 NA, Chisholm Papers, vol. 19, Chisholm interview with Power, 1962. Bliss, *Right Honourable Men*, 140: 'King's greatest weakness was his inability to write or deliver a good speech in public.'

51 King diary, 19 Nov. 1941.

52 Granatstein, *Canada's War*, 207. English, 'French Lieutenant,' 191.

53 Gibson, 'Cabinet of 1935,' 114. Neatby, 'French Canada,' 5. Neatby, *King*, 2: 402. Bliss, *Right Honourable Men*, 142.

54 King diary, 20 Sept. 1926. Chisholm, 'Never,' 5.

55 Pope, *Memoirs*, 277.

56 Interview with Mrs R. Ouimet, 1992. See also NA, Chisholm Papers, vol. 19, Chisholm interview with Mrs R. Ouimet, 1962.

57 Claude Couture, *Le mythe de la modernisation du Québec: Des années 1930 à la révolution tranquille* (Montreal: Méridien 1991), 30. Genest, 'L'élection,' 110–11. Linteau et al., *Québec*, 2: 725. Dickinson and Young, *Quebec*, 245. Ronald Rudin, 'Revisionism and the Search for a Normal Society: A Critique of Recent Quebec Historical Writing,' Canadian Historical Review (*CHR*) 73

(1992), 30–60. Neatby, 'Unity,' 55. Monière, *Idéologies*, 260. Betcherman, *Swastika*, 27.
58 Jones, *Hégémonie libérale*, ii.

Chapter 1: Finding a Place to Stand

1 Neatby, 'French Canada,' 5.
2 Israël Tarte, in *La Patrie*, 22 June 1896; quoted in Jones, *Hégémonie libérale*, 54–9, 40.
3 Carman Miller, *Painting the Map Red: Canada and the South African War, 1899–1902* (Montreal: McGill-Queen's University Press, 1993), 16–30.
4 *Debates*, House of Commons, 30 June 1905, 8822.
5 NA, Lapointe Papers, vol. 9, file 31, Laurier speech at Athens, Ont., 13 Oct. 1905. Bernier, 'Lapointe,' 61, 147. Power, in Ward, ed., *Power*, 31.
6 NA, Laurier Papers, vol. 327, reel c-813, 87781, E. Michaud, a Rivière-du-Loup businessman, to Laurier, 8 July 1904, suggests that Lapointe has little support and will be easily beaten.
7 NA, Lapointe Papers, vol. 1, 003, Laurier to Lapointe, 29 Dec. 1908.
8 Ibid., 090, Lapointe to C.W. Robillard, 9 Nov. 1918: One person asked Lapointe to investigate a political adversary, but he refused.
9 Power, in Ward, ed., *Power*, 6. Bélanger, *Sévigny*, 61, 86.
10 NA, Lapointe Papers, vol. 1, 029, Laurier to Lapointe, 14 July 1914. Réal Bélanger, *Wilfrid Laurier: Quand la politique devient passion* (Quebec City: Université Laval 1986), 391. Bernier, 'Lapointe,' 13, 35.
11 Carl Berger, *Sense of Power*, 260. On Borden's opposition to bilingualism, see R.C. Brown, *Robert Laird Borden: A Biography*, vol. 1; *1854–1914* (Toronto: Macmillan 1975), 251.
12 Dandurand, describing Laurier's views, in Hamelin, ed., *Dandurand*, 144. Groulx, *Histoire du Canada français*, 2: 329.
13 *Debates*, House of Commons, 26 Feb. 1913, 4231–43. Brown and Cook, *Canada*, 208–10.
14 Bourassa, in Filteau, *Le Québec*, 23. Berger, *Sense of Power*, 235, 264.
15 Dandurand, in Hamelin, ed., *Dandurand*, 171, 210. Laurendeau, *Crise*, 16.
16 *Debates*, House of Commons, 28 Jan. 1916, 391.
17 Ibid., 8 May 1916, 3618.
18 NA, Skelton Papers, vol. 10, file 20, O.D. Skelton, *The Language Issue in Canada* (Kingston: Jackson Press, Bulletin of the Departments of History and Political and Economic Science in Queen's University, no. 23, April 1917), 24.
19 *Debates*, House of Commons, 20 June 1917, 2584.

20 Power, in Ward, ed., *Power*, 80, 99.

21 *Debates*, House of Commons, 20 June 1917, 2585.

22 NA, Laurier Papers, vol. 720, reel c-916, 199409, Lapointe to Laurier, 16 Jan. 1918. NA, Lapointe Papers, vol. 1, 0072, Laurier to Lapointe, 23 Dec. 1917. On benefits of conscription see Granatstein and Hitsman, *Broken Promises*, 98.

23 NA, Laurier Papers, vol. 721, reel c-916, 199962-5, Lapointe to Laurier and reply, 9, 11 March 1918. NA, Lapointe Papers, vol. 1, 0073, Laurier to Lapointe, 18 Jan. 1918.

24 *Le Soleil*, 'Les députés du Québec ... ,' 6 April 1918, 1.

25 *Debates*, House of Commons, 5 April 1918, 423–5.

26 Lionel Groulx, *Mes mémoires*, vol. 3 (Montreal: Fides 1970), 305.

27 NA, Laurier Papers, vol. 703, reel c-911, 193479, Lapointe to Laurier, 21 Oct. 1916: Quebecers were anxious to defeat the ministers. Bélanger, *Sévigny*, 323.

28 *Debates*, House of Commons, 20 June 1917, 2586–92.

29 Burke, Speech to the Electors of Bristol, 13 Oct. 1774.

30 *Le Soleil*, 'Lapointe parle ...,' 23 Dec. 1919, 1.

31 Ferns and Ostry, *Age of Mackenzie King*, 236–42.

32 King diary, 23 Aug. 1917.

33 King diary, 26 Oct. 1917. NA, Lapointe Papers, vol. 1, 0068, Laurier to Lapointe, 29 Oct. 1917.

34 NA, Lapointe Papers, vol. 1, 0053, Rodolphe Lemieux to Lapointe, 3 June 1917.

35 'Le déclin de notre influence,' *La Patrie*, 26 Feb. 1913, 4. 'Notre influence à Ottawa,' *Le Devoir*, 28 Feb. 1913, 1. 'Nous avions raison,' *Le Soleil*, 26 June 1919, 4. Le 'Cabinet unioniste n'est dans la pratique qu'un Cabinet de coalition CONTRE Québec'; 'Ces unionistes,' *Le Soleil*, 13 Oct. 1917, 4. Groulx, *Histoire*, 2: 316–17. Bélanger, *Sévigny*, 165, 176, 301.

36 NA, Liberal Party of Canada Papers, vol. 1215, Lapointe speech in 'The National Liberal Convention,' 1919, 88.

37 NA, Lapointe Papers, vol. 6, file 4A, letters from the public congratulate Lapointe for his support of the Catholic unions, April 1921. Lapointe, 'L'industrie canadienne et l'avenir national ...,' *Le Soleil*, 8 June 1921, 12.

38 Power, in Ward, ed., *Power*, 376. King diary, 18 Jan. 1920. Thompson and Seager, *Canada*, 21–5. Neatby, 'French Canada'.

39 NA, Lapointe Papers, vol. 1, 013–19, Taschereau to Gouin, reported by the provincial Liberal member for Kamouraska, Adolphe Stein, in a letter to Gouin, 27 April 1914. See also ibid., 012, Lapointe to Gouin, 23 April 1914.

40 *Debates*, House of Commons, 28 Jan. 1916, 392–7.

41 NA, Lapointe Papers, vol. 1, 0118, Armand Lavergne to Henri Pouliot, 3 Oct. 1919.

42 Whitaker, *Government Party*, 6. Wade, *French Canadians*, 2: 774.

43 *Gazette*, 13 Feb. 1917, in NA, Lapointe Papers, vol. 82 A.

44 King diary, 18–22 Feb. 1919.

45 Ibid., 6 Sept. 1921.

46 Ferns and Ostry, *Age of Mackenzie King*, 320.

47 King diary, 26 May, 9 Aug., 16 April 1919.

48 NA, Liberal Party of Canada Papers, vol. 1215, 'The National Liberal Convention,' 88. On Lapointe leading the left-wing, see Jacques Bureau, quoted in McGee, *Québec-Est*, 181.

49 NA, Lapointe Papers, vol. 1, 0087, Laurier to Lapointe, 5 Nov. 1918.

50 NA, Chisholm Papers, vol. 19, Chisholm interview with C. Power, 1962. Power, Ward, ed., *Power*, 376.

51 NA, Sifton Papers, reel c-593, King to Sifton, 3 July 1914. Later, at the Imperial Conference, 19 Oct. 1926, 10: NA, RG 7 G21, Governor General's Numbered Files, vol. 671, no. 54713.

52 Dawson, *King*, 1: 307. Saint-Aubin, *King*, 131. Brown and Cook, *Canada*, 330. Ferns and Ostry, *Age of Mackenzie King*, 321–2. Bernier, 'Lapointe,' 6, 134. Rumilly, *Histoire*, 27: 100.

53 Power, in Ward, ed., *Power*, 376. Bychok, 'Lapointe,' 9.

54 NA, Lapointe Papers, vol. 72, *Quebec, A monthly journal devoted to Quebec interests*, published in Britain, Nov. 1929, 228.

55 King diary, 5 Aug. 1919. See also King to R. Lemieux, 12 Feb. 1932, in Ferns and Ostry, *Age of Mackenzie King*, 320.

56 D-Hist., 000.9 (D118), biography of Lapointe by P. Aylen on CBC radio, 26 Nov. 1941, referring to King speech in 1939.

57 King diary, Pickersgill and Forster, *King Record*, 4: 354.

58 King diary, 3 Nov. 1917, 22 Oct., 17 Sept. 1918, 9 Aug. 1919, 27 Feb., 26 Nov. 1920, 3 Sept. 1921.

59 NA, Lapointe Papers, vol. 1, 150, G.A. McGaughey (North Bay) to Charles Murphy, 18 Nov. 1919.

60 NA, King Papers, MG 26 J1, vol. 43, 37705, J. Bureau to King, 19 Dec. 1919.

61 King diary, 18 Jan. 1920.

62 'M. Ernest Lapointe,' *Le Soleil*, 9 Oct. 1919, 4. 'Echo de la grande convention libérale,' ibid., 21 Oct. 1919, 4.

63 'La victoire de Québec-Est,' *Le Soleil*, 28 Oct. 1919, 4. McGee, *Québec-Est*, 177.

64 King diary, 18 Feb., 4 March 1919.

65 Dawson, *King*, 1: 294.

66 King diary, 7 Oct. 1919.

67 'Mr. Ernest Lapointe dans l'Ouest,' *Le Soleil*, 2 Oct. 1920, 4. 'Lapointe ... ,' ibid., 9 Oct. 1920, 4.

68 NA, Lapointe Papers, vol. 1, 096 to 230. *Le Soleil,* Jan. 1920 to Dec. 1921.

69 'On attend un nouveau Cartier,' *Le Soleil*, 11 Sept. 1920, 4. 'No French Canadian need apply,' ibid., 7 Nov. 1921, 4.

70 NA, Borden papers, reel c-4205, 3588-98, memo of talks with Lapointe, Gouin, Lemieux, 20, 24–5 July 1919.

71 Ibid., reel c-4350, 68578, Herbert Ames, the ranking Canadian on the League's permanent staff, to Borden, 15 Dec. 1919.

72 *Debates,* House of Commons, 5 April 1918. 'C'est de bon augure,' *Le Soleil*, 6 Aug. 1919, 1.

73 Laurier quoted in H.B. Neatby, *Laurier and a Liberal Quebec* (Toronto: McClelland and Stewart 1973), 137.

74 King diary, 18–22 Feb. 1919.

75 NA, Lapointe Papers, vol. 82-B, Lapointe speech, 'On individualism,' quoted in the *Daily Telegraph*, 1918. King diary, 9 Aug. 1919.

76 'M. Lapointe,' *Le Soleil*, 20 Oct. 1919, 4.

Chapter 2: Lapointe, Gouin, and King's Early Cabinets

1 Jones, *Hégémonie libérale*, 170. Power, in Ward, ed., *Power*, 77. Graham, *Meighen*, 1: 242–50.

2 On the Maritimes, see E.R. Forbes, *The Maritime Rights Movement, 1919–1927: A Study in Canadian Regionalism* (Montreal: McGill-Queen's University Press 1979). On the Progressives, see W.L. Morton, *The Progressive Party in Canada* (Toronto: University of Toronto Press 1950).

3 King diary, 25 March 1919. Dawson, *King*, 1: 307.

4 King diary, 19 Oct. 1921. On King's 'system,' see Neatby, *King*, 2: 4.

5 King diary, 4 Sept., 8 Dec. 1921.

6 Interview with Mrs R. Ouimet, 19 Sept. 1992. King diary, 13, 22–3 Dec. 1921. Gibson, 'Cabinet of 1921,' 63–103, 166.

7 Whitaker, *Government Party*, 37.

8 King diary, 29 Dec. 1921. Gibson, 'Cabinet of 1921,' 74.

9 King diary, 23 Dec. 1921, 14 Dec. 1922.

10 Ibid., 4, 22 Dec. 1921.

11 Rumilly, *Histoire*, 27: 91. Neatby, 'French Canada,' 7.

12 King diary, 21 April 1923. F.J.K. Griezic, 'The Honourable T.A. Crerar: The Political Career of a Western Liberal Progressive in the 1920s,' in S. Trofimenkoff, ed. *The Twenties in Western Canada* (Ottawa: Museum of Man 1972), 114, 123; Rea, *T.A. Crerar*.

13 NA, Skelton Papers, vol. 11, file 11, diary, 11 Nov. 1923, 171. Gouin died a few years later, in March 1929.
14 King diary, 6 Jan. 1924. On fears of coup see ibid., 19 Oct., 26 Nov., 23 Dec. 1921.
15 Ibid., 3 Jan. 1924.
16 Regenstreif, 'Threat to Leadership,' 272. The Toronto Liberal was W.D. Gregory in a letter to H. Bourassa, 30 Oct. 1925: NA, Bourassa Papers, reel m-721.
17 Dandurand asked King to resign: King diary, 5 Nov. 1925. Ibid., 2 Sept. 1924, 24 Sept., 29 Oct. 1925.
18 Dafoe, in Regenstreif, 'Threat to Leadership,' 285. According to Regenstreif, 279, Lapointe held the key to the situation.
19 NA, Chisholm Papers, vol. 19, Chisholm interview with Power, 1962. In the words of J.W. Pickersgill, Lapointe 'saved Mackenzie King's bacon'; ibid, Chisholm interview with Pickersgill, 1962.
20 NA, Skelton Papers, vol. 3, file 8, Skelton to King, 3 Nov. 1925.
21 King diary, 2 Nov. 1925, 7–8 Jan., 6 Feb., 26 March 1926.
22 NA, Skelton Papers, vol. 11, Skelton diary, 15 March 1926.
23 J.W. Dafoe, quoted in NA, Skelton Papers, vol. 11, file 16, Skelton's diary, 23 June 1926. Sifton, quoted in ibid.
24 'L'enquête des douanes,' *Le Soleil*, 28 May 1926, 4. Ibid., 'M. Stevens ...,' 25 Aug. 1926, 16. After the election, the Vancouver organization of bootleggers was revealed: 'Vancouver en était donc aussi!' ibid., 24 Nov. 1926, 4. *Debates*, House of Commons, 18 Jan. 1926, 218.
25 Power, in Ward, ed., *Power*, 114. NA, Lapointe Papers, vol. 2, 937–69, Rapport des procédés (of inquiry), 5–7 Aug. 1926.
26 King, in 'King...,' *Montreal Star*, 24 July 1926, 1.
27 King diary, 3 Feb., 7 May 1926, 17–21 June, 20 Sept. 1926.
28 Ibid., 23 Sept. 1926. 'Certainly I have a place in their hearts,' he wrote earlier: ibid., 3 Sept. 1926.
29 NA, Meighen Papers, vol. 128, reel c-3471, 76213-16, Manion to Meighen and reply, 23–8 July 1924. Dandurand, in Hamelin, ed., *Dandurand*, 235. Rumilly, *Histoire*, 28: 196.
30 King diary, 28 Jan. 1924, 1, 30 Sept. 1925. On Lapointe helping Bureau: NA, Lapointe Papers, vol. 2, 733, Lapointe to Bureau, 27 April 1925.
31 King diary, 21 Sept. 1926.
32 Ibid., 19 Dec. 1927; Laflamme was appointed.
33 Ibid., 9–10 Jan. 1928. NA, Lapointe Papers, vol. 2, 1036-50.
34 *Debates*, House of Commons, 1 May 1922. 'Une foule immense acclame les chefs libéraux,' *Le Soleil*, 19 Jan. 1923, 1. Power, in Ward, ed., *Power*, 37.

35 King diary, 20 Sept. 1926, 22 Sept. 1921, 10 Feb. 1922, 4 Jan. 1928.

36 NA, Gouin Papers, vol. 67, Gouin diary, 5–9 Jan. 1928.

37 King diary, 1 Sept. 1925, 11 Aug. 1924.

38 Ibid., 14 Jan. 1924, 5 Oct. 1925, 9 Nov. 1922.

39 Ibid., 3 Dec. 1929. 22, 28–9 Nov. 1929.

40 NA, Lapointe Papers, vol. 4, 2065–71, Lapointe to King, 30 Nov. 1929, 3 Dec. 1929. King diary, 6 Dec. 1929.

41 King diary, 30 Dec. 1929. NA, Lapointe Papers, vol. 4, 2097, Lapointe to Fortin, (from the *Sherbrooke Tribune*), 31 Dec. 1929.

42 King diary, 29 Dec. 1922, 11 May, 16 June, 7 Aug. 1926, 31 Aug. 1927, 21 Jan. 1930. *Debates*, House of Commons, 30 June 1926, 5209.

43 A. Lavergne, in *Homme libre*, 15 Aug. 1925. *Courrier fédéral*, 30 Nov. 1925, defended Lapointe. Both articles may be found in NA, Lapointe Papers, vol. 73, file 1.

44 Lapointe, 'Lapointe,' in *Le Soleil*, 22 Feb. 1922, 1. 'Quelle influence,' ibid., 17 May 1927, 4.

45 *Debates*, House of Commons, 6 March 1928, 1055.

46 NA, King Papers, vol. 102, reel c-2266, 86559, Lapointe to King, 23 May 1924, seeking francophones at statistics office.

47 King diary, 27, 16 July, 17 June 1929, 29 July 1930.

48 'Aux communes,' *Le Soleil*, 13 Jan. 1926.

49 King diary, 10 April 1926, 2 Oct. 1928. Also NA, Lapointe Papers, vol. 82, 'Meighen...,' *Montreal Standard*, 23 May 1925. Graham in *Meighen*, 1: 181, explains that Meighen had 'no time' to learn French as well as Lapointe learned English.

50 *Debates*, House of Commons, 15 May 1924, 2183.

51 *Debates*, House of Commons, 8 July 1924, 4196–204. See also ibid, 7 June 1922, 2607. Ibid., 18 Jan. 1926, 220. Ibid., 6 March 1928, 1036. 'Lapointe,' *Le Soleil*, 27 Sept. 1921, 1.

52 *Debates*, House of Commons, 29 April 1925, 2587–90. Ibid, 15 May 1924, 2183.

53 Yves Roby, *Les Québécois et les investissements américains (1918–1929)* (Quebec City: Université Laval 1976), 4, 81–117, 143.

54 NA, Lapointe Papers, vol. 2, 1255, 1319, Lapointe to Bourassa, 6 Sept. 1927, and Bourassa to Cannon, 20 Sept. 1927. Ibid., vol. 2, 909, Premier John Brownlee of Alberta to O.M. Biggar (Ottawa's legal representative), 7 April 1926. Ibid., King to Brownlee, 21 May 1926. King diary, 7 July 1928.

55 NA, Lapointe Papers, vol. 3, 1102, King's secretary to Lapointe, 31 Jan. 1927. King diary, 25 May, 21–2 June 1926, 27 April, 2 May 1930.

56 King diary, 25 May 1926.

57 NA, Woodsworth Papers, vol. 2, Lapointe to J.S. Woodsworth, 22 Jan. 1926, agrees to consider suggestions re immigration act, naturalization act, and Criminal Code but will refer questions of old age pensions and pensions for the unemployed to King. *Debates.*, House of Commons, 23 May 1929, 2738. King diary, 26 Jan. 1926.

58 NA, T. Casgrain Papers, vol. 1, Lapointe to Casgrain, 1929. *Debates*, House of Commons, 7 June 1929, 3362. On the vote see 'Respect aux droits des provinces,' *Le Soleil*, 27 Oct. 1927, 1.

59 NA, Lapointe Papers, vol. 7, file 21, speech, 8 Feb. 1928. 'Une nouvelle victoire pour nos deputés sur le divorce,' *Le Soleil*, 24 May 1921, 1. *Debates*, House of Commons, 8 April 1930, 1345. Ibid., 7 May 1929, 2297. Ibid., 28 May 1929, 2891. Ibid., 9 May 1930, 1913.

60 King diary, 11 March 1930. Five years earlier, King had voted for a divorce bill opposed by all Roman Catholic MPs that had carried by forty votes: ibid., 26 Feb. 1925.

61 King diary, 11 Feb. 1930.

62 NA, Skelton Papers, vol. 11, Skelton diary, 3 Nov. 1927. Skelton blamed the 'tory prejudices – let well enough alone,' of the two premiers. Neatby, *King*, 2: 235.

63 NA, Lapointe Papers, vol. 7, file 24, Minutes of meeting, 4 Nov. 1927. Ibid., vol. 3, 1119. Quebecers seemed to agree with Lapointe: 'Graves problèmes,' *Le Soleil*, 10 Nov. 1927, 4. *Debates*, House of Commons, 30 March 1925, 1707.

64 *Debates*, House of Commons, 18 Feb. 1925, 303. Ibid., 20 March 1924, 516. Ibid., 9 March 1927, 1033. 'Il se démasquent enfin!' *Le Soleil*, 31 March 1920, 4.

65 NA, Lapointe Papers, vol. 7, file 24, Minutes of meeting, 4 Nov. 1927. King diary, 4 Nov. 1927, 16 Feb. 1925.

66 King diary, 5 Feb. 1924 (spending), 15 Sept. 1927 (appointment), 22 May, 12 Dec. 1928 (legal questions).

67 On appointment of judges in Quebec: NA, Lapointe Papers, vol. 4, 1975, King to Lapointe, 4 Oct. 1929. On water power and Alberta natural resources: ibid., vol. 3, 1508, Cannon to King, 18 April 1928. On the St Lawrence Seaway project: ibid., vol. 3, 1736, MP J. Laflamme to Lapointe, 7 Jan. 1929. King Diary, 12 Dec. 1928.

68 King diary, 8 June, 9–11 Sept. 1919.

69 NA, Bourassa Papers, reel m-721, Gregory to Bourassa, 6 Nov. 1925.

70 King diary, 15 Nov. 1928.

71 Ibid., 9 Oct. 1926. *Le Soleil*, 7 to 14 Sept. 1926.

72 *Debates*, House of Commons, 18 Jan. 1926, 223.
73 King diary, 7 March 1929. Stacey, *Conflict*, vol. 2: 45.
74 King diary, 22 Dec. 1919.
75 NA, Skelton Papers, vol. 12, file 1, Skelton diary, 27 Feb. 1929: wrote that Robb had been sceptical of King's leadership.
76 NA, Lapointe Papers, vol. 3, 1089, Dandurand to Lapointe, 10 Jan. 1927. King diary, 7 March 1928.
77 King diary, 11 April 1929. Also, ibid., 19 Feb. 1929.
78 *Debates*, House of Commons, 14 Feb. 1927, 283. Ibid., 14 March 1924, 312. Interview with J.W. Pickersgill, 27 Dec. 1991.

Chapter 3: Autonomy in the Empire: A Sure-Fire Reliable

1 See Wigley, *Transition*. C.P. Stacey, 'From Meighen to King: The Reversal of Canadian External Policies, 1921–23,' *Transactions of the Royal Society of Canada* (Ottawa 1969), 233–46.
2 Lower, *Colony to Nation*. Dawson, *King*, vol. 1. Neatby, *King*, vol. 2. Creighton, *Forked Road*. Morton, in a review of Neatby, *King*, vol. 2, in *CHR* 45 (1964), 320. Thompson and Seager, *Canada*. Granatstein, *Britain's Weakness*.
3 *Debates*, House of Commons, 27 April 1921, 2722. 'Québec-Est ...,' *Le Soleil*, 30 Nov. 1921, 1. Dandurand, in Hamelin, ed., *Dandurand*, 269.
4 NA, RG 7, Governor General's Numbered Files, vol. 16, Colonial Secretary Churchill to governor general, 15 Sept. 1922. *Documents on Canadian External Relations* (*DCER*), 3: 74.
5 King diary, 16 Sept 1922.
6 NA, Governor General's Numbered Files, vol. 10, Governor General to Secretary of State for Colonies, 18 Sept. 1922. *DCER*, 3: 78.
7 King diary, 20 Sept., 26 Oct. 1922.
8 Stacey, *Conflict*, 2: 27. Thompson and Seager, *Canada*, 44. Hilliker, *Affaires extérieures*, 103.
9 King diary, 17–20 Sept. 1922, 20 Oct. 1923.
10 NA, King Papers, reel c-2244, 61951-4, Fielding to King, 18 Sept. 1922.
11 Ibid., vol. 76, reel c-2246, 64224, Lapointe to King, 19 Sept. 1922. King diary, 19 Sept. 1922.
12 NA, King Papers, vol. 76, reel c-2246, 64227, Lapointe to King, 20 Sept. 1922.
13 Ibid., reel c-2244, 61968, Fielding to King, 26 Sept. 1922.
14 NA, Lapointe Papers, vol. 2, 0598, R. Lemieux to Lapointe, 12 Oct. 1922. King diary, 18 Sept., 20, 28 Oct. 1922.

15 King diary, 17–19 Sept. 1922.

16 'Restons chez nous,' *Le Soleil,* 19 Sept. 1922, 4. Ibid., 19–24 Sept. 1922. 'Vues divergentes ... ,' ibid., 19 Sept. 1922, 1. Rumilly, *Histoire,* 26: 132. Stacey, *Conflict,* 2: 28.

17 *Debates,* House of Commons, 9 June 1924, 2971.

18 Lapointe quoted in 'Lapointe,' *Le Soleil,* 22 Feb. 1922, 12. Anonymous authour 'Lapointe,' *Action française* (1924), 148.

19 Lapointe, 'La situation internationale,' 11.

20 Lapointe in 'L'autonomie,' *Le Soleil,* 17 June 1924, 4. 'Lausanne,' ibid., 10 June 1924, 4. *Debates,* House of Commons, 9 June 1924, 2969–75. Lapointe, 'La situation internationale,' 12.

21 King diary, 29 Oct. 1922, 13 April 1924.

22 Quoted in Lapointe, 'La situation internationale,' 9.

23 NA, RG 7, Governor General's Numbered Files, vol. 111, Geddes to King, 14 Feb. 1923, and King reply to Geddes, 21 Feb. 1923; Geddes to King, 23 Feb. 1923, and King reply, 28 Feb. 1923. This correspondence is also in the *Canadian Sessional Papers,* 1923, no. 111a, 10–16, and *DCER,* 3: 651–3.

24 Dawson, *King,* 1: 434. Stacey, *Conflict,* 2: 53. *Le Soleil,* 2–5 March 1923.

25 Interview with Mr and Mrs R. Ouimet, 19 Sept. 1992.

26 'Le traité du flétan ... ,' *Le Soleil,* 3 June 1924, 1.

27 Wigley, *Transition,* 176. Hilliker, *Ministère,* 1: 105. Thompson and Seager, *Canada,* 51.

28 Stacey, *Conflict,* 2: 50.

29 Geddes to Byng, 9 March 1923, *DCER,* 3: 645. *Debates,* Senate of Canada, 29 June 1923, 1249. *Debates,* House of Commons, 20 March 1923, 1305.

30 King to Lloyd George, 8 August 1922, quoted in Stacey, *Conflict,* 2: 34.

31 'Le Canada est-il une nation maintenant?' *Le Soleil,* 15 April 1921, 1. NA, King Papers, vol. 76, reel c-2246, 64174, Lapointe to King, 8 July 1922, to remind him to bring up the treaty while in Washington, D.C.

32 King diary, 28 Feb., 1 March 1923.

33 *Debates,* House of Commons, 27 June 1923, 4454.

34 Ibid., 2 May 1923. Correspondence concerning these treaties may be found in *Canadian Sessional Papers,* 1923, No. 111a, 10–16, or *DCER,* 3: 785–94.

35 'L'autonomie,' *Le Soleil,* 6 March 1923, 1.

36 'Lapointe et la presse anglaise,' ibid., 5 July 1923, 4.

37 Dandurand, in Hamelin, ed., *Dandurand,* 264.

38 NA, King Papers, vol. 88, reel c-2254, 74788-93, King to Lapointe and reply, 1–3 March 1923: King asked to be wired as soon as the treaty was signed, 'mentioning names of signatories.'

39 *Debates*, House of Commons, 27 June 1923, 4473.

40 Lapointe, 'La situation internationale,' 8.

41 *Debates*, House of Commons, 27 June 1923, 4456–60.

42 D-Hist., 000.9 (D118), Biography of Lapointe read by Peter Aylen on CBC Radio, 26 Nov. 1941. Béland, in 'Deux hommes politiques,' *Le Soleil*, 22 Jan. 1924, 4.

43 NA, Meighen Papers, vol. 60, reel c-3438, 34878-83, Borden to Meighen and Meighen reply, 21, 27 March 1923.

44 *Debates*, House of Commons, 27 June 1923, 4452.

45 NA, RG 7, Governor General's Numbered Files, vol. 672, Minutes of Imperial Conference of 1926, 25 Oct. Also Lapointe, 'La situation internationale,' 9–10. NA, King Papers, vol. 102, reel-c 2266, 86570, King to Lapointe, 6 June 1924: congratulating Lapointe on the signing of a second treaty (about smuggling) with the United States.

46 Richard Jebb, *The Empire in Eclipse* (London 1926), 66.

47 NA, Foster Papers, Balfour to Foster, 5 May 1927: 'Nothing new has been done.' G. Foster, General W.A. Griesbach, *Debates*, Senate of Canada, 6 April 1927, 288–302. Glazebrook, *External Relations*, 2: 91. Wigley, *Transition*, 278.

48 Thompson and Seager, *Canada*, 48. Stacey, *Conflict*, 2: 86.

49 Glazebrook, *External Affairs*, 2: 90. Wade, *French Canadians*, 2: 805. Lower, *Colony to Nation*, 484.

50 Prime Minister Jan Smuts of South Africa said that Skelton 'should be satisfied – certainly this is Canada's Conference.' NA, Skelton Papers, vol. 11, file 11, diary, 7 Nov. 1923, 157.

51 Dafoe to Dawson, 23 May 1935, quoted in Ramsay Cook, 'J.W. Dafoe at the Imperial Conference, 1923,' *CHR* 61 (1960), 21.

52 Statement to Imperial Conference, 8 Oct. 1923, quoted in Thompson and Seager, *Canada*, 47.

53 King diary, 20 June 1929.

54 NA, Skelton Papers, vol. 3, file 16, Skelton wrote to his wife, 14–16 Oct. 1926, that on the ship to London Lapointe was ill and that, with King buried in 'that damned correspondence,' 'I've still not managed in all this week to get my two chiefs together for a review of Conference matters.'

55 NA, Skelton Papers, vol. 11, file 11, 97, diary, 22 Oct., 2 Nov. 1923: 'Mr. King follows largely my memoranda.' Confirmed by King in his diary, 11 Sept. 1923. On Skelton's opposition to a common imperial foreign policy, see King diary, 21 Jan. 1922.

56 King diary, 11 Sept. 1929. But he continued to oppose a common imperial foreign policy: King to Baldwin, 10 Jan. 1929, *DCER*, 4: 57.

57 Hillmer, 'Pursuit of Peace,' 150. Thompson and Seager, *Canada*, 41. Hilliker, *Affaires extérieures*, 1: 102. Pickersgill, *King Record*, 1: 6–7. Stacey, 'Laurier, King and External Affairs,' 85.

58 'Sommes-nous une nation?' *Le Soleil*, 10 Sept. 1919, 3: 'L'attitude du gouvernement canadien semble plutôt un jeu destiné à amener la centralisation vers le gouvernement impérial.' *Debates*, House of Commons, 27 April 1921.

59 NA, Skelton Papers, vol. 11, file 11, 5, diary, 30 July 1923: Lapointe, Béland, Bureau, and Dandurand were 'opposed to any cooperation whatever with the U.K.' On Lapointe's views of the conference, see *Le Soleil*, 18 Sept. 1923. *Debates*, House of Commons, 9 June 1924, 2969–75.

60 *Debates*, House of Commons, 19 March 1923, 1288.

61 King diary, 9 March 1926.

62 NA, Lapointe Papers, vol. 2, 1026, Bourassa to Lapointe, 21 Nov. 1926.

63 Ibid., vol. 7, file 27.1, Bourassa quoted in news clip, 22 Dec. 1927. Also NA, Bourassa Papers, Bourassa to Gregory, 20 Sept. 1926.

64 'M. Lapointe comme guide, il n'y a rien à craindre,' *Le Soleil*, 11 Oct. 1926, 1. Ibid., Oct.–Dec. 1926. The paper spoke of the 'rôle prépondérant que le ministre de la justice joue aujourd'hui dans le mouvement des destinées nationales.'

65 NA, Skelton Papers, vol. 3, file 16, Skelton to his wife, 28 Oct. 1926.

66 Ibid., vol. 3, file 17, Skelton to his wife, 10–12 Nov. 1926: He was overworked, and 'the fact that certain other people [King] give all their time to dining and talking with Lord this or Lady that and to diary writing or 5 minutes a day to preparing for conference matters makes everything pretty hard.'

67 D.B. McCrae to J.W. Dafoe, 21 Nov. 1926, in C.P. Stacey, ed., *Historical Documents of Canada*, Vol. V, *The Arts of War and Peace, 1914–45* (Toronto: Macmillan 1972), 454–5.

68 Meighen asked if Canada was bound by Britain's signature, and Lapointe replied 'No': *Debates*, House of Commons, 25 Jan. 1926, 382. Ibid, 1 Feb. 1926, 587. According to these treaties, officially signed in London in December 1925, Belgium, France, and Germany accepted their existing borders, which Britain and Italy agreed to guarantee.

69 NA, Lapointe Papers, vol. 9, file 33, Minutes of Conference, 4 Nov. 1926.

70 Ibid. *Debates*, House of Commons, 30 March 1927.

71 NA, Lapointe Papers, vol. 9, file 33, Minutes of Conference, 4 Nov. 1926, 6.

72 *Debates*, House of Commons, 30 March 1927, 1696–9. Ibid., 12 April 1928, 1944–9. Lapointe, 'La situation internationale,' 8–13.

73 King diary, 19 Oct. 1925. NA, Skelton Papers, vol. 3, file 8, R. Campney to A. Haydon (both Liberal strategists), 27 Sept. 1925.

74 King diary, 30 Jan. 1928.

75 NA, Lapointe Papers, vol. 3, 1237, Lapointe to Skelton, 5 Aug. 1927. See also NA, King Papers, vol. 144, reel c-2297, 122755, Lapointe to King, 5 Aug. 1927.

76 NA, Lapointe Papers, vol. 3, 1578, Skelton to Lapointe, 17 Nov. 1928. NA, Skelton Papers, vol. 3, file 26, 9 Oct. 1929.

77 NA, Lapointe Papers, vol. 76, file 15, Skelton to King (copy to Lapointe), 23 Dec. 1929.

78 NA, Lapointe Papers, vol. 6, file 9, Minutes of the 9th meeting, Conference on the Operation of Dominion Legislation and Merchant Shipping Legislation, 22 Oct. 1929, 11–17.

79 Ibid., vol. 76, file 15, 12, Skelton to King, 23 Dec. 1929. Lapointe was the 'best informed member of the Conference,' Skelton added.

80 NA, King Papers, vol. 308, reel c-4864, 261213, Malcolm MacDonald to King, 27 Feb. 1941. Maurice Ollivier in NA, Chisholm Papers, vol. 19, interview with Chisholm, 1962.

81 NA, Dandurand Papers, vol. 4, July 1930. A Liberal–party English–language pamphlet in the election campaign, 'Achievements in External Affairs, 1922–1930,' focused on the role of King: NA, Liberal Party of Canada Papers, vol. 1215.

82 Lapointe, 'La situation internationale,' 3. 'La France y croit aussi,' *Le Soleil*, 12 Jan. 1928, editorial, 4. King diary, 18 March 1929. Canadian legations were established in the United States (1926), Paris (1928), and Tokyo (1929).

83 NA, Lapointe Papers, vol. 3, 1693, Theo. Feilder, editor in chief, *Empire Mail*, London, to Lapointe, 31 Dec. 1928.

Chapter 4: Autonomy and the League

1 League of Nations, *League of Nations Official Journal – Special Supplements and Resolutions 1920–21* (London 1920).

2 Dandurand in League of Nations, *Records 5th Assembly Plenary Meetings* 1923, 2 Oct. 1924, 221. See also Veatch, *League*, 50.

3 Lapointe in League of Nations, *Records 3rd Assembly Minutes, 1 to 6 Committee* 1922, 14 Sept. 1922, 23–4. Borden believed that if Article X had been stricken, as Canada proposed, 'it is quite possible that the treaty would have been ratified by the Senate of the United States:' NA, Borden Papers, reel

c-4350, 68569, Borden to Doherty (Canadian delegate 1920–1), 30 Nov. 1920.

4 NA, Borden Papers, reel c-4350, 68577, Borden to Rowell, 30 Dec. 1920. League of Nations, *League of Nations Official Journal, 1920*, 9. League of Nations, *Records 2nd Assembly Minutes 1 to 3 Committee*, 1st Committee, 11th meeting, 30 Sept. 1921.

5 League of Nations, *Records 3rd Assembly Minutes 1 to 6 Committee* 1st Committee, 14 Sept. 1922, 23–4.

6 League of Nations, *Records of 3rd Assembly, Plenary Meetings, Debates* 1922. At the 15th meeting, 23 Sept. 1922, France's rebuttal was followed by 'loud applause.' The French delegate did note that he was pleased that Lapointe no longer sought deletion.

7 NA, King Papers, reel c-2252, 73316, Gouin to King, 1 Oct. 1923. League of Nations, *Records 4th Assembly, Plenary Meetings, Debates* 1923, 15th meeting, 24 Sept. 1924. See also Dandurand in Hamelin, ed., *Dandurand*, 348.

8 Stacey, *Conflict*, 2: 57.

9 Lapointe, in 'Des milliers de personnes acclament la politique libérale à Loretteville,' *Le Soleil*, 3 Oct. 1921, 1. *Debates*, House of Commons, 21 Feb. 1921: Béland, Denis, Stein, 164, 543–53.

10 Eayrs, *Defence*, 1: 8.

11 King to Riddell, 1928; quoted in Veatch, *League*, 54–5. King was referring to the threat of economic sanctions contained in Article XVI of the Covenant. See also Dawson, *King*, 1: 402.

12 King diary, 24 June 1919.

13 *Debates*, House of Commons, 20–2 June 1920, 3984, 3991.

14 *Debates*, House of Commons, 19 June 1922, 3188.

15 NA, King Papers, vol. 72, reel c-2244, 61936-41, Fielding to King, 15 Sept. 1922.

16 H.L. Keenleyside, in Keenleyside, *Memoirs*, 429.

17 *Debates*, House of Commons, Feb. 1921, 158–1966, speaking against Article x: Béland, Lemieux, Fournier, Trahan, Vien, Michaud, Deslauriers, and Lapointe (3170). On articles in *Le Soleil* 1919–26, see particularly Sept. 1919 to Aug. 1920.

18 'Avec les honorables Lapointe et Fielding,' *Le Soleil*, 16 Sept. 1922, 4. 'Foster et Doherty en voyage,' ibid., 9 Nov. 1920, 4. 'Ce que la Ligue coûte au Canada,' ibid., 11 Nov. 1920, 4.

19 NA, Meighen Papers, reel c-3228, 19309, Doherty to Meighen, 26 July 1921. Ibid., reel c-3429, 24607, Foster to Meighen, 26 July 1921. The Canadian delegation was among the smallest in 1921: League of Nations, *Records 2nd Assembly, Plenary Meetings, Debates* 1921, 4.

20 Veatch, *League*, 20, 41, 43.

21 NA, Chisholm Papers, vol. 19, Chisholm interview with Riddell, c. 1962.

22 Lapointe compared the former obligations to the British Empire, when Canada had no say, with Canadian obligations to the League and concluded that 'les engagements contractés par nous librement offrent certainement moins de danger:' Lapointe, 'La situation internationale,' 16–17. Lucien Cannon did not agree: *Debates*, House of Commons, 9 Sept. 1919, 140.

23 M. Politis, the Greek representative at Paris, quoted in Lapointe, 'La situation internationale,' 5.

24 NA, King Papers, vol. 76, reel c-2246, 64207-18, King to Lapointe, 19 Aug. 1922; Lapointe to King, 21 Aug. 1922: Lapointe did not want to upset France. *Debates*, House of Commons, 2 March 1926, 1447. Reparation payments and rearmament along the French–German border also caused tension: NA, Lapointe Papers, vol. 3, 1250, secretary of state for Dominion Affairs to King, 20 Aug. 1927. *Le Soleil* strongly supported France.

25 NA, King Papers, vol. 74, reel c-2244, 61903, King to Fielding, 3 Aug. 1922.

26 Ibid., vol. 76, reel c-2246, 64188, Lapointe to King, 9 Aug. 1922.

27 Lapointe to King, 12 June 1923, *DCER*, 3: 534.

28 Sir Joseph Pope to Secretary General, 19 June 1923, ibid., 534-5. Other countries showed little more interest.

29 NA, Chisholm Papers, vol. 19, Chisholm interview with W.A. Riddell: 'King never liked the League of Nations, and he told me one day he thought we were likely to withdraw from it (in 1924) ... but Lapointe was a pretty staunch supporter of the League.'

30 King to Secretary General, League of Nations, 9 March 1925, *DCER*, 3: 552.

31 NA, Dandurand Papers, vol. 5, Secretary of state for colonies (Leo Amery) to governor general, 19 Dec. 1924.

32 King to Baldwin, 28 Dec. 1924; quoted in Stacey, *Conflict*, 2: 62.

33 King to Amery, Dominions secretary, 23 Jan. 1929, *DCER*, 4: 639–40. Amery, to King, 9 Feb. 1929, ibid., 640.

34 Eayrs, *Defence*, 1: 10.

35 Veatch, *League*, 185, 51, 59–61.

36 Stacey, *Conflict*, 2: 62.

37 King, signing the treaty, considered that 'nothing more honorable or important could come a man's way in a lifetime': King diary, 28 July 1928. Lapointe was also pleased: *Debates*, House of Commons, 8 April 1929, 1313. But for King the 'event of real historic interest' was the presentation of the invitation recognizing Canadian nationality': King diary, 22 May 1928.

38 King diary, 2 Feb., 7 March 1925.

39 Ibid., 25 May 1927.

40 Lapointe, 'La situation internationale,' 17.

41 Lapointe, *Debates*, House of Commons, 19 June 1922, 3188: 'Il n'est pas vrai que les préparations de guerre assurent la paix; c'est le contraire qui est le cas.' See also 'Alliance,' *Le Soleil*, 11 April 1923, 1.

42 Lapointe, 'La situation internationale,' 17. *Debates*, House of Commons, 9 April 1930, 1378.

43 Dandurand in Hamelin, ed., *Dandurand. Debates*, Senate of Canada, 13 April 1927, 396–9.

44 Skelton to King, 12 Dec. 1928, in Hilliker, *Affaires extérieures*, 1: 149. Veatch, *League*, 69.

45 Lapointe, 'La situation internationale,' 12.

46 NA, RG 7, Governor General's Numbered Files, Minutes of Imperial Conference of 1926, 4, 9 Nov. Lapointe announced that Canada favoured 'considering further the principle of compulsory arbitration' but agreed to postpone accepting it.

47 Veatch, *League*, 113, 185.

48 NA, Lapointe Papers, vol. 2, 652, Lapointe to Choquette (the lawyer for the Canadian soldier Coderre), 30 June 1924.

49 NA, Dandurand Papers, vol. 3, early draft of memoirs, 372.

50 Veatch, *League*, 59. Dandurand and British Foreign Office legal expert Sir Cecil Hurst exchanged views on this in late 1928.

51 Skelton quoted in Veatch, *League*, 65.

52 NA, Skelton Papers, vol. 3, file 22, Skelton to his wife, 4 Sept. 1928.

53 The other four non-permanent seats would be named by the League Assembly. 'L'hon. M. Lapointe a revendiqué les droits du Canada,' *Le Soleil*, 14 Nov. 1922, 1. Canadian effectiveness was limited, particularly because of jurisdictional uncertainty as between the dominion and provincial governments: H.H. Wrong report, 30 Nov. 1938, *DCER*, 6: 636–48.

54 See Dandurand, in Hamelin, ed., *Dandurand*, 306.

55 Neatby, *King*, 2: 195.

56 Ibid., 194. Neatby, 'French Canada,' 10, Veatch, *League*, 16. Stacey, *Conflict*, 2: 65.

57 Veatch, *League*, 18, 33, 38. Neatby, *King*, 3: 8–9. Bercuson and Granatstein, *Dictionary*, 108.

58 King diary, 4 Sept. 1928.

59 Skelton commented that King feared that the costs of the League were 'excessive': Skelton to Pope, 13 Dec. 1924, *DCER*, 3: 451. King complained in his diary that 'it is almost a farce' the way Dandurand opens and closes the Senate to permit himself to go to the League Council: King diary, 19 March 1929. On his sacrificing his summer, see King diary, 29 May, 14 July 1928.

60 NA, Lapointe Papers, vol. 8, file 27.6, Skelton to Lapointe, 16 June 1927: King's views presented by Skelton in a memo.

61 King diary, 8 June 1927.

62 NA, Skelton Papers, vol. 11, diary, 7 June 1927.

63 Ibid., 13 March 1926.

64 King diary, 10 Aug. 1927.

65 NA, King Papers, vol. 144, reel c-2297, 122759, Lapointe to King, 12 Aug. 1927.

66 Dandurand in Hamelin, ed., *Dandurand*, 298. Lapointe to Skelton, 5 July 1927, in *DCER*, 4: 623.

67 Lapointe, 'La situation internationale,' 14.

68 Rumilly, *Histoire*, 29: 131.

69 'Autonomie et souveraineté,' *Le Soleil*, 21 Nov. 1927, editorial. 4. 'L'effet le plus important de l'élection de M. Dandurand,' ibid., 12 Oct. 1925, 1. 'Un siège au Conseil de la S.D.N.,' ibid., 8 Sept. 1927, 4. 'Le Canada au Conseil ... ,' ibid., 16 Sept. 1927, 4. Dandurand in Hamelin, ed., *Dandurand*, 298.

70 NA, Skelton Papers, vol. 11, diary, 7 June 1927. NA, Lapointe Papers, vol. 8, file 27.6, Skelton to Lapointe, 16 June 1927.

71 NA, Lapointe Papers, vol. 10, file 52, Skelton report to King, 29 Sept. 1927.

72 King diary, 4 Sept. 1927.

73 NA, Chisholm Papers, vol. 19, Chisholm interview with Riddell, c. 1962.

74 Quoted in J.L. Granatstein et al., *Twentieth Century Canada*, 2nd ed. (Toronto: McGraw–Hill Ryerson 1986), 203.

75 King diary, 26 Dec. 1926, 29 May 1928, 26 May 1930.

Chapter 5: A Stronger Voice and Popular Support

1 King diary, 27 May 1930.

2 Ibid., 29 July 1930.

3 NA, Lapointe Papers, vol. 4, 2088, Oscar Drouin to Lapointe, 27 Dec. 1929.

4 Power, in Ward, ed., *Power*, 115.

5 King diary, 16 Jan. 1930. Power, in Ward, ed., *Power*, 115 *Le Soleil*, editorials after Liberal defeat, 28–30 July 1930.

6 King diary, 20 Sept. 1930.

7 Ibid., 22–6 Nov. 1932. Ibid., 29 July, 10 Sept. 1930.

8 NA, Lapointe Papers, vol. 5, 2591, Drouin to Lapointe, 11 June 1935. On the results, see McGee, *Québec-Est*, 234.

9 *Le Soleil*, 3 Aug. to 11 Sept. 1935.

10 King diary, 26 May 1937.

11 King diary, 29 July, 2 Aug. 1930, 6 Feb. 1936, 28 July 1931.

12 Ibid., 17 Oct. 1935. King added that Lapointe 'has not stood up for the League of Nations as I think he should have.' Ibid., 8 Jan. 1936.
13 Ibid., 17–21 Oct. 1935.
14 Ibid., 2 June 1930, 17 Oct. 1935.
15 Gibson, 'Cabinet of 1935,' 134–41.
16 Power in Ward, ed., *Power*, 334, 377.
17 King diary, 20 July 1932.
18 'L'influence de Québec à Ottawa,' *Le Soleil*, 17 Nov. 1934, 4. English, 'French Lieutenant,' 185.
19 'Bienvenue à nos ministres,' *Le Soleil*, 13 Aug. 1936, 4. NA, Lapointe Papers, vol. 11, file 1, Lapointe to G. Pelletier, 2 May 1938.
20 *Debates*, House of Commons, 13 Feb. 1934, 510–12.
21 See Whitaker, *Government Party*, 405.
22 Rumilly, *Duplessis*, 104, 121. King compared Taschereau to Upper Canada's 'Family Compact': King diary, 11 June 1936.
23 NA, Lapointe Papers, vol. 5, 2578–80, Taschereau to Lapointe, 23 Aug. 1934, and Lapointe's reply, 31 Aug. 1934.
24 Power, in Ward, ed., *Power*, 343. See also Power to King, 27 Aug. 1931, quoted in Bychok, 'Lapointe,' 38.
25 Thérèse Casgrain, *Une femme chez les hommes* (Montreal: Du Jour 1971), 125.
26 Genest, *Godbout*, 109–12. Patricia Reid, 'Action Libérale Nationale, 1934–1939,' MA thesis, Queen's University, 1966, 47, 248.
27 Power, in Ward, ed., *Power*, 333–4. Martin, *Public Life*, 1: 167.
28 NA, Lapointe Papers, vol. 30, file 124, Lapointe to J. Archambault, 8 Dec. 1935. Whitaker, *Government Party*, 284. Vigod, *Taschereau*, 233. Rumilly, *Histoire*, 34: 148.
29 NA, King Papers, vol. 197, reel c-3673, 167207, King to Lapointe, 9 Dec. 1933: King had been asked to write Lapointe to put in a word on behalf of a person seeking favours from Taschereau's Liberals.
30 NA, Lapointe Papers, vol. 34, file 157, Judge P.A. Choquette to Lapointe, 8 Jan. 1936, and 29 Feb. 1936. Ibid., vol. 11, file 2, Lapointe to N. Laliberté, 15 Sept. 1940. Ibid., vol. 32, file 145. Ibid., vol. 31, file 128, about thirty letters to Lapointe between 1936 and 1939. Whitaker, *Government Party*, 277–85.
31 NA, Lapointe Papers, vol. 64, file B6. 'Les responsabilités et servitudes de l'homme d'État canadien,' 27 April 1936.
32 *Debates*, House of Commons, 14 Feb. 1938. King diary, 1 July 1938. See also NA, Chisholm Papers, vol. 19, Chisholm interviews with T.A. Crerar, A. Laurendeau, and J.W. Pickersgill.
33 Interview with J.W. Pickersgill, 27 Dec. 1991.

34 King diary, 11 Aug. 1933, 12, 23 Dec. 1936, 21 Jan. 1932, 18 May 1934.

35 King diary, 26 April, 27 May 1933.

36 Power, in Ward, ed., *Power*, 124.

37 King diary, 16 Dec. 1930, 6 Jan., 7 March 1931, 5 July 1935. NA, King Papers, vol. 192, reel c-2328, 160973, Taschereau to King, 13 June 1931.

38 NA, King Papers, vol. 207, reel c-3681, 178009, King to Lapointe, Sept. 24, 1935: Lapointe, during a meeting, had gone into nervous shock, remaining unconscious for an hour after plaster from the roof collapsed, hitting his leg.

39 Mme Lapointe to King, 1936–8, in King Papers, vol. 22.

40 King diary, 26 March, 19, 25 Aug. 1936.

41 NA, Lapointe Papers, vol. 12, file 13, Bourassa to Lapointe, 26 Jan., 2 Feb. 1937. 'Que de déclamations grotesques!' Bourassa wrote, referring to Groulx's 'Hommage à Jacques Cartier' speech.

42 King diary, 2–4 July 1935. 'L'affaiblissement de l'autorité,' *Le Soleil*, 18 June 1935, 4.

43 NA, Skelton Papers, vol. 4, file 20, Skelton to his wife, 23 June 1935.

44 Eugene Forsey, 'Quebec on the Road to Fascism,' *Canadian Forum* 17 (1937), 9–15. E. Delisle, *Le traitre et le Juif: Lionel Groulx, le Devoir et le délire du nationalisme d'extrême droite dans la province de Québec, 1924–1939* (Outremont: L'Étincelle, 1992), 27, 78. 'Le fanatisme exploite le faux fascisme,' *Le Soleil*, 17 Jan. 1938, 4. 'Fascisme,' *Le Canada*, 18 Nov. 1936, 3.

45 NA, Lapointe Papers, vol. 22, file 71, Adrien Arcand to Lapointe, 5 Feb. 1938.

46 *Debates*, House of Commons, 2 May 1938, 2489. Ibid., 4 Feb. 1938, 178. Ibid., 29 June 1938, 4522. 'Le fascisme québécois,' *Le Soleil*, 2 Feb. 1938, 4. On anglophone exaggerations, see Horn, 'Lost Causes,' 141; Thompson and Seager, *Canada*, 323. M. Horn, 'Lost Causes: The League for Social Reconstruction and the CCF in Quebec in the 1930s and 1940s.' *Journal of Canadian Studies* 2 no. 19 (summer 1984), 132–56.

47 Martin Robin, *Shades of Right: Nativist and Fascist Politics in Canada, 1920–40* (Toronto: University of Toronto Press 1992); Pierre Trépanier, review of this book in *Revue d'histoire de l'Amerique Française* (*RHAF*), 46 (1992), 349. Lapointe received many letters from English-Canadian groups and individuals opposed to Catholics, to Jews, and to Japanese immigration: NA, Lapointe Papers, vol. 25, file 86.

48 King diary, 25–7 Sept. 1928.

49 'W. Churchill admire l'oeuvre du fascisme,' *Le Canada*, 21 Jan. 1927, 1.

50 *Mail and Empire*, 11 Jan. 1934; quoted in Thompson and Seager, *Canada*, 322. *Globe and Mail*, 2 Dec. 1937, quoted in Peck, *Spain*, 30.

51 Victor C. Soucisse, 'Revolt in Quebec,' *Maclean's*, 1 July 1936, 10–11, 37–8, quoted in Bychok, 'Lapointe,' 90.
52 Neatby, King, vol. III, 186.
53 NA, Lapointe Papers, vol. 28, file 112, June–Sept. 1936.
54 *Debates*, House of Commons, 22 June 1934, 4221.
55 Ibid., 27 Feb. 1933, 2510 (Turnbull); ibid., 16 June 1936, 3829 (Tommy Church).
56 Dunning preferred having either language on bills, but never both: Dunning to Lapointe, 20 Feb. 1936, quoted in Bychok, 'Lapointe,' 76. 'Lapointe revendique les droits de sa race,' *Le Soleil*, 12 June 1936, 1. 'Le parti libéral sauvegarde les droits de la minorité ... ,' ibid., 17 June 1938, 1.
57 'L'anglais de M. Lapointe,' *Le Soleil*, 26 Jan. 1934, 4.
58 See the fifty letters in NA, Lapointe Papers, vol. 32, file 41; also there are sixty more individual letters from 1937, in ibid., vol. 32, file 142.
59 NA, Lapointe Papers, vol. 12, file 12: Lapointe sought use of French in the Quebec City phone book (1936–9). On agricultural services, see ibid., vol. 11, file 4, Lapointe to J.D. MacLean, 31 March 1936, and vol. 18, file 46. Ibid., vol. 33, file 147, Lapointe to Rogers, 6 Nov. 1936, on Trois-Rivières. On CP telegraph forms, see ibid., vol. 23, file 73, A. Maheux, Université Laval archivist, to Lapointe, 7 April 1941. Ibid., vol. 33, file 146, Lapointe to Dunning, 17 Dec. 1937: Lapointe sought a second telephone for the commission. *Debates*, House of Commons, 1 July 1931, 3215: Lapointe wanted the person refusing to write in French fired.
60 NA, Lapointe papers, vol. 11, file 6, Lapointe to King, 25 June 1936: department heads and principal officers (eight of thirty-nine), chairmen and heads of commissions (none of twenty-two), and assistant deputy ministers (three of twenty-three).
61 NA, Lapointe Papers, vol. 26, file 92b, Lapointe to Crerar, 6 April 1937, 17 April 1937, and 15 May 1940; Lapointe to Gardiner, 6 Feb. 1936. The minister of national defence, Ian Mackenzie, kept Lapointe informed of the search for a superintendent at Valcartier and eventually named Lapointe's choice, Belleau, to the post: ibid., vol. 19, file 53, Mackenzie to Lapointe, 17 Jan. 1936. G. Lanctôt was named dominion archivist in 1938 at Lapointe's request.
62 NA, King Papers, vol. 207, reel c-3681, 177999, Lapointe to King, 19 July 1935: Bennett had translated his address, and Lapointe warned King that the Liberals could not do less.
63 King diary, 22 April 1937. At the Department of External Affairs, English was the language of communication, and some anglophones resented serving under francophones: Hilliker, *Affaires extérieures*, 1: 137. Also Stacey, *Conflict*, 2: 96; King diary, 11 April 1928.

64 NA, Lapointe Papers, vol. 26, file 92, Th.-A. Fontaine, MP for St Hyacinthe, to Lapointe and reply, 19, 24 Sept. 1936.

65 Ibid., Charles Parent, MP, to Lapointe, 9 Oct. 1936, and about twenty-five other MPs.

66 King diary, 27 Nov. 1936, 14 Jan. 1930.

67 *Debates*, House of Commons, 5 June 1934, 3666, 25 June 1935, 4002.

68 NA, Lapointe Papers, vol. 65, file C3, 'National Liberal Federation,' 20 May 1938, 2.

69 Ibid., vol. 64, file B6, 'Constitutional Change in Canada' (1935?), 2. 'R.B. Bennett émule d'Adolph Hitler,' *Le Soleil*, 10 Jan. 1935, 4. 'M. Lapointe, Champion des provinces,' ibid., 15 Feb. 1935, 1. 'MM. King et Lapointe dénoncent les lois hypocrites des tories,' ibid., 26 March 1935, 1.

70 The decisions of the Supreme Court and of the Judicial Committee of the Privy Council in 1937 and 1939 on the questions referred may be found in NA, Lapointe Papers, vol. 37, file 6.

71 NA, Lapointe Papers, vol. 15, file 33, Dandurand to Lapointe, 23 Feb. 1938. King diary, 29 April 1931. *Debates*, House of Commons, 8 Feb. 1935, 653. Ibid., 25 March 1935, 2047. Ibid., 10 June 1935, 3470. Ibid., 24 June 1935, 3959. Ibid., 15 March 1935, 1735. 'Un plaidoyer de M. Lapointe sur les droits des provinces,' *Le Soleil*, 9 Feb. 1938, 1.

72 Lapointe, *Debates*, House of Commons, 1 Feb. 1937, 443. NA, Lapointe Papers, vol. 19, file 48, Lapointe to all premiers, 13 Dec. 1935. *Debates*, House of Commons, 8 April 1938, 2215. 'Les appels au Conseil privé,' *Le Soleil*, 13 April 1938, 4.

73 NA, Dominion–Provincial Conferences, Conference of 1935, vol. 59. Also NA, Lapointe Papers, vol. 64, file B6, 'La constitution canadienne et le cheval de troie,' 2–9.

74 On amending the BNA Act for action relating to defaulting provincial governments: King diary, 18 March 1936.

75 Ibid., 10 Feb. 1932, 6 Sept. 1930.

76 Ibid., 8 Jan. 1937. Lapointe agreed on 11 January.

77 NA, Lapointe Papers, vol. 15 file 38, Lapointe to L.M. Gouin, 7 Jan. 1941.

78 Ibid., vol. 61, file A5, speech to Confédération des Travailleurs catholiques du Québec (1938?).

79 *Debates*, House of Commons, 25 Feb. 1938, 865. See also Martin, *Very Public Life*, vol. I, 219.

80 *Debates*, House of Commons, 24 March 1937, 2186. On the strike, see Irving Abella, ed., *On Strike: Six Key Labour Struggles in Canada, 1919–1949* (Toronto: Lorimer 1975), 93–125.

81 King diary, 15 April 1937.

82 Neatby, *King*, 3: 42. Thompson and Seager, *Canada*, 292.

83 See Neatby, *King*, 3: 235. Richard Jones, 'Le cadenas sur la porte!' *Cap aux Diamants*, vol. 1 (1985), 9–12.

84 *Debates*, House of Commons, 30 May 1938, 3449.

85 NA, Lapointe Papers, vol. 43, file 18.17, 2, Lapointe to Governor General in Council, July 1938.

86 NA, Lapointe Papers, vol. 37, file 6, 5, the official decision on the Albertan laws: letter to the governor general, 10 Aug. 1937. Ibid., vol. 20, file 57, Lieutenant Governor J.C. Bowen of Alberta asked Lapointe if he should reserve two of the laws, and Lapointe told him to reserve all four: 13 Sept. 1937 and 3 Oct. 1937. Ibid., vol. 20, file 57, J.C. Bowen, Alberta's lieutenant governor, to Lapointe, 10 Aug. 1937. See also King diary, 6 Aug. 1937, 554.

87 Bychok, 'Lapointe,' 134–5, 152. Interview with Paul Martin, 19 March 1992. In April 1938, while Lapointe was deciding on what action to take, Bennett had ridiculed the possibility that any 'philosophical discussions' were responsible for the delay. *Debates*, 27 April 1938, 2354.

88 A year after his decision on the Padlock Law he wrote King with regard to strategy in Quebec for the upcoming dominion election campaign: 'It is a ridiculous thing to say but we shall have to meet a strong campaign in our Province because of our refusal to take steps like those of Duplessis with his Padlock law, and for having repealed section 98, and so forth.' NA, King Papers, vol. 270, 229097, Lapointe to King, 19 June 1939.

89 Pickersgill, King's secretary at the time, remembered in an interview, 27 Dec. 1991, that he encouraged Lapointe to disallow it but that Lapointe replied that he could not do so, for political reasons.

90 On anglophone ministers' views, see King diary, 6 July 1938, 533; and *Debates*, House of Commons, 4 Feb. 1938. Montreal CCF and League for Social Reform (LSR) groups formed a Civil Liberties Union to petition Lapointe to disallow the Padlock Law.

91 King diary, 6 July 1938.

92 NA, Lapointe Papers, vol. 26, file 90, King to A. Jarvis, the man in question, 10 Nov. 1937.

93 King diary, 15 Feb. 1936.

94 Ibid., 22 March 1938.

95 NA, Skelton Papers, vol. 14, file 10, Skelton's wife to her mother, 20 Feb. 1931. On Skelton's role, see Veatch, *League*, 117.

96 Ernest Lapointe, 'Le Statut de Westminster,' 3. Ian Drummond, *British Economic Policy and the Empire, 1919–39* (New York: George Allen and Unwin 1972), 32, 97. See also Neatby, *King*, 3: 21. *Debates*, House of Commons, 26 March 1931, 320.

97 Hilliker, *Affaires extérieures*, 1: 218–19.

98 Roosevelt at Kingston, 18 Aug. 1938, in Stacey, *Conflict*, 2: 225–31.

99 Skelton believed that the British press should not read too much into the 'idly by' statement because Roosevelt also said that he hoped for peace in the world, or at least in the hemisphere: Skelton to Pearson, 21 Sept. 1938, *DCER*, 6: 608.

100 King diary, 31 July 1936.

101 Canada received no invitation to the conference of 1936 in Buenos Aires: Skelton to King, 19 Nov. 1936, *DCER*, 6: 665, but King told Parliament that if Canada had wanted an invitation, one would have been sent. On the arguments for and against participation, see Keenleyside memo, 8 Jan. 1937, ibid., 666. Some people recommended leaving the League to join the new Union: *Le Soleil*, July–Nov. 1936.

102 NA, Skelton Papers, vol. 4, file 21, Skelton to his wife, 16 Nov. 1935.

103 NA, Lapointe Papers, vol. 35, file 159A, King to Lapointe, 15 Nov. 1935. King diary, 15 Nov. 1935, 1017.

104 NA, Lapointe Papers, vol. 35, file 159A, Lapointe to King, 16 Nov. 1935.

105 Pope, *Memoirs*.

Chapter 6: The League, Lapointe, King, and Chaos

1 Skelton to King, 7 Jan. 1936, quoted in Irving Abella and Harold Troper, *None Is Too Many: Canada and the Jews of Europe, 1933–48* (Toronto: Lester and Orpen Dennys 1982), 15.

2 On the Canadian role during the crisis, see Veatch, *League*, 115–25. F.H. Soward, 'Forty Years On: The Cahan Blunder Re-examined,' *BC Studies* no. 32 (winter 1976–7), 126–38. D. Story, 'The Cahan Speech,' in Kim Nossal, ed., *An Acceptance of Paradox: Essays on Canadian Diplomacy in Honour of John Holmes* (Toronto: Canadian Institute of International Affairs 1982), 17–38.

3 *Debates*, House of Commons, 20 June 1934, 4122. Ibid., 8 July 1931, 3509. NA, Skelton Papers, vol. 4, file 15, Skelton to his wife, 10 March 1933. Lapointe had urged Bennett to support the conference, while Skelton considered it hopeless, and it accomplished very little.

4 Anonymous, 12 Nov. 1935, 'Sanctions in the Italo-Ethiopian Conflict,' *International Conciliation* no. 315 (Dec. 1935), 539–45.

5 Note by Skelton of conversation with Bennett, 10 Oct. 1935; in *DCER*, 5: 391.

6 Notes by Christie on discussions with Bennett, 13 Sept. 1935, quoted in Veatch, *League*, 147. See also King diary, 25 Oct. 1935.

7 Bothwell and English, 'Riddell Incident,' 271.
8 Skelton to L. Beaudry, acting under-secretary of state for External Affairs, 26 Nov. 1935, *DCER*, vol. V, 410.
9 Beaudry to Skelton, 28 Nov. 1935; Skelton to Lapointe, 29 Nov. 1935, *DCER*, 5: 411–13.
10 Lapointe, 1 Dec. 1935, quoted in Veatch, *League*, 161.
11 Riddell to King, 5 Dec. 1935, *DCER*, 5: 416–17.
12 Eayrs, *Defence*, 2: 26. Bothwell and English, 'Riddell Incident,' 280. Thompson and Seager, *Canada*, 311.
13 Veatch, *League*, 161.
14 Ibid., 169. See also Neatby, *King*, 3: 141.
15 Stacey, *Conflict*, 2: 186–7. See also Eayrs, *Defence*, 2: 4. Waite, 'French-Canadian Isolationism,' 137.
16 King to National Liberal Federation, 12 Dec. 1934, quoted in Veatch, *League*, 133. Also *Debates*, House of Commons, 1 April 1935, 1002.
17 King diary, 2 Oct. 1935.
18 King diary, 11, 15 Oct. 1935. King 'agreed with [Bennett] that [Britain] had been splendid on the League end.'
19 *Debates*, House of Commons, 27 March 1934, 1851. NA, Lapointe Papers, vol. 63, file B4, 'La SDN et la prévention de la guerre,' speech at Quebec City, 10 May 1935. On his appointment as president of the League of Nations Society in Canada, see ibid, vol. 5, 2511, C. Cowan to Lapointe, 24 Oct. 1933, Lapointe to C. Cowan, 28 Oct. 1933, 2513. Ibid., Lapointe to H.M. Tory, 28 Oct. 1933, 2512.
20 *Debates*, House of Commons, 15 March 1935, 1735. Ibid., 25 March 1938, 1777.
21 NA, Lapointe Papers, vol. 61, file A5, 8, speech to University Catholic Clubs, 'The Citizen and the World Scene,' 1935?
22 NA, Lapointe Papers, vol. 63, file B4, speech, 'The Value of the League,' 1932–5? Ibid., vol. 71, speech, 'Canadian responsibilities,' 21 Jan. 1934. Ibid., vol. 61, file A5, 7, speech to La Société Saint Jean-Baptiste, 'La Société des Nations,' 1933. Veatch, *League*, 128.
23 NA, Skelton Papers, vol. 4, file 21, Skelton to his wife, 2 Dec. 1935.
24 NA, Lapointe Papers, vol. 33, file 149, 'Press Opinion,' a review of Canadian editorial opinion prepared for the League of Nations Society in Canada, 9 Dec. 1935.
25 Ibid. See also Mackay and Rogers, *Canada Looks Abroad*, 107.
26 *Debates*, House of Commons, 11 Feb. 1936, 123–4.
27 'Eloquent plaidoyer pour la S.D.N.,' *Le Soleil*, 24 April 1934, 4. 'La Ligue des Nations,' ibid., 25 July 1935, 4. 'Nous avons tout à perdre à Genève,' ibid., 20 Feb. 1935, 4. 'Une propagande anti-italienne,' ibid., 18 June 1935, 4.

28 NA, Lapointe Papers, vol. 33, file 149, 'Press Opinion,' a review of Canadian editorial opinion prepared for the League of Nations Society in Canada, 9 Dec. 1935. Ibid., vol. 25, file 89, B. Gérin to Lapointe, 3 Dec. 1935. Dandurand also congratulated Lapointe, ibid., vol. 31, file 140, Dandurand to Lapointe, 4 Dec. 1935. One editorial noted that 'pour une fois, nous n'avons pas marché dans le sillage de Londres.' *Le Soleil,* 'N'exagérons pas,' 5 Dec. 1935, 4.

29 Power in Ward, ed., *Power,* 121.

30 Lapointe to Skelton, and Skelton to Lapointe, 29 Nov. 1935; quoted in *DCER,* 5: 413–14.

31 Veatch, *League,* 161.

32 King diary, 29 Nov. 1935. See also ibid., 14, 19 Aug. 1936.

33 Ibid., 22 Aug. 1935.

34 Speech of 9 Sept. 1935, in Stacey, *Conflict,* 2: 180.

35 King diary, 17, 19 Oct. 1935.

36 Ibid., 29 Oct. 1935.

37 King to Riddell, 29 Oct. 1935, *DCER,* 5: 403.

38 King diary, 29 Oct. 1935.

39 King to Riddell, 4 Nov. 1935, *DCER,* 5: 405–6. King told President Roosevelt that Riddell 'acted off his own bat in regard to the suggestion re further prohibitions' and admitted that he was annoyed: King diary, 8 Nov. 1935.

40 King diary, 29 Nov. 1935.

41 NA, Chisholm Papers, vol. 19, Chisholm interview with J.A. Hume, 27 April 1974. Ibid., Chisholm interview with Riddell: at a dinner several months after Riddell's unauthorized action, he found Lapointe less than friendly and very disappointed with Riddell.

42 See Eayrs, *Defence,* 2: 24.

43 'The British Government and Jingoes,' he wrote in his diary, 'won't like my exposure of their manoeuvre to use Canada – as the Times has been doing, as the active aggressive party in this matter.' And later: 'We have gone too far already in meddling in European affairs.' King diary, 2, 11, 18–19, 30 Dec. 1935.

44 Ibid., 26 Feb. 1936. See also King to Massey, 29 Feb. 1936, *DCER,* 6: 876.

45 *Debates,* House of Commons, 11 Feb. 1936. King diary, 11 June 1936.

46 *Debates,* House of Commons, 18 June 1936.

47 King, in *Records of the League of Nations,* Proceedings of the 17th Assembly, 29 Sept. 1936.

48 *Debates,* House of Commons, 10 June 1929, 3452. NA, Lapointe Papers, vol. 55, file 67, Adrien Arcand speech, quoted in *Le Fasciste canadien,* 1938.

49 NA, P. Casgrain Papers, vol. 1, Casgrain memo, Aug. 1936.

50 King diary, 1 Sept. 1936.

51 Hoar, *Mackenzie–Papineau Battalion*, 1. Peck, *Spain*, 2.

52 Hoar, *Mackenzie–Papineau Battalion*, 1.

53 NA, Lapointe Papers, vol. 22, file 70: Lapointe received many letters and petitions from the population. See also Hoar, *Mackenzie–Papineau Battalion*, 35. Frohn-Neilsen, 'Foreign Enlistment Act,' 55.

54 Frohn-Neilsen, 'Foreign Enlistment Act,' 24. Peck, *Spain*, x.

55 *Debates*, House of Commons, 19 March 1937, 2024.

56 Ibid., 2004.

57 Hoar, *Mackenzie–Papineau Battalion*, 106, 225. 'La loi,' *Le Soleil*, 8 Feb. 1939, 4, described the 'Mac–Paps' as a group of criminals who broke the law and who should not be glorified.

58 Thompson and Seager, *Canada*, 318. Stacey, *Conflict*, 2: 197. Mark Zuehlke, *The Gallant Cause: Canadians in the Spanish Civil War, 1936–1939* (Vancouver: Whitecap 1996), 121.

59 Genest, 'Élection 1939,' 12. See also Rumilly, *Histoire*, 36: 74.

60 Morton, *Canada and War*, 100. Hilliker, *Affaires extérieures*, 1: 238.

61 King diary, 5 Aug. 1936, 9 Feb. 1937.

62 King to J.L. Counsell (an American friend of King's), 13 April 1937, quoted in Hoar, *Mackenzie–Papineau Battalion*, 105.

63 NA, Lapointe Papers, vol. 22, file 70: Many anglophones wrote to Lapointe emphasizing that the conflict was between democratic free speech and fascism; however, they were willing to following Britain's policy. Peck, *Spain*, 10. Frohn-Neilsen, 'Foreign Enlistment Act,' 28, 35.

64 Peck, *Spain*, 10. 'Nombreux prêtres victimes des hordes communistes,' 10 Aug. 1936, *Le Soleil*, 1. The paper was also critical of Franco's fascism in July and August 1936. On support in Quebec for the Spanish government: see R. Martin, 'Le Congrès des métiers et du Travail et la guerre civile espagnole,' *RHAF* 33 no. 4 (1980), 575. Laurendeau, *Crise*, 11.

65 NA, Lapointe Papers, vol. 16, file 40, Duplessis to Wilfrid Lacroix, MP, 23 Jan. 1939. Duplessis, Trois-Rivières speech, quoted in *Le Devoir*, 26 Jan. 1937, quoted by Lapointe in *Debates*, House of Commons, 29 Jan. 1937.

66 King diary, 18 Dec. 1936.

67 Ibid., 5 July 1938.

68 Ibid., 3 May 1938.

Chapter 7: Nation to Colony?

1 Lapointe, *Records of the League of Nations*, Minutes of the 6th committee, 30 Sept. 1938.

2 NA, Lapointe Papers, vol. 62, file A8, Lapointe to the League of Nations Society in Canada, 'The League and World Cooperation,' 7 Nov. 1938, 1.

3 Ibid., speech to Kiwanis International Convention, Boston, 'International Cooperation,' 19 June 1939, 3. Ibid., vol. 63, file B2, speech to American audience, 'Canadian–American relations,' 1930? 3, 14.

4 MacDonald during a meeting of British ministers and officials on 19 March 1937, quoted in Hillmer, 'Pursuit of Peace,' 156.

5 King speech to the Imperial Conference of 1937, 21 May 1937. For Minutes see NA, Lapointe Papers, vol. 17, file 44B; NA, Robertson Papers, vols. 10–11; and DCER, 6: 162–5. See also Minister of Defence Ian Mackenzie's speech, 24 May 1937, 203, and T.A. Crerar quoted in Eayrs, Defence, 2: 55.

6 King speech to the Imperial Conference of 1937, 21 May 1937.

7 Chamberlain, Minutes of Imperial Conference, 7 June 1937. See also Neatby, King, 3: 214. Hillmer, 'Pursuit of Peace.'

8 Neatby, King, 3: 210.

9 Stacey, Conflict, 2: 206–7.

10 Eayrs, Defence, 2: 54. Hillmer, 'Pursuit of Peace,' 165.

11 Bertrand, 'Politique extérieure,' 10. Laurendeau, Crise, 12–13. Thompson and Seager, Canada, 315.

12 Hillmer, 'Pursuit of Peace,' 166. Neatby, King, 3: 212. See also Bothwell and Granatstein, in Bothwell ed., Canada and Quebec, 72.

13 King diary, 15 June 1937.

14 Ibid., 6 Aug., 24 Sept. 1936.

15 C.P. Stacey, 'The Divine Mission: Mackenzie King and Hitler,' CHR 16, no.4 (1980), 504.

16 King diary, 20 Oct. 1937.

17 Ibid., 7 June 1937.

18 Ibid., 31 May 1937. See also Stacey, 'Mission,' 511. DCER, 6: Nov. 1936, 729–43.

19 Maxime Raymond, Debates, House of Commons, 24 March 1938, 1652. 'M. King à la conférence impériale,' Le Devoir, 16 June 1937, 1. 'Le prix de la liberté,' Le Soleil, 11 Nov. 1937, 4.

20 NA, Lapointe Papers, vol. 12, file 13, Bourassa to Lapointe, 8 March 1938.

21 'L'honorable Ernest Lapointe,' Le Soleil, 8 Oct. 1936, 4. See also 'Canada et la guerre,' ibid., 28 May 1937, 4. 'La Conférence Impériale,' ibid., 13 May 1937, 4. 'Cette injure ne l'atteint pas,' ibid., 13 Dec. 1937, 4. 'Une consultation inutile,' ibid., 9 May 1936, 4.

22 NA, Lapointe Papers, vol. 65, file C2, 5-6, speech in Dec. 1937. Lapointe, in Le Canada, 20 Dec. 1937, quoted in Laurendeau, Crise, 18.

23 Debates, House of Commons, 4 Feb. 1938, 186.

24 The Liberal J.-N. Francoeur defeated the nationalist Paul Bouchard (9,910 votes to 5,239) on 27 Dec. 1937: Rumilly, Duplessis, 1: 408. 'Il y a armements et armements,' Le Soleil, 4 Jan. 1938, editorial, 4.

25 Dafoe, quoted in March 1936, in Thompson and Seager, *Canada*, 313. Also Mackay and Rogers, *Canada Looks Abroad*, 190. Hamelin, in Hamelin, ed., *Dandurand*, 9. Stacey, *Conflict*, 2: 233.

26 David Lenaric, 'Where Angels Fear to Tread: Neutralist and Non-Interventionist Sentiment in Inter-War English Canada,' PhD thesis, York University 1991, 286. Hillmer, 'O.D. Skelton,' 71, 78.

27 MacKay and Rogers, *Canada Looks Abroad*, 239. Bourassa told Lapointe that he considered this interpretation false and added that it was important not to lose ground won by Lapointe and King: NA, Lapointe Papers, vol. 12, file 13, Bourassa to Lapointe, 17 Feb. 1938. Skelton also feared that once 'the guns go off' 'old memories and old loyalties may carry the day:' Skelton memo, April 1937?, in Hillmer, 'Pursuit of Peace,' 153.

28 NA, Lapointe Papers, vol. 17, file 44B, Defence Minister Ian Mackenzie to the 5th meeting of the Imperial Conference of 1937, 24 May 1937. Also in *DCER*, 6: 196–203.

29 Canadian high commissioner to London Vincent Massey to King, 13 March 1936, in Neatby, *King*, 3: 180–1.

30 King diary, 10 March 1936.

31 *Le Soleil*, in 'Devant une double menace,' 5 Aug. 1936, 4, announced that the population of Quebec was 'unanimement hostile,' and francophones sent many letters to Lapointe opposing spending increases to help Britain: NA, Lapointe Papers, vol. 19, file 52. In Parliament, in February 1937, some French Canadians opposed increased defence spending, but most agreed to accept it for the defence of Canada. King did not stay to listen to these speeches because they were in French: King diary, 18 Feb. 1937.

32 King diary, 26 Aug. 1936.

33 *Debates*, House of Commons, 23 Feb. 1937, 1170.

34 *Debates*, House of Commons, 4 Feb. 1937, 547–62. See also NA, Lapointe Papers, vol, 64, file B6, speech, 'Une question nationale: Le Canada doit-il se défendre ou se croiser les bras?' 1937, 11.

35 NA, King Papers, vol. 219, reel c-3689, 188840, Lapointe to King, 14 April 1936. Ibid., 188861, Lapointe to King, 4 Sept. 1936, Lapointe was 'very, very sorry' that Governor General Lord Tweedsmuir had spoken on defence, as he was just about to speak on the question, 'but Tweedsmuir's intervention will make it extremely more difficult,' as Quebec would see any defence spending as having been forced on Canada by the British.

36 King diary, 18 Dec. 1936. King considered that it was 'absolutely necessary to make some provision in the estimates which would show that we were conscious of the dangerous conditions of any and every country in the world today.'

37 Ibid., 7 June 1937.
38 NA, King Papers, vol. 219, reel c-3689, 188840, Lapointe to King, 14 April
    1936. King also hoped that Britain would not act (King diary, 7 March
    1936), and Skelton agreed with Lapointe that Canada had no obligation to
    help Britain if war broke out: NA, Lapointe Papers, vol. 33, file 149a,
    Skelton memo to King (copy to Lapointe), 'Canada and the Rhineland,' 13
    March 1936.
39 King was relieved when Austria submitted without a fight and hoped that
    'Europe may still escape war': King diary, 11 March, 11 April 1938.
40 'A deux doigts de la guerre,' Le Soleil, 14 March 1938, 4.
41 Basil Rauch, From Munich to Pearl Harbor (New York: Creative Age Press
    1950), 75. Roosevelt had ensured Britain in 1938 that it could count on the
    United States 'for everything except troops and loans': Roosevelt, quoted in
    A.A. Offner, American Appeasement (Cambridge, Mass: Harvard University
    Press 1964), 58.
42 Skelton remarked in his diary that 'French public opinion according to the
    British ambassador [is] strongly adverse [sic] to war almost at any price': NA,
    Skelton Papers, vol. 13, Skelton diary, 25 Sept. 1938. See also Weinberg,
    'Munich,' 170.
43 Churchill quoted in Weinberg, 'Munich,' 174.
44 King diary, 21 Aug. 1941.
45 See Weinberg, in 'Munich,' 172. Hitler, according to Weinberg, had been
    unable to make the shift from propaganda to war 'as he had always in-
    tended.'
46 King diary, 23 Sept. 1938.
47 NA, Lapointe Papers, vol. 11, file 1, Lapointe to King, 24 Sept. 1938; King to
    Lapointe, 23 Sept. 1938.
48 King diary, 24–7 Sept. 1938.
49 Statement by the prime minister, 27 Sept. 1938, DCER, 6: 1097.
50 King to Chamberlain, 29 Sept. 1938, ibid., 1099. The agreement was made
    public the following day. On King, see Loring Christie, in Granatstein and
    Bothwell, 'Self-Evident National Duty,' 223.
51 Stacey, Conflict, 2: 218.
52 Granatstein and Bothwell, 'Self-Evident National Duty,' 221–2. Neatby,
    'Unity,' 68.
53 Neatby, King, 3: 291. Neatby, 'French Canada,' 11.
54 Stacey, Conflict, 2: 217.
55 Hillmer and Granatstein, Empire to Umpire, 145.
56 King diary, 31 Aug., 13, 23 Sept. 1938.
57 Ibid., 27–8 Sept. 1938.

58 *Debates*, House of Commons, 24 May 1938, 3294.

59 King diary, 20 May 1938.

60 Ibid., 31 Aug. 1938.

61 Ibid., 14 March 1938. King to Dominions Secretary, 28 June 1938, *DCER*, 6: 217.

62 'L'opinion universelle admire Chamberlain,' *Le Soleil*, 15 Sept. 1938, 1. 'Le Pacte de Munich sème la joie dans le monde entier,' ibid., 30 Sept. 1930, 1.

63 'Pas cette fois!' ibid., 28 Sept. 1938, 4.

64 King diary, 27 Sept. 1938.

65 Ibid., 23 Sept. 1938.

66 Skelton commented that the increasing acceptance of intervention was encouraged by a dislike of Hitler but added that 'it would be sympathy for Britain that would be the determining force' if Canada entered a European war: NA, Skelton Papers, vol. 5, file 5, Skelton memo to King, 24 Sept. 1938.

67 Ibid., vol. 13, diary, 23 Sept. 1938. In his diary, 27 Sept. 1938, he added that he 'began to fear [King] had leaned too far toward imperialists.'

68 On Skelton's decreasing influence, see Hilliker, *Affaires extérieures*, 1: 244. When King told cabinet that most people would insist that Canada support Britain, Skelton concluded: 'My fourteen years effort here wasted': NA, Skelton Papers, vol. 13, diary, 20 May 1938. See also King diary, 31 August, 13 Nov. 1938, 28 April 1939.

69 King diary, 21, 26 Aug. 1939.

70 NA, Skelton Papers, vol. 13, diary, 24 Sept. 1938.

71 Power, quoted in Stacey, *Conflict*, 2: 216.

72 NA, Skelton Papers, vol. 13, diary, 26 Sept. 1938.

73 NA, King Papers, vol. 262, reel c-3740, 223110, King to Wrong, 22 Sept. 1938. On Lapointe's proposition, see the permanent delegate to the League of Nations, Hume Wrong, to King, 20 Sept. 1938, in *DCER*, 6: 943–4.

74 NA, Lapointe Papers, vol. 63, file B4, radio address to the United States, 'The League and the Possibility of War,' 25 Sept. 1938, 2.

75 After the Riddell affair, King suspected Skelton's loyalty after his five-year association with Bennett; during the Munich crisis King clearly refused his advice: King diary, 11 Feb. 1936.

76 Ibid., 11 June 1937. During the same trip Lapointe was named to the (Imperial) Privy Council and became the Right Honourable Ernest Lapointe.

Chapter 8: Fighting King and Cabinet

1 King diary, 14 Nov., 16 Dec. 1938.

2 Ibid., 24 Nov. 1938. Neatby, in *King*, vol. 3: 305, adds that 'the eventual policy showed more expediency than King would have admitted. The onus was shifted to the provincial governments by asking them how many Jewish refugees they would admit.'

3 King diary, 29 Nov. 1938.

4 *Debates*, House of Commons, 16 Jan. 1939, 52. He was quoting a speech of Sir Wilfrid Laurier's.

5 King diary, 24 May, 14 June 1940, 6 Feb. 1941.

6 King complained that they lacked vision, experience, and knowledge: King diary, 6 Feb. 1941.

7 During a strike at Arvida, King was surprised to find Macdonald 'so strong in his attitude against labour. I expected the opposite from him:' King diary, 29 July 1941.

8 Lapointe preferred an immediate election, as he believed that there was no danger of war, but King, in his diary, 11 Aug. 1939, decided not to announce the election because he believed the chances of war too great, and Lapointe accepted this decision.

9 King diary, 5 Sept. 1940, 6 Feb. 1941.

10 NA, Lapointe Papers, vol. 64, file 86, Lapointe speech at King banquet, quoting King from Lapointe's banquet, 8 Aug. 1939.

11 NA, King Papers, vol. 270, Lapointe to King, 19 June 1939, 229097. Lapointe said that if King wanted financial details he should see Power or Cardin, adding that the Liberal campaign in Quebec would have to focus on three themes: Ottawa's fight against communism; unemployment relief and Duplessis's obstruction of it; and military expenditures and war policy.

12 Ibid., vol. 294, 248676, King to Power, 25 March 1940. See also Chisholm, 'Never,' 20. Lapointe finally beat the independent nationalist candidate Paul Bouchard 17,914 to 12,302, according to McGee, *Québec-Est*, 272.

13 Jean Laponce, in 'Ruling Elites in a Multilingual Society: Quebec within Canada,' in M. Czudnowski, ed., *Political Elites and Social Change: Studies of Elite Roles and Attitudes* (Dekalb: Northern Illinois University Press 1983), 45, also calculates that French Canadians, rather than Quebecers, made up the following proportion of caucus in each of these election years: 1917 – 67 per cent, 1921 – 47 per cent, 1925 – 54 per cent, 1926 – 49 per cent, 1930 – 48 per cent, 1935 – 29 per cent, and 1940 – 30 per cent.

14 King also noted that Lapointe and Dandurand had decided 'before I was informed' not to replace Rinfret until after the next election: King diary, 19 July 1939. Also ibid., 2 July 1940, 6 Feb., 4 Nov. 1941. Lapointe to Dexter, 25 Oct. 1940, quoted in Bychok, 'Lapointe,' 247.

15 *Le Devoir*, 7 May 1938; quoted in Genest, 'L'élection,' 30.

16 Before organizing a trip to English Canada, Godbout asked Lapointe if this would be a good idea, and Lapointe approved: NA, Lapointe Papers, vol. 35, file 161, Godbout to Lapointe, 29 July 1941. See also Genest, *Godbout.*

17 King diary, 3 April, 9 May, 31 Oct. 1940. NA, Lapointe Papers, vol. 23, file 75, Lapointe to J. Fortin, 28 Jan. 1941.

18 King diary, 29 Nov. 1938.

19 NA, Lapointe Papers, vol. 23, file 78, Godbout to Lapointe and Lapointe to Godbout, 21 Nov. 1939.

20 'Respect aux Chefs ... ,' *Le Soleil,* 6 July 1939, 4.

21 NA, Lapointe Papers, vol. 65, file C4, campaign speech, 22 Feb. 1940.

22 Ibid., Lapointe speech, 13 March 1940.

23 Rumilly, *Histoire,* 38: 119.

24 Power, in Ward, ed., *Power,* 123.

25 Athanase David, a prominent provincial Liberal, wrote Lapointe that he had seen Henri Bourassa and had been impressed with the 'considerable influence you have on him': NA, Lapointe Papers, vol. 18, file 47.A, David to Lapointe, 7 Sept. 1939.

26 E.M. Forster, *Two Cheers for Democracy* (London: Arnold, 1951), 227.

27 The prime minister again complained of his poor speech and that Lapointe had been great, as always: King diary, 8 Aug. 1939. Pickersgill, *King Record,* 1: 33, describes how King, after hearing Churchill, regretted that he himself was not a better speaker.

28 T.A. Crerar to Grant Dexter, 12 Oct. 1940, quoted in Bychok, 'Lapointe,' 247.

29 NA, Chisholm Papers, vol. 19.8, Chisholm interview with Riddell, c. 1962.

30 Dexter's account of conversation with Lapointe, 25 Oct. 1940, quoted in Bychok, 'Lapointe,' 247.

31 Dexter in Granatstein, *Canada's War,* 106. Lapointe asked to be relieved of his responsibilities: NA, King Papers, vol. 290, reel c-4570, 245068, Lapointe to King, June 1940.

32 King diary, 11 July 1940. NA, King Papers, vol. 298, reel c-4576, 252901, R. Valin, Lapointe's doctor, to King, 12 July 1940, informing King that Lapointe urgently needed a month's rest.

33 Granatstein, *Canada's War,* 106.

34 NA, Meighen Papers, vol. 160, reel c-3557, 98012, R.B. Hanson to Meighen, 18 July 1940.

35 King diary, 22 May, 11 July 1940. King had remarked earlier that Skelton was working too hard: ibid., 1 Feb. 1940.

36 Bychok, 'Lapointe,' 248. Lapointe did not miss many Cabinet War Committee (CWC) meetings after returning from his three-week holiday in July 1940. The following numbers indicate how many of the eighty-four meetings

between 13 August 1940 and 31 October 1941 each minister attended: King (78), Crerar (74), Ralston (73), Ilsley (73), Macdonald (70), Lapointe (64), Howe (61), Power (57), Gardiner (37), and Dandurand (14).

37 King diary, 18, 20 Feb. 1939, 14 May, 2 Aug. 1940.

38 Lapointe, during his interview with Grant Dexter, 25 Oct. 1940, quoted in Bychok, 'Lapointe,' 248.

39 Ibid., 244.

40 King diary, 22 June, 14 July 1941.

41 King wrote in his diary that he believed that it would take a miracle for Britain to win the war if the Soviet Union collapsed, and five days later he believed that it would be a miracle if the Soviet Union did not collapse: King diary, 10, 15 Oct. 1941.

42 Ibid., 24 June, 26 Sept. 1940.

43 Ibid., 29 Nov. 1938, 1 Feb., 29 March, 25 June, 5 Sept. 1940.

44 NA, Lapointe Papers, vol. 26, file 96, King to Lapointe, 12 Aug. 1940. During a ceremony to celebrate Lapointe's thirty-five years in Parliament, King praised Lapointe's loyal services in 1919 and 1925: 'Éloge du T.H. Ernest Lapointe par ses témoins,' Le Soleil, 20 Feb. 1939, 1. King diary, 18 Feb. 1939.

45 King speech, 18 Feb. 1939, quoted in Bychok, 'Lapointe,' 211. King diary, 8 March 1941.

46 King diary, 20–2 Jan. 1941. King did raise the question in the CWC and the anglophone colleagues, notably Macdonald, were as opposed as King: NA, Privy Council, CWC Minutes, 20 Jan. 1941, 10.

47 Bakvis, Regional Ministers, 52. D. Owram, The Government Generation: Canadian Intellectuals and the State, 1900–45 (Toronto: University of Toronto Press 1986), ix, 147, 240. Linteau et al., Québec, 152.

48 NA, King Papers, vol. 270, 229145, Lapointe to King, 24 Oct. 1939.

49 NA, Lapointe Papers, vol. 33, file 147, Lapointe to King (a copy was sent to all ministers), 8 Dec. 1939.

50 King diary, 5 Sept. 1940.

51 Stacey, Official History, 44. J.L. Granatstein, The Generals: The Canadian Army's Senior Commanders in the Second World War (Toronto: Stoddart 1993), 237–57.

52 NA, National Defence Papers, vol. 5812, HQS 8798, Lapointe to Ralston, 3 July 1941: 'Our English-speaking friends have no idea of the difficult situation young French Canadians find themselves in when they are not very proficient in English, are in unfamiliar surroundings and are even some-times considered by some of their fellow-officers as poor country relations.'

53 King diary, 28 Dec. 1939.

54 NA, Lapointe Papers, vol. 42, file 18.13, King to all ministers, 16 Dec. 1939. King also asked that each minister calculate the percentage of French

Canadians in his department. Lapointe replied that sixty-two of 134 employees in Justice were French Canadian: ibid., 'Department of Justice: List of Employees,' 1939.

55 'Pour l'unité nationale,' *Le Soleil*, 28 Sept. 1940, editorial, 4.

56 NA, Lapointe Papers, vol. 35, file 163, Rodrigue Cardinal Villeneuve to Lapointe, 21 July 1941. Groulx, *Histoire*, 2: 339. Letters to Lapointe in April and May 1940: NA, Lapointe Papers, vol. 33, file 147.

57 NA, Lapointe Papers, vol. 33, file 147, Drouin to Lapointe, 3 Oct. 1941; Drouin also complained to Howe, 3 Oct. 1941. Ibid., Lapointe to Howe, 3 Dec. 1940 and 23 Dec. 1940. King described in his diary an incident in cabinet that opposed Cardin and Howe, each criticizing the other for delaying action on public-works projects in Lapointe's riding: King diary, 28 March 1939.

58 CWC Minutes, 26 Sept. 1940.

59 Howe defended his action with the unconvincing argument that action was urgent. Lapointe pointed out that, if he needed to act quickly, local people should have been preferred: Lapointe to Howe, 1 June 1940; Howe reply, 8 June 1940; Lapointe reply, 10 June 1940: NA, Lapointe Papers, vol. 33, file 147.

60 Ibid., Howe to Lapointe, 8 May 1941; Lapointe reply, 9 May 1941. See also Pariseau and Bernier, *Canadiens français*, 1: 144.

61 King diary, 19 Sept. 1940.

62 NA, Lapointe Papers, vol. 33, file 147, Lapointe to Ilsley, 20 Oct. 1941.

63 Ibid., Lapointe to King, 20 Oct. 1941.

64 King diary, 29 Nov. 1940; Bychok, 'Lapointe,' 253.

65 NA, Lapointe Papers, vol. 22, file 69, Villeneuve to Lapointe, 14 Dec. 1939; Lapointe to Ilsley, 16 Dec. 1939.

66 Ibid., Lapointe to Ilsley, 3 Jan. 1940.

67 Ibid., vol. 15, file 35, Lapointe to King, 12 Feb. 1941.

68 King diary, 30 May 1941.

69 CWC Minutes, 28 July 1941, 2.

70 NA, Lapointe Papers, vol. 11, file 7, A. Charpentier to Lapointe, 4 Aug. 1941.

71 CWC Minutes, 28 July 1941. King diary, 26–7 July 1941. The province refused to pay the bill from National Defence for the troops, arguing that Ottawa (McLarty and Howe) had insisted on sending them: NA, National Defence Papers, vol. 6518, HQ 363–63.

72 NA, King Papers, vol. 307, reel c-4864, 259677, Lapointe to King, no date: Lapointe added: 'Godbout says that he will not let Quebec be slandered before the world.'

73 'Sabotage et grève à Arvida,' *Le Soleil*, 30 July 1941, 4 'Sabotage et grève à Arvida,' *Le Soleil*, 30 July 1941, 4. King diary, 26, 31 July 1941.

74 NA, Lapointe Papers, vol. 23, file 78, R.L. Cadiz, RCMP memo to Lapointe, 28 Oct. 1941. See also ibid., vol. 11, file 7, C. Vaillancourt, from the Fédération des Caisses populaires du Québec, to Howe. King diary, 26 July 1941.

75 King diary, 29 July 1941. King added that 'if not for Lapointe, I would have had a particularly difficult time in getting the complete understanding and support for my views, which he so completely shares.'

76 NA, National Defence Papers, vol. 6518, HQS 363-63-1, Officer M.S. Campbell's report concluded that 'the disturbance is due to an irresponsible element,' probably sabotage, and recommended that the men return to work immediately.

77 NA, Lapointe Papers, vol. 19, file 54, Lapointe to McLarty, 30 July 1941. McLarty argued that because of the urgency of the situation there was only one agent available: ibid., McLarty to Lapointe, 31 July 1941; Lapointe to McLarty, 6 Aug. 1941.

78 King diary, 18 Jan. 1941.

79 Lapointe, quoted by Grant Dexter, 25 Oct. 1940, in Bychok, 'Lapointe,' 248.

80 For different interpretations of the failure of this conference, see Rumilly, *Duplessis*, 1: 586–7, and Creighton, *Forked Road*, 51.

81 King diary, 30 May 1941. See also ibid., 15–18 Jan. 1941.

82 A magazine suggested that Lapointe should become prime minister in a Union government: *Canadian Magazine* (April 1938), in NA, Lapointe Papers, vol. 12, file 15. In July 1940 King did offer to bring opposition leaders into the CWC, but they opposed the idea: King diary, 2, 12 July 1940. On Lapointe's opposition, see *Debates*, House of Commons, 24 Feb. 1941, 998, and '... cabinet d'union,' *Le Soleil*, 25 Feb. 1941, 1.

83 See Pickersgill, *King Record*, vol. I, 74.

84 Lapointe, *Debates*, House of Commons, 10 March 1939, 1814–15; ibid., 15 Feb. 1939, 996–7.

85 King diary, 25 Aug. 1939.

86 Creighton, *Forked Road*, 43. Stacey, *Conflict*, 2: 307–17.

Chapter 9: Sacred Pledges: The No-Conscription Pact

1 NA, Lapointe Papers, vol. 62, file A8, speech to the League of Nations Society in Canada, 'The League and World Cooperation,' 7 Nov. 1938, 6, 7, 14. The *Winnipeg Free Press* criticized the speech, upsetting Lapointe: ibid., vol. 33, file 149, Lapointe to R.B. Inch, Society National Secretary, 17 Nov. 1938.

2   King diary, 8 Nov. 1940, 21 Aug. 1941.

3   *Debates*, House of Commons, 16 Jan. 1939, 54.

4   NA, Skelton Papers, vol. 13, diary, 2 Feb. 1939.

5   C. Hull, *The Memoirs of Cordell Hull*, vol. 1 (London: Hodder and Stoughton 1948), 615.

6   *Debates*, House of Commons, 20, 31 March 1939, 2043, 2464–71.

7   Ibid., 2464–70.

8   Hillmer and Granatstein, *Empire to Umpire*, 147. The British high commissioner wrote that King 'explained to me how he and Lapointe are working together acting, as it were, as two props of a bridge.' Sir G. Campbell to Dominions Office, 19 April 1939, quoted in Bothwell and Hillmer, eds., *In-Between Time*, 174. See also Stacey, *Conflict*, 2: 242–3. Neatby, *King*, 3: 300–1.

9   Granatstein in Bothwell, *Canada and Quebec*, 72.

10   Neatby, 'Unity,' 65. See Hillmer, 'Pursuit of Peace,' 153. Granatstein, *Canada's War*, 5. Granatstein and Bothwell, 'Self-Evident National Duty,' 213. Eayrs, *Defence*, 2: 74–5. Stacey, *Conflict*, 2: 237, blames King's 'isolationist staff and his French-Canadian colleagues' for hesitation.

11   Granatstein and Bothwell, 'Self-Evident National Duty,' 236.

12   King diary, 27 Jan. 1939, 14 Jan. 1940.

13   Ibid., 31 March 1939.

14   Ibid. King had also recorded in his diary, 19 August 1936, that Lapointe had become convinced after a European trip that 'we were in for a terrible war,' but he kept hope.

15   Ibid., 21 March 1939. Neatby, in *King*, 3: 298–9, notes that the first sentence of this extract was approved by cabinet, but King decided, just before delivery, to add the second, which went much further towards a commitment to help Britain. Skelton was opposed, but Lapointe was willing to accept it.

16   *Debates*, House of Commons, 31 March 1939, 2468–9. Lapointe added that no expeditionary force should be sent.

17   *Debates*, House of Commons, 30 March 1939, 2426.

18   NA, Lapointe Papers, vol. 23, file 79A, Le Cercle Maurras de Québec to Lapointe, 29 March 1939. *Le Soleil*, 31 March–1 April 1939. 'A la guerre, messieurs?' *Le Devoir*, 23 March 1939, 1.

19   NA, Lapointe Papers, vol. 23, file 79A: twelve francophones wrote to Lapointe, six opposing participation and six approving the no-conscription promise. *Le Soleil*, 16–17 March, 3 April 1939.

20   'Civil War if Canada Neutral–Lapointe,' *Globe and Mail*, 1 April 1939, 1. See also Neatby, *King*, vol. III, 303.

21 Sir G. Campbell to the Dominions Office, 19 April 1939, in Bothwell and Hillmer, eds., *In-Between Time*, 174.

22 *Debates*, House of Commons, 21 Jan. 1942, 4551.

23 NA, Lapointe Papers, vol. 23, file 79A, E. Sanderson, Confederation Life Association, Toronto, to Lapointe, 1 April 1939. This file contains twenty-three other letters from anglophones, all congratulating Lapointe for announcing Canada's intention to be with Britain and two calling for conscription. The Ontario legislature, on 23 March 1939, called for mobilization of manpower.

24 King diary, 27 Jan. 1939.

25 Ibid.

26 Lapointe to the CTCC, 21 Jan. 1939, quoted in Laurendeau, *Crise*, 21.

27 King diary, 27 Jan. 1939.

28 NA, Skelton Papers, vol. 13, diary, 2 Feb. 1939.

29 King diary, 27 Jan. 1939.

30 Ibid., 13 Feb. 1939.

31 Ibid., 20 Feb. 1939.

32 Ibid., 31 March 1939.

33 The prime minister believed that 'the King's visit had helped immensely reuniting Canada for this crisis': King diary, 26 Aug. 1939, 915.

34 Ibid., 25 April 1939.

35 Rumilly, *Duplessis*, 1: 513. French Canadians did not oppose the visit as much as *Life* magazine suggested: Lapointe, *Debates*, House of Commons, 29 May 1939, 4756.

36 King diary, 24 Aug. 1939.

37 Stacey, *Conflict*, 2: 263 and 256. See also Thompson and Seager, *Canada*, 329. Granatstein and Hitsman, *Broken Promises*, 133. Neatby, 'National Unity,' 54–70. Morton, *Histoire militaire*, 256. Bercuson and Granatstein, *Dictionary*, 108.

38 Granatstein, *Canada's War*, 2, 18.

39 Creighton, *Forked Road*, 2.

40 Waite, 'French-Canadian Isolationism,' 143. See also Slobodin, 'Tangled Web,' 497–9. Hooker, 'Defence of Unity,' 7, 33, 236.

41 Brunet, *Québec*, 270. Monière, *Idéologies*, 286.

42 Bertrand, 'Politique extérieure,' 2, 25, 29. See also Genest, 'L'élection,' 2, 43.

43 Laurendeau, *Crise*, 32.

44 *Debates*, House of Commons, 8 Sept. 1939, 19–40.

45 King diary, 31 Dec. 1939.

46 *Debates*, House of Commons, 9 Sept. 1939, 66–8.
47 See the memo of J.P. Moffat, American minister in Canada, to the secretary of state, 21 Dec. 1940, quoted in Bothwell and Hillmer, eds., *In-Between Time*, 99.
48 See Sir G. Campbell to Dominions Office, 20 Sept. 1939, in Bothwell and Hillmer, eds., *In-Between Time*, 186.
49 *Globe and Mail*, quoted in Stacey, *Conflict*, 2: 262.
50 NA, Chisholm Papers, vol. 19, Chisholm interview with J.A. Hume, 27 April 1974.
51 Granatstein, *Canada's War*, 16.
52 Pickersgill, *Memoir*, 177.
53 *Debates*, House of Commons, 9 Sept. 1939, 64.
54 *Debates*, 9 Sept. 1939, 69–73. The Conservative member for Lethbridge agreed that conscription was necessary.
55 King diary, 1 July 1939. On English-Canadian motivation to fight, see Granatstein, *Canada's War*, 19. Stacey, *Conflict*, 2: 277. Morton, *Canada and War*, 104.
56 NA, Skelton Papers, vol. 5, file 12, 'Canada and the Polish War: A Personal Note,' 25 Aug. 1939, 1. Skelton to H. Wrong, 2 March 1939, quoted in Stacey, *Conflict*, 2: 266.
57 King diary, 28 Sept. 1938.
58 R.A. Divine, *The Reluctant Belligerent* (Austin: University of Texas Press 1965), 212. Roosevelt promised that he would do all he could to keep out of the war: *Public Papers and Addresses of FDR*, 1939 vol., 457.
59 MP Maxime Raymond estimated that 90 per cent of francophones opposed the war. See Rumilly, *Histoire*, 38: 11, 24. Power, in Ward, ed., *Power*, 346. Laurendeau, *Crise*, 37.
60 'A chaque jour son inquiétude,' *Le Soleil*, 19 Aug. 1939, 4. Also 'L'Angleterre et la France en lice,' ibid., 4 Sept. 1939.
61 'Hitler victime de Staline,' *Le Soleil*, 24 Aug. 1939, 4.
62 King diary, 25–6 April, 22 Aug. 1939.
63 NA, Lapointe Papers, vol. 23, file 78, Power memo to Lapointe, 1 Sept. 1939. Jean Hamelin, *Histoire du catholicisme québécois: le XXe siècle*, vol. 2 (Montreal: Boréal 1984), 15–20.
64 See NA, King Papers, vol. 270, 'French-Canadian Press and the War,' 4 Oct. 1939, 229117–33.
65 *Debates*, House of Commons, 9 Sept. 1939, 69.
66 Cardin, Michaud, and Power also preferred to wait, and Euler, Howe, and McLarty agreed: King diary, 24 Aug. 1939.

67 Ibid., 30 Aug., 7 Sept. 1939.

68 Ibid., 30 Aug. 1939.

69 NA, King Papers, vol. 270, Lapointe to King, 31 Aug. 1939, 229104. He said that he was sending a 'few ideas which I would like you to consider when preparing your statement, if circumstances compel you to make it.' He also suggested quoting Roosevelt's speech of January 1939, to the effect that when the time comes people have to fight for freedom, which King did.

70 Pickersgill, in *Memoir*, 173, remembered the confusion when King arrived with the text, not realizing that it would need to be translated. He assumed that Lapointe would do it as he read.

71 NA, Audio-visual tape 8618 1983-0065/088-90, speeches by King, Lapointe, Rogers, and Power, 3 Sept. 1939.

72 King to Skelton, 2 Nov. 1939, *DCER*, 7: 192.

73 NA, King Papers, vol. 290, reel c-4570, 245114, Lapointe to King, 2 Nov. 1940. Ibid., vol. 307, c4864, 259696, Lapointe to King, 29 Aug. 1941.

74 NA, Lapointe Papers, vol. 23, file 79A, J.W. Dafoe to Lapointe, 10 Sept. 1939. Pickersgill emphasized that Lapointe's speech was an appeal to emotions: interview with J.W. Pickersgill, 27 Dec. 1991. See also Martin, *Very Public Life*, 1: 243.

75 Laurendeau, *Crise*, 30.

76 Paul Sauriol, quoted in Laurendeau, *Crise*, 29. Gravel, 'Québec militaire,' 80.

77 Power, in Ward, ed., *Power*, 130. Former minister Lucien Cannon believed that Quebec supported the war and that MPs were unnecessarily nervous: NA, Lapointe Papers, vol. 18, file 46, Cannon to Power, 13 Sept. 1939.

78 'M. Lapointe dans la lutte,' *Le Soleil*, 30 Sept. 1939, 1.

79 King diary, 25, 28 Sept. 1939.

80 Power, in Ward, ed., *Power*, 347–8.

81 'Ce que l'on dit à Toronto,' *Le Soleil*, 30 Sept. 1939, 4.

82 Genest, *Godbout*, 121.

83 Genest, 'L'élection,' 52, 137. Before the election, the Union Nationale had seventy-three of the ninety seats.

84 NA, Skelton Papers, vol. 5, file 13, Lapointe to Skelton, 28 Oct. 1939.

85 Archives nationales du Québec (ANQ), Godbout speech, 1939, video 87–135.

86 Creighton, *Forked Road*, 8. Bychok, 'Lapointe,' 225. Jones, *Duplessis*, 10. Rumilly, *Histoire*, 38: 48.

87 Granatstein, *Canada's War*, 201.

88 Bliss, *Right Honourable Men*, 148.
89 René Durocher, 'Maurice Duplessis et sa conception de l'autonomie provinciale au début de sa carrière politique,' *RHAF* 23, no. 1 (June 1969), 33. See also Monière, *Idéologies*, 286. Rumilly, *Duplessis*, 1: 534.
90 Brunet, *Québec*, 270.
91 King diary, 25, 28 Sept. 1939.
92 NA, King Papers, vol. 265, reel c-3742, 225312, B. Claxton to A. Heeney, 3 Oct. 1939. He considered the resignation threat 'politically inexpedient,' as it would lead to problems if Duplessis wins, 'as seems likely.' Surprisingly, D.J. Bercuson, in *True Patriot: The Life of Brooke Claxton, 1878–1960* (Toronto: Oxford University Press 1992), 90, writes that Claxton realized the 'opportunity' to rebuff the nationalists and hoped that Ottawa would intervene 'without compromise.'
93 King diary, 12 Oct. 1939. *Le Devoir*, 11 Oct. 1939. Genest, 'L'élection,' 52.
94 Power, in Ward, ed., *Power*, 347. This interpretation is repeated by Granatstein, *Canada's War*, 29, and Creighton, *Forked Road*, 8.
95 King diary, 26 Oct. 1939.
96 Ibid., 25 Sept. 1939.
97 NA, Lapointe Papers, vol. 65, file C3, Lapointe speech, 9 Oct. 1939, 3, 13, 15.
98 Ibid., Lapointe speech, 22 Oct. 1939, 3.
99 Ibid., vol. 18, file 46, Pickersgill to Lapointe, 21 April 1939.
100 'L'Honorable Ernest Lapointe,' *Le Soleil*, 6 Oct. 1939, 4. 'Wilfrid Laurier ... ,' ibid., 17 Oct. 1939, 1.
101 NA, Lapointe Papers, vol. 63, file B5, 'French-Canadian press on the Quebec provincial election.' Genest, 'L'élection.'
102 Laurendeau, *Crise*, 43–5. Rumilly, *Duplessis*, 1: 572.
103 NA, Chisholm Papers, vol. 19, Chisholm interview with Daniel Johnson, 1962.
104 NA, Lapointe Papers, vol. 63, file B5, 'French-Canadian press on the Quebec provincial election.'
105 Bychok, 'Lapointe,' 229. Other newspapers, such as the *Vancouver Sun*, 26 Oct. 1939, realized the importance of the no-conscription policy: see Granatstein and Hitsman, *Broken Promises*, 136.
106 NA, Lapointe Papers, vol. 63, file B5, 'French-Canadian press on the Quebec provincial election.'
107 NA, King Papers, vol. 266, reel c-3742, 225954, Justice T.C. Davis, Court of Appeals, Saskatchewan, to King, 26 Oct. 1939.
108 King diary, 25 Oct., 3 Nov., 31 Dec. 1939.

109 Dexter memo, 25 Oct. 1940, quoted in Bychok, 'Lapointe,' 276. And Lapointe, quoted by Dexter after a conversation, 25 Oct. 1940, quoted in Granatstein, *Canada's War*, 40, note 115.

110 King diary, 27 Sept. 1939.

111 NA, King Papers, vol. 270, King to Lapointe, 6 Oct. 1939, 229135.

112 Ibid., King to Lapointe, 25 Oct. 1939, 229147.

113 King diary, 25 Oct. 1939: Lapointe 'will have a place second to none in Canadian history.' The election 'has given them all, especially Lapointe, an exceedingly high place in public regard ... I venture to say that Lapointe's place today is as far in esteem as that of Sir Wilfrid in the best of his day.'

114 NA, Lapointe Papers, vol. 27, file 106, Hepburn to Lapointe, 4 Dec. 1939.

115 King diary, 18, 22 Jan. 1940. Pickersgill, *King Record*, 1: 63: Lapointe wanted to encourage a 'King v. Hepburn' confrontation in the election, but King preferred to put more emphasis on his colleagues.

116 NA, Lapointe Papers, vol. 65, file C4, Lapointe speech, 23 March 1940, 11.

117 Ibid., 1. See also Lapointe's speeches in *Le Soleil*, 'La conscription,' 5 March 1940, 4. 'L'indéfectible champion du Canada français,' ibid., 13 March 1940, 3.

Chapter 10: French Canada and the Fall of France

1 NA, Chisholm Papers, vol. 19, Coldwell, interviewed by Elspeth Chisholm, June 1963.

2 King diary, 24 May, 16, 23–4 June, 31 Oct. 1940.

3 Ibid., 24 May 1940.

4 Winston Churchill, *The Second World War*, vol. 2, *Their Finest Hour* (New York: Bantam Books 1962, first pub. 1949), 198–206.

5 *Debates*, House of Commons, 5 July 1940, 1359.

6 CWC Minutes, 17 Sept. 1940, 2.

7 King diary, 25 Sept. 1940.

8 CWC Minutes, 11 July 1940, 2.

9 King diary, 19 June 1940. King continued to oppose British requests to use force: ibid., 20–1 June 1940.

10 Ibid., 26 July 1940.

11 Ibid., 26 July 1940. CWC Minutes, 31 July 1940, 3. The CWC referred another Churchill request for French gold to Lapointe, Ralston, and Ilsley: CWC Minutes, 27 Aug., 9, 5 Sept., 5, 24 Oct. 1940, 5.

12 King diary, 19 Oct. 1940.

13 CWC Minutes, 12 July, 1, 1 Oct., 7, 5 Nov. 1940, 1–3.

14 NA, Lapointe Papers, vol. 13, file 23, Charpentier to Georges Pelletier of *Le Devoir*, 7 Feb. 1941.

15 Ibid., vol. 24, file 82, Canadian High Commissioner in London Vincent Massey to Norman Robertson, 18 Feb. 1941, and Robertson to King, 19 Feb. 1941.

16 CWC Minutes, 2 Jan. 1941, 7. Dupuy made three trips between November 1940 and August 1941.

17 King diary, 30 May 1941. CWC Minutes, 20 May 1941.

18 CWC Minutes, 13 Aug., 5, 10 Sept., 4, 29 Dec. 1941, 3.

19 NA, Department of External Affairs, vol. 2824, 1299-40C, Dupuy to King, 4 Sept. 1942.

20 NA, Lapointe Papers, vol. 24, file 82, C.J. Burchell, Canadian high commissioner to Australia, to Robertson, 9 July 1941.

21 NA, Ralston Papers, vol. 1, diary, 7 Jan. 1941.

22 King diary, 14 Feb. 1941.

23 Ibid., 1, 24–6 Dec. 1941. The Chiefs of Staff Committee recommended, on 21 August 1941, occupation of the islands by Canadian forces: NA, Howe Papers, vol. 56.

24 Thomson, *Vive le Québec libre*, 65–7.

25 Stacey, *Conflict*, vol. II, 300.

26 Creighton, *Forked Road*, 55–6.

27 Laurendeau, *Crise*, 54–5. Dionne, 'La presse écrite.'

28 Rumilly, *Histoire*, 38: 185, 230–9. Rumilly, *Duplessis*, 1: 580–8.

29 Some recognize Lapointe's role: J.F. Hilliker, 'The Canadian Government and the Free French: Perceptions and Constraints, 1940–44,' *International History Review* 2, no. 1 (1980), 87–108; Thomson, *Vive le Québec libre*, and Bychok, 'Lapointe.'

30 King diary, 3, 23 June, 2–4 July 1940. A Canadian mission reported Pétain having some independence (CWC Minutes, 26 Dec. 1940, 4), but King believed that if the war were lost it would be because of the 'rottenness' of certain French leaders. Pickersgill, *King Record*, vol. 1, 52. Thomson, *Vive le Québec libre*, 75.

31 Lapointe, in interview with Grant Dexter, 12 Oct. 1940, quoted in Bychok, 'Lapointe,' 249.

32 NA, Lapointe Papers, vol. 66, file C6, 2, radio speech to France, 26 Oct. 1940. Ibid., vol. 66, file C6, 'War Savings Bonds and Stamps,' 26 May 1940.

33 NA, Skelton Papers, vol. 5, file 14, diary, 30 May 1940.

34 'The Hand of Pétain but the Voice of Hitler,' *Ottawa Journal*, 8 July 1940, 1. Stacey, *Conflict*, vol. II, 302.

35 NA, Ralston Papers, vol. 1, diary, 11 Dec. 1940, 6 Jan. 1941.

36 NA, Lapointe Papers, vol. 24, file 82, Ralston to Lapointe, 4 June 1941. Poll of 633 workers at Quebec Power Corporation.

37 Philippe Prévost, *La France et le Canada: d'une après guerre à l'autre (1918–1944)* (St Boniface, Man.: Éditions du blé 1994), 325. Dionne, 'La presse écrite.'

38 King diary, 7 Oct. 1940.

39 NA, Lapointe Papers, vol. 24, file 82, C. Melançon to Lapointe, 7 and 10 Nov. 1941. de Miribel, in Thomson, *Vive le Québec libre*, 34.

40 *Le Soleil*, 17, 25, 27 June, 10 July, 13 Sept., 26 Oct., 2 Nov. 1940, 28 Jan., 5, 27 May, 11 June, 13 Aug. 1941.

41 A 1942 poll asked who best defended the interests of France: 45 per cent in Quebec chose de Gaulle, 46 per cent Pétain: Dionne, 'La presse écrite,' 79.

42 CWC Minutes, 17 Sept. 1940, 2.

43 *DCER*, 8: 785 (Lapointe quoted in Skelton memo to King, 18 Oct. 1940). Pickersgill, in *King Record*, 1: 147, says that Skelton favoured the action, but the documents in *DCER* suggest that he did not.

44 King diary, 19 Oct. 1940.

45 Ibid., 3, 9 Feb. 1941. The gold remained in Canada.

46 CWC Minutes, 26 Sept. 1940, 2.

47 NA, Lapointe Papers, vol. 24, file 82, Ralston to Lapointe, 27 Sept. 1940, Lapointe to Ralston, 30 Sept. 1940.

48 CWC Minutes, 29 May 1940, 6.

49 NA, Lapointe Papers, vol. 24, file 82, King to Lapointe, 2 Oct. 1940.

50 Ibid., vol. 66, file C6, radio speech to France, 26 Oct. 1940. The speech was heard in other countries, and Lapointe received letters on it from Britain and the United States: ibid., vol. 24, file 81, Lapointe to A. Frigon, Directeur général adjoint Radio Canada, Montréal, Oct. 30 1940.

51 Ibid., vol. 24, file 82, Robertson to King, 19 Feb. 1941.

52 Quoted in Thomson, *Vive le Québec libre*, 41–2.

53 *DCER*, vol. VIII, 617, Robertson to King, 25 Sept. 1941.

54 CWC Minutes, 27 May 1941, 13 Aug. 1941, 5.

55 NA, Lapointe Papers, vol. 66, file C6, radio speech to France, Sept. 1941, 12. He added his support for the Free French in another speech: ibid., 'Faisons le pointe,' 15 May 1941, 2.

56 Ibid., vol. 61, file A3, Lapointe speech, 'The War,' 24 Sept. 1941, 11.

57 Larry Hannant, 'Fear Sweeps Nation: Fifth Column Crisis,' *Beaver* 73, no. 6 (1993), 24–5.

58 CWC Minutes, 22 May 1940, 5. J.L. Granatstein, *A Man of Influence: Norman A. Robertson and Canadian Statescraft, 1929–68* (Toronto: Deneau 1981),

80–109. Jean Côté, *Adrien Arcand* (Montreal: Méridien 1991), 97. Betcherman, *Swastika*, 145. 'Arcand,' *Le Soleil*, 30 May 1940, 1. 'Communistes,' ibid., 5 June 1940, 1.

59 Stacey, *Conflict*, 2: 190. See also Granatstein and Bothwell, 'Self-Evident National Duty,' 213. R. Bothwell, I. Drummond, and J. English, *Canada, 1900–1945* (Toronto: University of Toronto Press 1987), 299. Bychok, in 'Lapointe,' 159–60, recognizes and perhaps exaggerates Lapointe's role.

60 King diary, 16, 21–4 Nov. 1939. For the weekly RCMP reports, and internments in 1939–40, see NA, Robertson Papers, vol. 12.

61 NA, Lapointe Papers, vol. 16, file 40, Lapointe to King, 20 Dec. 1939.

62 Pickersgill, *King Record*, 1: 36–40.

63 NA, Lapointe Papers, vol. 16, file 40, McLarty to Lapointe, 22 Dec. 1939.

64 King diary, 3 Jan. 1940.

65 *Debates*, House of Commons, 21 June 1940, 1013. Ibid., 27 June 1940, 1221. Ibid., 27 Feb. 1941, 1110.

66 Power, in Ward, ed., *Power*, 351.

67 *Debates*, House of Commons, 20 May 1940, 21. Ibid., 23 May 1940, 148. NA, King Papers, vol. 290, reel c-4570, 245096–8, Lapointe to King, King reply, 30 May 1940.

68 Lapointe, quoted in Larry Hannant, 'Fifth-Column Crisis,' *Beaver* 73 no. 6 (Dec. 1993), 25–7.

69 NA, Lapointe Papers, vol. 23, file 78, S.T. Wood, RCMP Commissioner, to Lapointe, 4 July 1940.

70 *Life Magazine*, 5 May 1941, 108, in ibid., Raymond, *Debates*, House of Commons, 8 May 1941, 2712.

71 NA, Lapointe Papers, vol. 14, file 27, Taschereau to Lapointe, 14 June 1941.

72 Ibid., vol. 16, file 40, Lapointe to King, 20 Dec. 1939.

73 Pickersgill, *Memoirs*, 198.

74 NA, King Papers, vol. 243, Minutes of 'Meeting of Cabinet with representatives of the Ontario legislature,' 3 Oct. 1939, 302540.

75 Ibid., vol. 265, reel c3742, 225586, Conant to Lapointe, replies, 1, 5, 15 Sept. 1939, 229109–14.

76 CWC Minutes, 28 July 1941, 3.

77 *Debates*, House of Commons, 3 Dec. 1940, 666. Ibid., 9 Sept. 1939, 66. When the Soviet Union entered the war on the side of the Allies, Lapointe's approach changed, but communists continued to be interned: ibid., 10 Nov. 1941, 4287.

78 'Le *Globe and Mail* et M. Lapointe,' *Le Droit*, 4 March 1941.

79 'His Whim Is Law,' *Canadian Tribune*, 26 April 1941, in NA, Lapointe Papers, vol. 13, file 22. *Debates*, House of Commons, 4 March 1941.

80 NA, Lapointe Papers, vol. 16, file 40, Lapointe reply to A. Larkin, daughter of P. Larkin, 27 Oct. 1941.

81 *Debates*, House of Commons, 4 March 1941, 1256. Ibid., 14 May 1941, 2873. Ibid., 9 June 1941, 3755.

82 Lapointe ordered the RCMP to bring certain people to trial: NA, Lapointe Papers, vol. 14, file 25, Lapointe to Wood, 20 June 1940. He also obtained the release of G. Gilet as a favour to Cardinal Villeneuve: ibid., vol. 23, file 6, Villeneuve to Lapointe, 5 Sept. 1941, and Lapointe reply, 8 Sept. 1941.

83 King diary, 24 May 1940.

84 *Debates*, House of Commons, 18 June 1940, 854, 902. On the application of the NRMA, see D. Byers, 'Canada's Zombies: A Portrait of Canadian Conscripts and Their Experience during the Second World War,' *Journal of the CHA* (Ottawa: Canadian Historical Society 1997), 175–203.

85 Granatstein, *Canada's War*, 100.

86 Stacey, *Conflict*, 2: 371. Creighton, *Forked Road*, 39.

87 Brunet, *Québec*, 270. See also Rumilly, *Duplessis*, 1: 572. Monière, *Idéologies*, 287.

88 King diary, 17–18 June 1940.

89 Ibid., 17 June 1940.

90 Lapointe also insisted that mobilization of wealth should be included: CWC Minutes, 17 June 1940, 2.

91 Ibid., 27 June 1940, 2. See also Lapointe, *Debates*, House of Commons, 18 June 1940, 902.

92 King diary, 30 May, 5 June 1940.

93 Laurendeau, *Crise*, 59.

94 NA, Lapointe Papers, vol. 18, file 47, J.F. Pouliot, MP for Rivière du Loup, to Lapointe, 24 June 1940. 'Mobilisation,' *Le Soleil*, 18 June 1940, 1. 'Mise en garde,' ibid., 18 June 1940, 1. 'Lapointe reste à son poste,' ibid., 3 Aug. 1940, 4.

95 NA, Lapointe Papers, vol. 15, file 30, René Chaloult, MPP for Lotbinière, to elector Paul-E. Gagnon, 15 Aug. 1940.

96 King diary, 19 June 1940.

97 Laurendeau, *Crise*, 57–9. Five well-known Quebec nationalists signed a letter opposing Houde's internment and sought assurance that no conscripts would go overseas. Lapointe replied that such guarantees were already in the bill: NA, Lapointe Papers, vol. 47, file 18.30, Philippe Hamel, J.-E. Grégoire, René Chaloult, Paul Bouchard, and Louis Even to Lapointe, Lapointe reply, 9, 14 Aug. 1940.

98 King diary, 3–5 Aug. 1940.

99 *Debates*, House of Commons, 18 June 1940, 889.

100 King diary, 17 June 1940.

101 CWC Minutes, 17 June 1940, 2.

102 Ibid., 29 July 1941, 1–4. See also journalist Grant Dexter, quoted in Rea, 'Conscription,' 13.

103 Stacey, *Conflict*, 2: 372.

104 Creighton, *Forked Road*, 58. Slobodin, 'Tangled Web,' 490–8.

105 S. Durflinger, 'City at War: The Effects of the Second World War on Verdun, Quebec,' PhD thesis, McGill University, 1997, writes that 'as a whole, Verdunites remained remarkably united in pursuing a vigourous war effort.' Charles Spina, 'War by Other Means: Quebec's Contribution to Canada's War,' MA thesis, University of Ottawa, 1981, 89, 177, 187, 198.

106 NA, Lapointe Papers, vol. 84A, Major Goforth, DND report, 'Quebec's recruiting problem,' 25 June 1941. Ibid., vol. 18, file 46, Lapointe to Power and Power to Lapointe, 7 May 1941. According to Goforth's report, 6.5 per cent of junior officers were French-speaking, and 17 per cent of personnel. See also J. Pariseau, 'La participation des Canadiens français à l'effort des deux guerres mondiales,' *Revue canadienne de défense* 13 no. 2 (1983), 47–8. Pariseau and Bernier, *Canadiens français*, 125.

107 NA, Lapointe Papers, vol. 60, file 94B, Godbout to Lapointe, 17 May 1941, Lapointe reply, 23 May 1941. Godbout sought statistics, but Lapointe replied that none were kept, adding that Macdonald, Power, and Ralston were all satisfied with Quebec's voluntary enrolment. Serge Bernier, 'Participation des Canadiens français: évaluation et tentative de quantification,' in *Bulletin d'histoire politique: La participation des Canadiens français et la Deuxième Guerre mondiale: mythes et réalités* 3 nos. 3–4 (Montreal: AQHP/Septentrion 1995), 20. Gravel, 'Quebec militaire,' 82–108. Bakvis, *Regional Ministers*, 52. Pariseau and Bernier, *Canadiens français*, 147.

108 King, writing for the New York *Outlook*, 25 July 1917, quoted in Granatstein and Hitsman, *Broken Promises*, 69–70.

109 King, quoted in an interview, 28 Feb. 1942, by journalist Grant Dexter, quoted in A. Levine, 'Grant Dexter,' *Beaver* 72, no. 6 (1992), 23. Pickersgill, *Memoirs*, 217.

110 CWC Minutes, 9 May 1941, 5.

111 King diary, 8–9 Oct., 4 Dec. 1940, 25 Dec. 1941.

112 *Debates*, House of Commons, 8 May 1941, 2712. Ibid., 3 Dec. 1940, 665. NA, Lapointe Papers, vol. 61, file A3, 'The War,' 24 Sept. 1941. Ibid., vol. 66, file C6, 'French Canada's War Effort,' 23 June 1941.

113 King diary, 27 Jan. 1941.

114 CWC Minutes, 9 May 1941, 5: Lapointe sought a clear stand against overseas conscription, as existed in Australia and South Africa, to end the increased pressure. King agreed, but Ralston preferred not to rule it out. Ibid., 23, 30 April 1941.

115 NA, Department of National Defence (DND) Papers, vol. 5812, HQS 8798, Brig. Gen. M. Pope to DND, 29 Sept. 1941. After Lapointe promised that DND would increase French-Canadian representation in the department, Cardinal Villeneuve had told Pope that 'Mr. Lapointe's announcement of the Department's policy had created the most favourable impression throughout the province.'

116 Lapointe, 'Faisons le point!'

117 Ibid., 8–9. See also NA, Lapointe Papers, vol. 66, file C6, Lapointe radio address, 'The War,' 8 July 1941. Ibid., Lapointe radio address, 'L'emprunt de la victoire,' 1 June 1941. Ibid., vol. 62, file A8, Lapointe speech, 'Appel de fonds,' 21 March 1941.

118 CWC Minutes, 30 May 1941, 5. Lapointe, 'Faisons le point!' 5. See also *Debates*, House of Commons, 24 Feb. 1941, 995–6; NA, Lapointe Papers, vol. 66, file C6, Lapointe radio speech, Sept. 1941.

119 D-Hist., 001.9, notes on meeting of senior army officers and Minister of Defence Rogers, 20 April 1940: they also agreed that sending a third division overseas would be undesirable 'from the military point of view' because a smaller formation promptly maintained was more effective than a large army under strength.

120 CWC Minutes, 26 Feb. 1941, 10. Ibid., 28 Sept. 1939, 3.

121 General Crerar to Ralston, 24 Sept. 1940, quoted in Granatstein and Hitsman, *Broken Promises*, 149.

122 NA, Lapointe Papers, vol. 68. H. Carl Goldenberg, Associate Director-General, Department of Munitions and Supply, Economic and Statistics Branch, letter to Ralston, attached to report 'Memorandum on Man-Power,' 12 June 1941. Ralston told the British press that volunteers were 'coming very well indeed.' NA, Ralston Papers, vol. 64, interview with press, 14 Oct. 1941.

123 D-Hist., 723.012 (D1), Ralston to King, 5 Jan. 1941.

124 CWC Minutes, 5 June 1941, 4.

125 NA, King Papers, vol. 307, reel c-4864, 259684, Cardinal Villeneuve to Lapointe, 21 July 1941. Villeneuve was upset that the impressive French-Canadian participation was not recognized.

126 NA, Lapointe Papers, vol. 14, file 24, Drouin to Lapointe, 29 April 1941.

127 Pariseau and Bernier, *Canadiens français*, 121.

128 *Public Opinion Quarterly*, 453.

129 NA, Lapointe Papers, vol. 78, file 42, DND memo no. 22, Summary of Intelligence from military districts, 25–31 May 1941. Also NA, P. Casgrain Papers, vol. 14, Casgrain to DND, reply, 16 April 1941.

130 NA, Lapointe Papers, vol. 74, file 3. On papers defending Quebec, see the *Winnipeg Free Press*, 'Quebec Is in the Fight,' 26 March 1941. *Saturday Night*,

24 May, 19 July 1941, criticized the *Globe and Mail* for its conscription campaign.

131 Dexter, quoted in Granatstein, *Canada's War*, 209.

132 NA, DND Papers, vol. 2069, HQS 54-27-3-55: several francophones, between July and September 1942, sought and received permission to join the Free French.

133 King diary, 27 June, 2, 15 July 1941.

134 NA, Lapointe Papers, vol. 18, file 47, Pattullo to Lapointe, 11 July 1941, and Lapointe reply, 8 Aug. 1941; R.B. Hanson to Lapointe, 29 July 1941.

135 Ibid., R.H. Gregory to Lapointe, 21 June 1941.

136 Ibid., George C. Macdonald, Montreal accountant, to Lapointe, 6 June 1941, reply, 14 June 1941.

137 Dexter memo of conversation with King and Bruce Hutchison, 28 Feb. 1942, quoted in Allan Levine, 'Grant Dexter on Parliament Hill,' *Beaver* 72 no. 6 (Dec. 1942), 21–2. CWC Minutes, 9 May 1941, 4. Ibid., 10 Sept. 1941, 4. Ibid., 9 Oct. 1940, 1. Churchill's speech at Glasgow, 9 Feb. 1941, quoted in Rea, 'Conscription,' 12.

138 CWC Minutes, 20 May 1941, 3.

139 NA, King Papers, vol. 307, reel c-4864, 259724, Lapointe to King, 5 Nov. 1941: Lapointe remarked that 'the conscription issue is prominently debated. I should seize the first opportunity to strongly express my views.' He also insisted that King maintain his decision not to declare war on Finland, Hungary, and Romania; however, on 7 December 1941 Canada did follow Britain's lead.

140 *DCER*, 7: 420–7, Lapointe to Massey, 13 June 1941; King to Massey, 14 June 1941; King to Churchill, 22 June 1941.

141 King finally did visit England, but his reluctance to make such trips was again obvious when he wrote to Lapointe from London to express his delight that Prime Minister Fraser of New Zealand agreed that Commonwealth leaders should remain in their own countries as much as possible: NA, Lapointe Papers, vol. 11, file 1, King to Lapointe, 29 Aug. 1941.

Epilogue: King without Lapointe

1 King diary, 31 Oct., 15 Nov. 1941.

2 Ibid., 11, 19, 30 Nov. 1941. NA, King Papers, vol. 299, reel c-4860, 254806, King to Athlone, 26 Nov. 1941.

3 King diary, 19 Nov., 1, 2 Dec. 1941. Pickersgill, *King Record*, 1: 356.

4 King diary, 20 Nov., 1 Dec. 1941.

5 Ibid., 26, 30 Nov. 1941.

6 *Debates*, House of Commons, 21 Jan. 1942, 4548–9.

7 'Hommage à Lapointe,' *Le Soleil*, 26 Nov. 1941, 19. 'L'Honorable Ernest Lapointe et ses détracteurs,' *Le Canada*, 25 Oct. 1941, 4. Léopold Richer, *Nos chefs*, 45–8.

8 *Debates*, House of Commons, 21 Jan. 1942, 4553–4.

9 Godbout, in 'Declaration,' *Le Soleil*, 26 Nov. 1941, 9.

10 King diary, 29 Nov. 1941.

11 Ibid., 19, 20, 29, 30 Nov. 1941. Pickersgill, *King Record*, 1: 290. Pickersgill, *Memoirs*, 213. King told Godbout that Dandurand was not young, Cardin not in shape, and Power not a French-Canadian, and Casgrain lacked experience: King Papers, vol. 305, reel c-4863, 25794, King to Godbout, 30 Nov. 1941.

12 NA, King Papers, vol. 305, reel c-4863, 25794, King to Godbout, 30 Nov. 1941.

13 King diary, 4, 5 Dec. 1941.

14 Neatby, 'French Canada,' 11. King diary, 5 July 1940.

15 Granatstein, *Canada's War*, 107.

16 Nolan, *King's War*, 78. One anglophone historian who has recently questioned the 'fanciful image of St. Laurent' as 'Uncle Louis' is Michael Bliss, who argues that 'the real St. Laurent was aristocratic, aloof, and, whenever removed from Ottawa, out of touch.' Bliss, *Right Honourable Men*, 181.

17 Rumilly, *Duplessis*, vol. 1, 605.

18 J.-G. Genest, 'Adélard Godbout,' PhD thesis, Université Laval, 1977, 436–7.

19 Laurendeau, *Crise*, 65.

20 Power, in Ward, ed., *Power*, 133, 393–4. See also Dawson, *Conscription*, 62. René Lévesque highlights the contrast between St Laurent and Lapointe, who came from and was associated with a small town: interview in NA, Chisholm Papers, vol. 19.10, 1962.

21 In Dale C. Thomson, *Louis St. Laurent: Canadian* (Toronto: Macmillan 1967), 128.

22 *Public Opinion Quarterly*, 1945, 88. Asked which minister was doing the best job, 28 per cent named Ilsley, 5 per cent Howe, and 3 per cent McNaughton.

23 Pariseau and Bernier, *Canadiens français*, 1: 156. See also Wade, *French Canadians*, 2: 954, and Thomson, *St. Laurent*, 10, 128.

24 Oscar Drouin, a leading figure in the Quebec East organization, sought a pledge from St Laurent to continue Lapointe's policies; St Laurent replied that he did not intend to replace Lapointe. Thomson, *St. Laurent*, 110. Power, in Ward, ed., *Power*, 133–8.

25 Neatby, 'French Canada,' 11.

26 NA, King Papers, vol. 446, reel c-11054, 407724, King to Mrs. Rose, a journalist writing on King's career, 7 July 1949.

27 Interview with J.W. Pickersgill, 11 April 1994.

28 C.P. Stacey, *Arms, Men and Governments: The War Policies of Canada, 1939–45* (Ottawa: Queen's Printer 1970), 400. Granatstein, *Canada's War*, 205. King diary, 7 Nov. 1941.

29 King diary, 2–4 Dec. 1941. On the fourth, Dandurand opposed Ralston, invoking Lapointe's memory. See also Granatstein and Hitsman, *Broken Promises*, 156.

30 King diary, 9, 23 Dec. 1941. Minister of Revenue Colin Gibson told cabinet that a friend had told him that King 'had only to say the word and Quebec would follow.' Ilsley, Macdonald, and Ralston preferred not to commit themselves to a no-conscription policy.

31 King diary, 14 Nov., 11, 18 Dec. 1941.

32 Dexter memo of meeting with journalist Bruce Hutchison and King, 28 Feb. 1942, quoted in A. Levine, 'Grant Dexter on Parliament Hill,' *Beaver* 72, no. 6 (1992), 23.

33 NA, St Laurent Papers, vol. 249, King radio broadcast, 7 April 1942, 6. Granatstein, *Canada's War*, 226. King quoted in Ward, ed., *Power*, 135.

34 Granatstein, *Canada's War*, 236. Pickersgill, *King Record*, 1: 372.

35 Morton, *Canada and War*, 116.

36 Granatstein and Hitsman, *Broken Promises*, 163. Rea, 'Conscription,' 14. Stacey, *Official History*, vol. I, 122.

37 Creighton, *Forked Road*, 69.

38 Laurendeau, *Crise*, 113–14.

39 R. Lévesque interviewed by E. Chisholm for 1964 radio show: NA, Chisholm Papers, vol. 19.10.

40 Monière, *Idéologies*, 286. See also Laurendeau, *Crise*, 56–9, 65. Rumilly, *Duplessis*, 1: 605.

41 'La guerre ... ,' *Le Soleil*, 9 Dec. 1941, 4. Stacey, *Conflict*, 2: 322.

42 Polls cited in Claire Hoy, *Margin of Error: Pollsters and the Manipulation of Canadian Politics* (Toronto: McClelland and Stewart 1989), 19–20. On French-Canadian distrust of Ottawa, see Cook, *French-Canadian Question*, 55. Granatstein and Hitsman, *Broken Promises*, 179.

43 Laurendeau, *Crise*, 65. Elspeth Chisholm, 'Never,' 50. Fiset to J. Pierrepont Moffat, 19 Feb. 1942, quoted in Granatstein and Hitsman, *Broken Promises*, 167.

44 King diary, 5, 11, 18, 23 Dec. 1941.

45 NA, King Papers, vol. 424, A.D.P. Heeney memo to King, with copy of CWC Minutes, 2 March 1942.

46 NA, St Laurent Papers, vol. 249, St Laurent radio speech, 17 April 1942, 1.

47 NA, King Papers, vol. 335, reel c-6814, 288010, G. Murray to J.A. Hume, Secretary, Minister of National War Services. See also Thomson, *St. Laurent*, 120. Laurendeau, *Crise*, 81, 116.

48 Winston Churchill, *The Second World War: The Grand Alliance*, first pub. 1950 (New York: Bantam Books 1962), 511.

49 *Debates*, House of Commons, 9 Sept. 1939, 72. Interview with J.W. Pickersgill, 27 Dec. 1991.

50 King diary, 3 Dec. 1941. CWC Minutes, 3 Dec. 1941, 4. Granatstein and Hitsman, *Broken Promises*, 158, point out that 'in retrospect, it is clear that the conscription crisis of 1944 became almost a certainty with this decision.'

51 CWC Minutes, 3 Dec. 1941, 3. See also Rea, 'Conscription,' 15.

52 King diary, 17 Sept. 1942.

53 Dawson, *Conscription*, 15, 62–4, 73–7. Norman Hillmer and Roger Sarty, 'The Mythology of Canada's War, 1939–45,' *History and Social Science Teacher* 20 no. 2 (1984–5), 73.

54 Rea, 'Conscription,' 18–19.

55 King diary, 22 Nov. 1944. John Swettenham, *McNaughton*, vol. 3, *1944–66* (Toronto: Ryerson Press 1969), 44.

56 Stacey, *Arms, Men and Governments*, 53, 432, 459. See also Stacey, *Conflict*, 2: 257. Creighton, *Forked Road*, 68, 96.

57 Bliss, *Right Honourable Men*, 150, 182: King 'would never have allowed himself to lose touch with the mood of the country as St. Laurent had.' Granatstein and Hitsman, *Broken Promises*, 238, 264. Rea, 'Conscription,' 19. Dawson, *Conscription*, 15, 64, 122–4. Morton, *Histoire militaire*, 272, 295. Nolan, *King's War*, 3.

58 J.M.S. Careless, *Canada: A Story of Challenge* (Toronto: Macmillan 1965), 386–7.

59 Pariseau and Bernier, *Canadiens français*, 124. See also Rumilly, *Histoire*, 41: 152–75. Gravel, 'Québec militaire,' 105–6.

60 Brunet, *Québec*, 271. Linteau et al., *Québec*, 2: 137–9.

61 Robert Lahaise, *La fin d'un Québec traditionnel, 1914–1939*, vol. 1, *Histoire du Canada à notre état français* (Montreal: Hexagone 1994), 19.

62 Laurendeau, *Crise*, 8, 153. See also Linteau et al., *Québec*, 132, 723. Brunet, *Québec*, 270.

63 *Public Opinion Quarterly*, 591. Gravel, 'Quebec militaire,' 106.

64 *Debates*, House of Commons, 5 Dec. 1944, 6831.

65 King diary, 6 Dec. 1944.
66 St Laurent to G. Dexter, 21 July 1942, quoted in Granatstein, *Canada's War*, 243. Thomson, *St. Laurent*, 138.
67 *Debates*, House of Commons, 29 Nov. 1944, 2344.
68 Ibid., 21 Jan. 1942, 4550.
69 King diary, 3 Aug. 1941.

Works Cited

Primary Sources

Archives

Archives Nationales du Québec.

Directorate of History (D-Hist.), Department of National Defence.

Personal collection of Mr and Mrs R. Ouimet.

National Archives of Canada (Manuscript Group)

Bennett Papers. MG 26 K.
Borden Papers. MG 26 G.
Bourassa Papers. MG 27 II E1.
P. Casgrain Papers. MG 27 III B2.
T. Casgrain Papers. MG 32 C25.
Chisholm Papers. MG 31 E50.
Dandurand Papers. MG 27 III B3.
Foster Papers. MG 27 II D7.
Gouin Papers. MG 27 III B4.
Howe Papers. MG 27 III B20.
Inch Papers. MG 30 C187.
King Papers. MG 26 J1-J18.
   King diary. MG 26 J13.
   Cabinet War Committee (CWC) Minutes, 1939–42.
   MG 26 J4. vols. 423–4.

Lapointe Papers. MG 27 III B10.
Laurier Papers. MG 26 H.
Lemieux Papers. MG 27 II B10.
Liberal Party of Canada Papers. MG 28 IV 3, vol. 1215.
Meighen Papers. MG 26 I.
Picard Papers. MG 27 III C10.
Power Papers. MG 27 III B19.
Ralston Papers. MG 27 III B11.
Ralston diary. Vols. 63–4.
Robertson Papers. MG 30 E163.
St Laurent Papers. MG 26 L.
Sifton Papers. MG 27.
Skelton Papers. MG 30 D33.
  Skelton diary. Vols. 10–13.
Woodsworth Papers. MG 27 III C7.

National Archives of Canada (Record Group)

Dominion–Provincial Conferences. RG 47.
External Affairs. RG 25.
Governor General's Office. RG 7.
Justice. RG 13.
National Defence. RG 24.
Privy Council. RG 2 (Cabinet War Committee Minutes).

Published Sources

Articles and Books

Debates, House of Commons. 1904–1942. I used the French version for this
  study; however, all quotations in English refer to the English-language
  version.
Debates, Senate of Canada. 1923–7.
Documents on Canadian External Relations (DCER). Vols. 3–8. 1919–41. Ottawa:
  Department of External Affairs, 1970–6.
Lapointe, Ernest. 'Faisons le point!' Published speech on Radio Canada, 15 May
  1941 (Ottawa: Queen's Printer 1941). Also in NA, Lapointe Papers.
– 'La situation internationale du Canada.' Published speech to the Cercle
  universitaire de Montréal, 29 Oct. 1927 (Montreal 1928). Also published in
  Revue trimestrielle canadienne (Dec. 1927). Also in NA, Lapointe Papers, vol. 7,
  file 27.1.

– 'Le Statut de Westminster et l'évolution nationale du Canada.' Published speech to the Cercle universitaire de Montréal, 16 Jan. 1932 (Montreal 1932). Also published in *Revue trimestrielle canadienne* (March 1932). Also in NA, Lapointe Papers, vol. 71.

League of Nations, *Records of 1st–19th Assemblies,* Plenary Meetings and Meetings of Committees, Geneva, 1920–38.

Riddell, Walter A., ed. *Documents on Canadian Foreign Policy, 1917–1939.* Toronto, Oxford University Press, 1962.

Roosevelt, Franklin D. *Public Papers and Addresses of Franklin D. Roosevelt.* 1938 vol: *The Continuing Struggle for Liberation.* New York, 1941.

– *Public Papers and Addresses of Franklin D. Roosevelt.* 1939 vol: *War and Neutrality.* New York, 1941.

Newspapers and Magazines

Canadian Forum.
Le Devoir.
Globe and Mail.
Maclean's.
La Presse.
Public Opinion Quarterly. Vols. 1938–45. New York, 1939–45.
Le Soleil. 1919–42.

Interviews

Interview with Paul Martin, 19 March 1992.
Interview with Mr and Mrs A.R. Menzies (son-in-law and daughter of O.D. Skelton), 25 Nov. 1993.
Interview with Mr and Mrs R. Ouimet (son-in-law and daughter of Ernest Lapointe), 2 May 1992 and 19 Sept. 1992.
Interview with J.W. Pickersgill, 27 Dec. 1991 and 11 April 1994.

Secondary Sources

Anonyme. 'M. Ernest Lapointe.' *Action française* (Sept. 1924), 145–9.

Bakvis, Herman. *Regional Ministers: Power and Influence in the Canadian Cabinet.* Toronto: University of Toronto Press 1991.

Bélanger, Réal. *L'impossible défi: Albert Sévigny et les Conservateurs fédéraux (1902–1918).* Quebec, Presses de l'Université Laval 1983.

Bercuson, David J., and Granatstein, J.L. *Dictionary of Canadian Military History.* Toronto: Oxford University Press 1992.

Berger, Carl. *The Sense of Power: Studies in the Ideas of Canadian Imperialism, 1867–1914.* Toronto: University of Toronto Press 1970.

Bernier, Paul. 'Les débuts de la carrière d'Ernest Lapointe (1904–1919).' MA thesis, Université Laval, 1977.

Bertrand, Denis. 'La politique extérieure du Canada et la réaction canadienne française à la veille de la deuxième grande guerre.' PhD thesis, Université de Montréal, 1965.

Betcherman, Lita-Rose. *The Swastika and the Maple Leaf: Fascist Movements in Canada in the Thirties.* Don Mills: Fitzhenry and Whiteside 1975.

Bliss, Michael. *Right Honourable Men: The Descent of Canadian Politics from Macdonald to Mulroney.* Toronto: HarperCollins 1994.

Bothwell, Robert, ed. *Canada and Quebec: One Country, Two Histories.* Vancouver: UBC Press 1995.

Bothwell, Robert, and Hillmer, Norman, eds. *The In-Between Time: Canadian External Policy in the 1930s.* Toronto: Copp Clark 1975.

Bothwell, Robert, and English, John. 'Dirty Work at the Crossroads: New Perspectives on the Riddell Incident.' *CHA Historical Papers* (1972), 263–85.

Brown, Robert Craig, and Cook, Ramsay. *Canada 1896–1921: A Nation Transformed.* Toronto: McClelland and Stewart 1976.

Brunet, Michel. *Québec, Canada anglais: deux itinéraires, un affrontement.* Collection constantes, vol. 12. Montreal: Editions HMH 1968.

Bychok, Paul. '"La muraille qui vous protege": Ernest Lapointe and French-Canada, 1935–1941.' MA thesis, Queen's University, 1985.

Chisholm, Elspeth. '"Never": Ernest Lapointe and Conscription, 1935–1944.' *Canada: An Historical Magazine* 3, no. 3 (March 1976), 3–21; 3, no. 4 (June 1976), 40–53.

Cook, Ramsay. *Canada and the French Canadian Question.* First pub. 1966. Toronto: Macmillan, 1969.

– 'The Evolution of Nationalism in Quebec.' *British Journal of Canadian Studies* 4, no. 2 (1989), 306–17.

– 'J.W. Dafoe at the Imperial Conference, 1923.' *CHR* 61, no. 1 (March 1960), 19–40.

Creighton, Donald. *The Forked Road: Canada 1939–1957.* Toronto: McClelland and Stewart 1976.

Dahl, Robert A. *Modern Political Analysis.* First pub. 1963. 3rd ed. Englewood Cliffs, NJ: Prentice Hall 1976.

Dawson, R. MacGregor. *The Conscription Crisis of 1944.* Toronto: University of Toronto Press 1961.

– *William Lyon Mackenzie King.* Vol. 1. *A Political Biography, 1874–1923.* Toronto: University of Toronto Press 1958.

Dickinson, John A., and Young, Brian. *A Short History of Quebec*. 2nd ed. Toronto: Copp Clark Pitman 1993.

Dionne, Stéphane. 'La presse écrite Canadienne-française et de Gaulle de 1940 à 1946.' MA thesis, Université de Montréal, 1990.

Eayrs, James. *In Defence of Canada*. Vol. 1. *From the Great War to the Great Depression*. Toronto: University of Toronto Press 1964.

– *In Defence of Canada*. Vol. 2: *Appeasement and Rearmament*. Toronto: University of Toronto Press 1967.

– '"A Low, Dishonest Decade": Aspects of Canadian External Policy, 1931–39.' In H.L. Keenleyside et al., eds., *The Growth of Canadian External Policies in External Affairs*, 59–80. Durham, NC: Duke University Press 1960.

English, John. 'The "French Lieutenant" in Ottawa.' In R. Kenneth Carty and W. Peter Ward, eds., *National Politics and Community in Canada*, 184–200. Vancouver: UBC Press 1986.

Esberey, Joy E. *Knight of the Holy Spirit: A Study of William Lyon Mackenzie King*. Toronto: University of Toronto Press 1980.

Ferns, H.S. 'Mackenzie King on Television.' *British Journal of Canadian Studies* 3, no. 2 (1988), 308–12.

Ferns, Henry S., and Ostry, Bernard. *The Age of Mackenzie King*. First pub. 1955. Toronto: James Lorimer 1976.

Filteau, Gérard. *Le Québec, le Canada et la guerre 1914–1918*. Montreal: L'Aurore 1977.

Frohn-Neilsen, Thor Erik. 'Canada's Foreign Enlistment Act: Mackenzie King's Expedient Response to the Spanish Civil War.' MA thesis, University of British Columbia, 1982.

Gaudreault, P.-M. 'Ernest Lapointe.' *La Revue dominicaine* 48, no. 1 (Jan. 1942), 1–9.

Genest, Jean-Guy. 'L'élection provinciale québécoise de 1939.' MA thesis, Université Laval, 1968.

– *Godbout*. Sillery: Septenrion 1996.

Gibson, Frederick W. 'The Cabinet of 1921.' In F.W. Gibson, ed., *Cabinet Formation and Bicultural Relations: Seven Case Studies*, 63–103. Studies of the Royal Commission on Bilingualism and Biculturalism. Ottawa: Queen's Printer 1970.

– 'The Cabinet of 1935.' In F.W. Gibson, ed., *Cabinet Formation and Bicultural Relations: Seven Case Studies*, 105–40. Studies of the Royal Commission on Bilingualism and Biculturalism. Ottawa: Queen's Printer 1970.

Glazebrook, G.P. de T. *A History of Canadian External Relations*. Vol. 2. *In the Empire and the World, 1914–1939*. First pub. 1966. Toronto: McClelland and Stewart 1970.

Graham, Roger. *Arthur Meighen.* Vol. 1. *The Door of Opportunity.* Toronto: Clarke, Irwin and Co. 1960.
- *Arthur Meighen.* Vol. 2. *And Fortune Fled.* Toronto: Clarke, Irwin and Co. 1963.
Granatstein, J.L. *Canada's War: The Politics of the Mackenzie King Government, 1939–1945.* Toronto: Oxford University Press 1945.
- *How Britain's Weakness Forced Canada into the Arms of the United States.* Toronto: University of Toronto Press 1989.
Granatstein, J.L. 'King and His Cabinet: The War Years.' In John English and J.O. Stubbs, eds., *Mackenzie King: Widening the Debate,* 173–90. Toronto: Macmillan 1977.
Granatstein, J.L., and Bothwell, R. '"A Self-Evident National Duty": Canadian Foreign Policy, 1935–1939.' *Journal of Imperial and Commonwealth History* 3, no. 2 (1975), 212–33.
Granatstein, J.L., and Hitsman, J.M. *Broken Promises: A History of Conscription in Canada.* First pub. 1977. Toronto: Copp Clark Pitman 1985.
Gravel, Jean-Yves. 'Les francophones dans les Forces Armées canadiennes.' In Jean-Yves Gravel, ed., *Le Quebec et la guerre,* 169–73. Montreal: Boréal 1974.
- 'Le Québec militaire, 1939–45.' In Jean-Yves Gravel, ed., *Le Quebec et la guerre,* 77–108. Montreal: Boréal 1974.
Groulx, Lionel. *Histoire du Canada français depuis la découverte.* Vol. 2. *Le Régime britannique au Canada.* First pub. 1960. Montreal: Fides 1976.
Hamelin, Marcel, ed. *Les mémoires du Sénateur Raoul Dandurand, 1861–1942.* Quebec City: Presses de l'Université Laval 1967.
Hilliker, John. *Le ministère des Affaires extérieures du Canada.* Vol. 1. *Les années de formation, 1909–1946.* Quebec City: Presses de l'Université Laval 1990.
Hillmer, Norman. 'The Anglo Canadian Neurosis: The Case of O.D. Skelton.' In Peter Lyon, ed., *Britain and Canada: Survey of a Changing Relationship,* 61–84. London, Frank Cass 1976.
- 'The Pursuit of Peace: Mackenzie King and the 1937 Imperial Conference.' In John English and J.O. Stubbs, eds., *Mackenzie King: Widening the Debate,* 149–72. Toronto: Macmillan 1977.
Hillmer, Norman, and Granatstein, J.L. *Empire to Umpire: Canada and the World to the 1990s.* Toronto: Copp Clark Longman 1994.
Hoar, Victor. *The Mackenzie-Papineau Battalion: Canadian Participation in the Spanish Civil War.* Toronto: Copp Clark 1969.
Hooker, Martha Ann. 'In Defence of Unity: Canada's Military Policies, 1935–44.' MA thesis, Carleton University, 1985.
Jones, Richard. 'Le cadenas sur la porte!' *Cap aux Diamants* 1, no. 3 (1985), 9–12.
- *Duplessis et le gouvernement de l'Union nationale.* CHA Booklet no. 35. Ottawa: Canadian Historical Association 1983.

– 'Politics and Culture: The French Canadians and the Second World War.' In Sidney Aster, ed., *The Second World War as a National Experience*, 82–91. Ottawa: Canadian Committee for the History of the Second World War 1981.

– *Vers une hégémonie libérale: Aperçu de la politique canadienne de Laurier à King.* Québec City: Presses de l'Université Laval 1980.

Keenleyside, H.L. *Memoirs of Hugh L. Keenleyside.* Vol. 1. *Hammer the Golden Day.* Toronto: McClelland and Stewart 1981.

Laurendeau, André. *La crise de la conscription, 1942.* Montreal: Du Jour 1962.

Lemieux, Vincent. *Eléments d'une théorie politique des voix.* Quebec City: Cahiers du Laboratoire politiques et d'études administratives, Université Laval, 1992.

Linteau, Paul-André, et al. *Histoire du Québec contemporain.* Vol. 2. *Le Québec depuis 1930.* Montreal: Boréal 1986.

Lloyd, Lorna. 'Le Sénateur Dandurand, pionnier du règlement pacifique des différends.' *Études internationales* 23, no. 3 (1992), 581–606.

Lower, A.R.M. *Colony to Nation: A History of Canada.* Toronto: Longmans, Green and Co. 1946.

McGee, J.C. *Laurier, Lapointe, Saint-Laurent: Histoire politique de Québec-Est.* Quebec City: Bélisle 1948.

MacKay, R.A., and Rogers, E.B. *Canada Looks Abroad.* Toronto: Oxford University Press 1938.

Martin, Paul. *A Very Public Life.* Vol. 1. *Far from Home.* Ottawa: Deneau 1983.

Monière, Denis. *Le développement des idéologies au Quebec: des origines à nos jours.* Ottawa: Québec-Amérique 1977.

Morton, Desmond. *Canada and War: A Military and Political History.* Toronto: Butterworths 1981.

– *Une histoire militaire du Canada: 1608–1991.* Sillery: Septentrion 1992.

Neatby, H.B. 'Mackenzie King and French Canada.' *Journal of Canadian Studies* 11, no. 1 (1976). 3–13.

– 'Mackenzie King and the Historians.' In John English and J.O. Stubbs, eds., *Mackenzie King: Widening the Debate*, 1–14. Toronto: Macmillan 1977.

– 'Mackenzie King and National Unity.' In Harvey L. Dyck and H. Peter Krosby, eds., *Empire and Nations*, 54–70. Toronto: University of Toronto Press 1969.

Neatby, H. Blair. *William Lyon Mackenzie King.* Vol. 2. *1924–1932, The Lonely Heights.* Toronto: University of Toronto Press 1963.

– *William Lyon Mackenzie King.* Vol. 3. *The Prism of Unity.* Toronto: University of Toronto Press 1976.

Nolan, Brian. *King's War: Mackenzie King and the Politics of War, 1939–1945.* Toronto: Random House 1988.

Pariseau, Jean, and Bernier, Serge. *Les Canadiens français et le bilinguisme dans les forces armées canadiennes.* Vol. 1. *1763–1969, le spectre d'une armée bicéphale.* Ottawa: Supply and Services 1987.

Peck, Mary Biggar, *Red Moon over Spain: Canadian Media Reaction to the Spanish Civil War, 1936–1939.* Ottawa: Steel Rail Publishing 1988.

Pickersgill, J.W. *The Mackenzie King Record.* Vol. 1. *1939–1944.* Toronto: University of Toronto Press 1960.

Pickersgill, J.W. 'Mackenzie King's Political Attitudes and Public Policies: A Personal Impression.' In John English and J.O. Stubbs, eds., *Mackenzie King: Widening the Debate,* 15–29. Toronto: Macmillan 1977.

– *Seeing Canada Whole: A Memoir.* Markham: Fitzhenry and Whiteside 1994.

Pickersgill, J.W., and Forster, D.F. *The Mackenzie King Record.* Vol. 2. *1944–1945.* Toronto: University of Toronto Press 1968.

– *The Mackenzie King Record.* Vol. 3. *1945–1946.* Toronto: University of Toronto Press 1970.

– *The Mackenzie King Record.* Vol. 4. *1947–1948.* Toronto: University of Toronto Press 1970.

Pope, Maurice. *Soldiers and Politicians: The Memoirs of Lt. General Maurice A. Pope.* Toronto: University of Toronto Press 1962.

Rea, J.E. 'The Conscription Crisis: What Really Happened?' *Beaver* 74, no. 2 (April 1994), 10–19.

Regenstreif, Peter S. 'A Threat to Leadership: C.A. Dunning and Mackenzie King.' *Dalhousie Review* 44 (1964–5), 272–89.

Richer, Léopold. *Nos chefs à Ottawa.* Montreal: éditions Albert Lévesque 1935.

Rumilly, Robert. *Histoire de la Province de Québec,* vols. XXIV–XXXVIII. Ottawa: Fides 1952–68.

– *Maurice Duplessis et son temps.* Vol. 1. *1890–1944.* Montreal: Fides 1973.

Slobodin, T.B. 'A Tangled Web: The Relationship between Mackenzie King's Foreign Policy and National Unity.' PhD thesis, Queen's University, 1982.

Stacey, C.P. *Canada and the Age of Conflict: A History of Canadian External Policies.* Vol. 1. *1867–1921.* First pub. 1977. Toronto: University of Toronto Press 1984.

– *Canada and the Age of Conflict: A History of Canadian External Policies.* Vol. 2. *1921–1948, The Mackenzie King Era.* First pub. 1981. Toronto: University of Toronto Press 1984.

Stacey, C.P. 'Laurier, King and External Affairs.' In J.S. Moir, ed., *Character and Circumstance, Essays in Honour of Donald Grant Creighton,* 80–95. Toronto: Macmillan 1970.

– *Official History of the Canadian Army in the Second World War.* Vol. 1. *Six Years of War: The Canadian Army in Canada, Britain and the Pacific.* Ottawa: Queen's Printer 1955.

Thompson, John Herd, and Seager, Allen. *Canada, 1922–1939: Decades of Discord.* Toronto: McClelland and Stewart 1985.

Thomson, Dale C. *Vive le Québec libre.* Toronto: Deneau, 1988.

Veatch, Richard. *Canada and the League of Nations.* Toronto: University of Toronto Press 1975.

Vigod, Bernard. *Quebec before Duplessis: The Political Career of Louis-Alexandre Taschereau.* Montreal: McGill-Queen's University Press 1986.

Wade, Mason. *The French Canadians, 1760–1960.* Vol. 2. *1911–1967.* Toronto: Macmillan 1976.

Ward, Norman, ed. *A Party Politician: The Memoirs of Chubby Power.* Toronto: Macmillan 1966.

Waite, P.B. 'French Canadian Isolationism and English Canada: An Elliptical Foreign Policy, 1935–1939.' *Journal of Canadian Studies* 18, no. 2 (summer 1983), 132–48.

Weinberg, Gerhard L. 'Munich after 50 Years.' *Foreign Affairs* 67 (1988), 165–82.

Whitaker, Reginald. *The Government Party: Organizing and Financing the Liberal Party of Canada, 1930–1958.* Toronto: University of Toronto Press 1977.

Wigley, Philip. *Canada and the Transition to Commonwealth: British–Canadian Relations, 1917–1926.* Cambridge: Cambridge University Press 1977.

Index

Hillmer, Norman, 7, 109, 116, 140
Hitler, Adolph, 109–10, 113–14,
117–19, 130, 136–9, 142, 145,
149–50, 164–5, 182
Houde, Camillien, 175
Howe, C.D., 133–5, 172–6, 182, 189,
193–4
Hughes, Charles Evans, 51–2
Hughes, Sam, 133
Hull, Cordell, 110, 139, 163
Hume, J.A., 148
Hyde Park Declaration, 137

Ilsley, J.L., 133–4, 150, 161, 169, 172,
176, 189, 193
Imperial Conference of 1923, 47,
55–6; of 1926, 13, 15, 47, 55–60,
78, 197; of 1937, 13, 15, 91,
107–13, 119–20, 198–9
International Labour Organization
(ILO), 69–70

Jarvis, A., 90
Johnson, Daniel, 155

Kemal, Mustapha, 47
King, James H., 39
King, William Lyon Mackenzie: in
Canadian historiography, 3–8;
political vision vis-à-vis Lapointe,
9–12; and the First World War, 22–
5; and the Liberal convention of
1919, 25–9; his role in Liberal
cabinets (1921–9), 33–41; views on
bilingualism, 41; and prairie natural
resources, 42; and federal social programs, 42–3, 87–8; and Dominion-
Provincial Conference of 1927, 43;
and St Lawrence seaway project, 44;
and Chanak crisis, 47–51; and

Halibut Treaty, 51–4; and Imperial
Conference of 1926, 55–60; and
Article X, 61–5; and Optional
Clause, 65–9; and search for seat on
League Council in 1927, 69–73; his
role in the federal Liberal party
(1930–8), 77–85; and francophones
in the civil service, 85–93, 131–7;
and Rowell–Sirois Commission, 88;
and strike at General Motors in
Oshawa (1937), 88–9; and Padlock
Law, 89–90; and Ethiopian crisis,
94–102; and Spanish Civil War,
102–6; and Imperial Conference of
1937, 107–13; and Munich crisis,
113–19; his role in federal Liberal
cabinets (1938–41), 123–31; and
strike at Arvida, 135; and invasion
of Czechoslovakia, 139–46; and
application of the no-neutrality,
no-conscription pact, 146–52; and
Quebec provincial election of 1939,
152–8; and Canadian relations with
Vichy France, 159–68; and the
Defence of Canada Regulations,
168–73; and NRMA, 173–6; and
conscription in 1941, 176–83; and
selection of Lapointe's successor,
186–9; and plebiscite of 1942,
189–93; and reinforcement crisis of
1944, 193–7

Lacasse, Gustave, 39
Lacombe, Liguori, 149
Lacroix, Wilfrid, 82
Laflamme, Napoléon, 38
Lafontaine, L.–H., 73
Landeryou, J.C., 149
Lapointe, Ernest: in Canadian
historiography, 4–8, 191–2; political